Market-Based Health Care

All Myth, No Reality

GRACE BUDRYS
DePaul University

ROWMAN & LITTLEFIELD
Lanham • Boulder • New York • London

Executive Editor: Rolf Janke
Editorial Assistant: Courtney Packard
Senior Marketing Manager: Amy Whitaker

Credits and acknowledgments for material borrowed from other sources, and reproduced with permission, appear on the appropriate page within the text.

Published by Rowman & Littlefield
An imprint of The Rowman & Littlefield Publishing Group, Inc.
4501 Forbes Boulevard, Suite 200, Lanham, Maryland 20706
www.rowman.com

6 Tinworth Street, London SE11 5AL, United Kingdom

British Library Cataloguing in Publication Information Available

Library of Congress Cataloging-in-Publication Data

Names: Budrys, Grace, 1943– author.
Title: Market-based health care : all myth, no reality / Grace Budrys.
Description: Lanham : Rowman & Littlefield, [2019] | Includes bibliographical references and index.
Identifiers: LCCN 2019007896 (print) | LCCN 2019008425 (ebook) | ISBN 9781538128374 (electronic) | ISBN 9781538128350 (cloth) | ISBN 9781538128367 (pbk.)
Subjects: | MESH: Delivery of Health Care—economics | Health Care Sector—economics | Health Care Reform | Private Sector—economics | National Health Programs—economics | United States
Classification: LCC RA412.2 (ebook) | LCC RA412.2 (print) | NLM W 84 AA1 | DDC 338.4/73621—dc23
LC record available at https://lccn.loc.gov/2019007896

Contents

Acknowledgments

I want to extend my appreciation to a number of people for their willingness to take the time to read and comment on early drafts of this book. Once I had assembled the facts, I was eager to share them but knew that my enthusiasm could get in the way of presenting all those facts in an orderly manner. I was fortunate to have friends and colleagues who were not only willing to help me accomplish that but were also experts in the field, meaning that they could evaluate how I was interpreting those facts. I am especially grateful to Michael Ash, Susan Sanders, and Gretchen Fleming for reactions to the central ideas presented in the book as well as the research backing up those ideas. I also wish to thank Dr. Bhupendra Khatri and Andrea Wynne for feedback and suggestions on early drafts.

I want to acknowledge the input of editors at Rowman & Littlefield. They have given me an enormous amount of assistance. They have, of course, improved the writing, plus accomplishing the monumental task of checking and rechecking the picky details in my citations without complaint.

Finally, I thank my husband, Dan Lortie, who not only read drafts but listened to me talk about the ideas that went into the book pretty much on a daily basis month after month.

1

Introduction

This book grew out of what I learned from my students over many years of teaching a course focusing on the US health care system. On the first day of class I would ask what they thought of US health care delivery arrangements. Most were not sure, but there were always a few students willing to tell me what their parents said about it, which generally went like this: Whenever the government gets its hands on something, it gets messed up. The only solution is to hand it all over to the private sector, which is efficient and would not waste our money imposing all kinds of unnecessary bureaucratic rules and regulations. I heard the same assessment year after year. My students did not use the term *privatization*, but that is clearly what they were advocating. Admittedly, these were the most vocal students, who may not represent the opinion of the majority. However, it is the loud voices that get heard. So it is to them and to anyone listening to them that I want to direct my comments.

Not prepared to point out the weaknesses in this stance or get into a proxy argument with their parents on the first day of class, I did not voice the thoughts going through my head in reaction to this assessment. Now that I am not teaching the class, I want to share all those pent-up, unvoiced reactions. I wish to do so because I believe that my students reflect the views not only of their parents but of neighbors and of many Americans, and I find that troubling.

What bothers me most about my students' notion that the private sector, meaning the business sector, would do a better job of organizing our health care arrangements is that it reveals a lack of understanding of how complex our health care system is. I propose to take a stab at unraveling some of that complexity in the chapters to follow. It would take many more books and much greater talents than I have to unravel it completely. However, it is also true that a lot of very smart people have been giving the issues involved a great deal of thought. It is my intention to use their observations to comment on the private sector or market-based, theoretical approach to health care and the health sector, contrasting that to market-based operations in practice.

Let's start with a basic point. Many Americans are proud to assert that we have a private sector, market-based system rather than the government-based system that some other countries have. That may be. But that is not same as saying that the flow of money is limited to the exchange between private sector companies and their customers. The public, meaning government, share of US health spending, including the monies that the government pays out for public insurance programs plus tax subsidies, means that the government is picking up 64 percent of the tab, projected to increase to 67 percent by 2024.[1] In short, it appears we have a publicly supported, market-based system when, as a matter of fact, we have a mixed system. It includes private sector organizations, both for-profit and nonprofit, and public sector or government organizations.

I find it interesting that those who argue that the private sector would do a better job of organizing our health care system tend to think that the discussion can end there. They generally do not explain how the shift to the private sector could or would occur. What forces could turn nonprofit and government hospitals and clinics over to the for-profit sector? Congress could simply give government-run organizations to the private sector by passing a law. That has certainly happened in some instances. But it cannot force nonprofit organizations, which own and operate the majority of hospitals and clinics in this country, to transfer ownership. And investors could not afford to buy out the entire nonprofit sector. They could buy some hospitals, clinics, and doctors' practices, but they could not afford to buy them all. Would private sector investors want to buy them all? If not, we would continue to have a mixed system. Thus the task facing advocates of a market-based approach to health care, and everyone listening to their pitch, is deciding the proportion of the health care system that should be market-based. Arguing in either/or terms, that health care operations should be government-run and/or owned or all private sector–run and/or owned, is just simplistic.

Another thing I wanted to ask my students but did not was, Are all the rules and regulations governing health care objectionable? Which ones would they have liked to see eliminated? How would they deal with sorting out which rules and regulations are objectionable and which are not? Would they base that on public opinion surveys or something else? Would they seek to find out why the rules were put into place to begin with, or would they move on without bothering to do that?

I did not want to get into discussion, on the first day of the course, of the results of public opinion surveys reporting that Americans like the law that prohibits insurance companies from denying coverage on the basis of pre-existing conditions. Survey respondents like coverage for persons under age 26 under parental plans. My students share that view. Americans really like Medicare, the government insurance program for persons over age 65. Health policy makers used to say it is the "third rail"—touch it as a politician and you die. It is that popular with recipients. (That has not stopped a few politicians from advocating privatization of Medicare, probably because they can get credit for taking the position that government should get out of the way even as they know that there is no chance of the proposal getting any traction. Yes, there is a private sector version, Medicare Advantage, but it did not come up at this stage of classroom discussion.) Survey results indicate that the majority of Americans think health care should be available to persons who do not have the money to pay for it. Then there are all the federal and state laws related to drugs, hospitals, and doctors. If you want to pick and choose certain laws, that is not the same as saying government should get out of the way.

How about the idea that private sector organizations are efficient and government organizations are not? That is really the core point of the position the students were taking. What I wanted to ask was, What do you mean by efficiency? How do you know whether an organization is or is not efficient? Economists define *efficiency* as an equilibrium reflecting an absence of waste, which occurs when suppliers produce only as much as is needed and buyers demand only as much as is needed. I don't think my students were relying on economic theory in charging government organizations with inefficiency. As far as I could tell, they were employing profitability as the primary indicator of efficiency. There was also something about the private sector being "lean and mean" and not employing so many people needlessly, the way the government does. (Now that is a charge that deserves a lot more attention, which we will get to in chapter 8.) If the private sector is so efficient, what about all the private sector organizations that have run into financial trouble? You know, like General Motors and Chrysler. The federal government stepped in to save them from bankruptcy, meaning the government owned them for a while. Turning private sector organizations over to the government is the opposite of the call for privatization. There is no word in English to describe it—"deprivatization" just doesn't seem to do it. Indeed, there is no shortage of examples of private sector companies closing their doors. Doesn't that suggest that they were inefficient in managing their affairs?

Critics might say that private sector organizations are allowed to fail and government organizations continue to be supported by taxpayer dollars. That not only ignores the GM and Chrysler stories but dismisses the financial failure of Wall Street organizations leading to the Great Recession of 2008. In those instances, the taxpayers did foot the bill, a very big bill.

It is important to recognize that lack of profitability, indicating extreme inefficiency, was what resulted in the government bailouts. However, the absence of profit cannot serve as an indicator of efficiency in the case of either government or nonprofit organizations, because they are not in the business of making a profit. But efficiency is constantly cited as a reason for turning to the private sector, so we will be getting back to it here and giving it much more attention in the chapters to follow.

WHERE DOES THE IDEA THAT THE GOVERNMENT SHOULD GET OUT OF THE WAY COME FROM?

The views expressed by my students caused me to spend time thinking about the source of the idea that the government should get out of the way. The answer, it turns out, is not that hard to figure out. And tracking down what the spokespersons for this position say can make for eye-opening reading.

What troubles me is that my students are far from alone in holding what can only be described as a superficial and uninformed assessment of a very complicated social institution. In evidence of that observation, I offer the statement made by Mr. Trump once he began taking steps to repeal and replace Obamacare: "Who knew health care was so complicated?" The answer is, of course, that a lot of people knew—legions of health researchers and health policy analysts for a start and many others who make the effort to read material that is sometimes by necessity detailed and dense.

I guess I should not be surprised that many people, from my students and their parents to the president, are ready to embrace what has become a widely accepted solution to the challenges presented by the health care system. Those who favor the private sector approach are unceasing in promoting it. The appeal as presented by proponents is that the solution is so simple and so clear that offering evidence in support of the argument is superfluous. I don't subscribe to that view. I believe that the argument and some of the evidence being cited require closer scrutiny.

The idea that the government should get out of the way has been part of the political conversation in this country since before passage of the Affordable Care Act (ACA, commonly known as Obamacare) in 2010. The Republican call for "repeal and replace" was a constant refrain in the media. It grew much louder in 2017, when Republicans gained control over two of the main branches of government: the executive branch and Congress. The "replace" proposals crafted by the Republican Congress in 2017 did not pass, so there is no point in dissecting them in any detail, though we will need to return to them briefly in chapter 8. It is worth noting, however, that the proposals did not go very far in proposing to get the government out of the way.

In the meantime, changes are being introduced by various government entities—the White House, the secretary of the Department of Health and Human Services, and governors in a number of states—with the explicit aim of rescinding portions of the ACA. We will discuss some of these in greater detail in chapter 4. I am not at all sure that these initiatives translate into getting the government out of the way.

The repeal-and-replace agenda was grounded in the commitment to a private sector approach to health care. It is an objective actively promoted by those who stand on the conservative side of the political divide. The political version of this commitment reflects a set of beliefs regarding the interplay between the individual and society. From the conservative perspective, individuals should have the right to make their own choices regarding how they live their lives and to take full responsibility. Proponents say that people should be able to do so without outside interference, most notably from government rules and regulations. This is the position taken by Tom Price, the briefly seated head of the Department of Health and Human Services, and by conservative think tanks including the Heritage Foundation and the American Enterprise Institute. The argument extends to the full range of choices that affect health status: buying health insurance, seeking medical care, engaging in healthy as opposed to unhealthy behaviors, and so on. There are some in the conservative camp who go further, asserting that health is not a right to be protected by government legislation. Ron Paul, an obstetrician and former representative from Texas, made that point in an interview with CNN host Wolf Blitzer. In response to Blitzer asking whether an uninsured man in a coma should be treated, Paul stated that having health insurance is "what freedom is all about, taking your own risk." When Blitzer asked whether the man should be allowed to die, Tea Party members in the audience cheered, shouting, "Yeah."[2]

At the center of the conservative position is commitment to the idea that health care is a consumer good like other consumer goods that are purchased in the market. Identifying oneself as a *consumer* in the market for health care services as opposed to identifying oneself as a *patient* in need of health care services is a core requirement for the market-based health care approach to work. The underlying premise behind the discussion presented in the remaining chapters of this book is that fulfilling the role of a health care consumer is not easy, for a whole host of reasons that are worth examining in some detail.

I want to make clear that my response to the argument presented by market-based health care proponents is not to suggest simply getting rid of market-based health. It is to say that because we have a complex, interrelated, and mixed system in this country that includes government, for-profit, and nonprofit health care organizations, getting government out of the way is unrealistic.

The challenge is to decide how big a role each of these sectors, for-private, nonprofit, and public, should play in our health care arrangements. I do not propose to offer a formula to accomplish this, although I will identify proposals being considered as of 2019 by those in a position to pass legislation resulting in significant policy changes. For my part, I propose to take the position that government support is crucial to the existence and operations of the private sector health care organizations. I intend to provide evidence showing that without taxpayer dollars, private sector organizations would have little interest and little reason to participate in health care markets. In short, the market for health care goods and services would shrivel.

Proponents of the market-based approach to health care are adamant in saying that transactions between buyers and sellers—without interference from third parties—will achieve an equilibrium price for health care goods and services. At the same time, they complain that their vision is not being realized because buyers are not doing a good job fulfilling the role assigned to them. That strikes me as a serious weakness in the market-based approach. If you can't count on buyers to hold up their end, can you really say that sellers are supplying health care goods and services in response to consumer demand?

It is for reasons such as this that I aim to challenge the idea that a market-based approach to health care is the solution to health care system problems. I intend to do this from the perspective of someone trained as a sociologist. As a sociologist interested in health care, I focus on the impact our health care arrangements and organizations have on people—groups of people differentiated by factors such as age, sex, race, income, and education. I follow health system change, paying special attention to the difference specific changes make in health outcomes—over time and in different regions of the country; to the structure in which health care delivery takes place, which involves factors related to the continuing rise in health care costs and who has access to care and who does not; and to the continuing struggle to establish what quality of care means. This kind of information is tracked by the government, interpreted by health policy experts, and made available to anyone who is interested.

Health policy analysts, who come from a wide range of disciplines, collect, review, and debate information on arrangements that work well and those that do not. However, policy analysts do not make policy. Politicians do. It is in the political arena that commitment to a market-based health care system receives its most forceful expression. It is interesting to note that advocates of a private sector approach invariably couch what they say in economics, invoking sophisticated concepts central to economic theory to bolster their argument. However, health economists are adamant in saying that the private sector approach does not work in the health care sector. At least one highly influential economist, William Hsiao (who is credited with creating the resource-based relative value scale system used by Medicare to determine physician fees and more recently with designing a single-payer plan for the state of Vermont) says that health economics is a separate field.[3] He says that it is certainly not something that can be explained by colleagues who deal in macroeconomics, the branch of economics that plays the biggest role on the public political stage. Macroeconomics deals in the workings of the economy at the aggregate level, focusing on such issues as Gross Domestic Product and fiscal and monetary policy, measuring such factors as inflation, unemployment, and industrial production. Health care is addressed at another level—microeconomics. This involves the behavior of individuals acting as consumers, the actions of firms or sellers, and the role of government. I will return to what health economists have to say in later chapters. I should note that they have a lot of interesting things to say.

I am ready to acknowledge that there are always exceptions to generalizations. For example, John Goodman is one of a handful of economists who favor the market-based approach to health care. He takes the position that this is just common sense. He puts it this way: "Wouldn't you be more likely to buy something if the price were lower? Of course."[4] Actually, I can think of many instances in which one would not make that choice. This is, however, the foundational idea behind the argument that consumers will make choices in the health care market that will cause prices to drop. Those who favor this approach invariably predict that it is sure to happen at some future time when conditions are ideal. One economist, Regina Herzlinger, who has been promoting market-based health care over the last couple of decades, goes further.[5] She has turned to celebrating the arrival of "consumer-driven" health care. I would argue that the celebration is premature.

It is also true that with a big enough platform for doing so, anyone can present an argument favoring a market-based approach and make it sound convincing, without reference to economic theory. For a particularly disquieting take on how that happens, I recommend Anand Giridharadas's book, *Winners Take All* (2018). He nominates the very rich as being primarily responsible for promoting the free-market approach. He says the rich are committed to promoting the value of the market-based approach to justify their wealth, which they say is the result of knowing the "right way to do it." The rich maintain that this is elemental because the public sector is failing. Giridharadas says that their success in promoting this view crowds out the public sector, reduces its legitimacy and efficacy in order to replace it with commitment to efficiency and markets. Getting everyone to buy into this perspective is, of course, exactly what makes the rich so rich. He goes on to say that market-based ideology has larger negative effects that the rich do not address. By draining money away from public social institutions, like health care, and shifting the money to the pockets of individuals, free-market ideology promotes increasing social inequality. He points to the detrimental consequences of social inequality expressed externally as political anger and internally as behavior resulting in shortened life expectancy. Giridharadas focuses on how the rich justify their advantaged position. They establish foundations aimed at reducing poverty and creating opportunity. They do not acknowledge that there would be no need for the foundations if the very rich were not responsible for the existence of tremendous social inequality. As I say, this is a disquieting assessment, one that deserves more attention than we can manage here. But I think it is a message well worth stopping to think about.

At this point, I want to make very clear that my criticism of the private sector approach is directed solely to health care. I have no interest in addressing the workings of the free-market model in other sectors of the economy. My basic objective is to explore the difference between market-based health care in the abstract—that is, what proponents say it will do—and the reality of our health care arrangements in point of fact. As things stand, I would argue that an enormous amount of effort, largely in the political arena, is going into trying to force health care reality to conform to the market-based health care theoretical model.

Each of the following chapters comes back to the claim that the private sector is more efficient than government. The question I propose to address in each case is, How is that claim working out? Coming up with answers requires wading through a lot of complexity. It often feels like tramping through very thick alphabet sludge that consists of endless acronyms in capital letters. It can be overwhelming but worth the effort for what it reveals. Comparing what advocates say about the virtues of the market-based model, which is theory, and what market-based health care looks like in practice results in an irreconcilable picture.

Another challenge in considering the way the health care system works is that it is undergoing a tremendous upheaval. While it is true that our health care arrangements have been undergoing continuing change due to advances in medicine and technological capacity all along, things are now, in some cases, moving in a direction that differs from the one in which they had been moving in the recent past. Moreover, things seem to be moving at an accelerated pace. The fact that the 2018 midterm elections brought health care to the center of debates between Republican and Democratic political aspirants and that the Democrats achieved significant gains in House of Representative races indicates that health care will be receiving a great deal of attention over the next few years. In short, be warned that the facts presented here may be fleeting.

The discussion is organized as follows. Chapter 2 consists of an exploration of the market-based model and what it promises to achieve in the health sector. Chapters 3 and 4 focus on health insurance arrangements, 5 on doctors, 6 on hospitals, and 7 on the pharmaceutical industry. Chapter 8 considers the development of health sector occupations and organizations in relation to the nation's economy as a whole. Chapter 9 ends the discussion with some concluding thoughts on the market-based health care approach. The epilogue comments on two bills before Congress offering alternatives to market-based health care.

The format I am employing relies on questions about the workings of parts of the health care system. I raise questions that I don't see being asked and addressed. There are more questions presented in earlier chapters and fewer questions as discussion proceeds, to avoid the repetition of what turn out to be very similar questions.

NOTES

1. David Himmelstein and Steffie Woolhandler, "The Current and Projected Taxpayer Share of U.S. Health Costs," *American Journal of Public Health* 106, no. 3 (2016): 449–52.

2. Amy Bingham, "Tea Party Debate Audience Cheered Idea of Letting Uninsured Patients Die," ABC News, September 13, 2011, https://abcnews.go.com/blogs/politics/2011/09/tea-party-debate-audience-cheered-idea-of-letting-uninsured -patients-die/.

3. William Hsiao and Peter Heller, "What Should Macroeconomists Know About Health Care Policy?" (working paper, International Monetary Fund. 2007).

4. John Goodman, *Priceless: Curing the Healthcare Crisis* (Oakland, CA: Independent Institute, 2012), 39.

5. Regina Herzlinger, *Market-Driven Health Care* (Cambridge, MA: Perseus Books, 1997).

2

The Market-Based
Health Care Model

The confidence expressed by those who advocate the market-based approach stems from its association with concepts embedded in economic theory, which are treated as indisputable and self-explanatory. However, because the assumptions on which the market-based theoretical approach is based are generally not articulated, they go unexamined. A prime example has to do with what *efficiency* means. What is the indicator of efficiency you have in mind? It's not enough to say, "Everyone knows that government organizations are inefficient," or "You can just see it to know it is true." That's not convincing, at least not convincing to me.

What *competition* means is also not as obvious as one might think at first glance. Do you think of it as a race? I do. Don't we all cheer at competitive sports events when our favorite team wins? There is supposed to be a winner, right? In my experience, market-based health care advocates are adamant in saying that competition does not work that way and should not work that way. Exactly how should it work?

Market-based health care at the theoretical level is grounded in ideas about supply and demand. It holds that the transactions between buyers and sellers determine the price and quantity of the goods and services available in the market. Consumer demand is a singularly important force necessary for the market to function the way market theory says it does. Indeed, market-based health care proponents claim that we have entered the era of "consumer-driven" health care.

To illustrate what this would look like, I offer a statement by Administrator Seema Verma, of the Centers for Medicare and Medicaid Services:

> It's time for a new era of consumerism in health care, with patients at the center of the delivery system. Patients should be empowered to make the best decisions about their care, and providers should have to compete for patients by offering them higher quality at lower cost.[1]

Another influential advocate of the consumer-driven idea is Secretary Alex Azar, of the Department of Health and Human Services (HHS). In speaking to an audience of hospital administrators of for-profit hospitals, he presented the following vision:

> Imagine a day when health care delivery in the United States functions the way other parts of our economy do. We as patients would pick providers with the level of information we have when using Amazon or Yelp.[2]

I expect that my students would welcome Verma's and Azar's approach. The underlying theoretical assumption is that the market can and will balance supply and demand for health care goods and services in response to the choices made by consumers. The likelihood of that happening is the subject of the chapters to follow.

I would like to mention a point that may have gone unnoticed in Azar's presentation, because he devoted only one sentence to it. He said, "We're looking at using Medicare and Medicaid to drive the value-based transformation of our entire health system." That is a version of a market-based approach that those who want to see the government getting out of the way might be surprised to hear. Exactly how the government interacts with the health care system deserves a closer look. It is a topic that is addressed in every chapter of the book.

Azar seems to treat employing government programs to shape the country's health care system as a radical idea. So it is interesting to consider what Robert Field, a well-informed health policy analyst, has to say on this topic. Field holds that the laws government has instituted and the funding it provides actually created the "free-market" health care system that exists in this country today:

Without the government's active role, health care in the United States would look nothing like it does today. Most significantly, the industry would be substantially smaller. . . . [T]he government has not stifled private health care, nor has it crowded out private companies from business opportunities. Quite to the contrary, it has built the foundation on which private health care rests.[3]

Before proceeding I would like to add a note on language. "Market-based" health care is the current (2019) label for the private sector, businesslike approach to the delivery of health care goods and services. In the past, the approach was labeled "for-profit." It has now been rebranded undoubtedly because "market-based" sounds more pleasing. I use the labels interchangeably. The message is the same regardless of which term is being used—private sector, for-profit, or market-based. Central to the vision is the idea that the market, in this case the market for health goods and services, should operate as a "free market" with few if any restraints. Especially objectionable are governmental restraints.

WHEN THE THEORETICAL MODEL AND REALITY ARE A MATCH

Economists as far back as Adam Smith used the agricultural sector to illustrate the basic features of a free market in operation. While most people these days do not know much about arrangements governing the distribution of agricultural products, many are familiar with a small-scale version of the agricultural sector, that is, the farmers' market. Its operations make the economic principles essential for understanding how the free market is supposed to work perfectly clear. The foundational mechanism is competition. What follows is an illustration of an ideal type—a model market that works pretty much like what Adam Smith was looking at when he outlined the workings and benefits of the free market. Its fundamental elements are easily identified.

I will assume that you have had the opportunity to go to a local farmers' market during the summer months to buy fruits and vegetables, maybe some bakery goods, and possibly all kinds of other homemade products. Consider the scene. There are lots of people milling about looking at the stands. There are *many sellers* displaying their offerings and *many buyers* moving from stand to stand to see what is on offer. Buyers are there because this is where they can get the freshest, most tasty produce at a good price. Sellers bring the produce that they believe will appeal to potential buyers. Buying and selling in a farmers' market takes place between individuals rather than larger, organized entities. The transactions are simple, straightforward, and transparent.

Free-market proponents assert that *consumer choice* is not only central to free-market operations but stands at the heart of an open and free society. This makes anything that interferes with market operations objectionable in principle.

Farmers' market buyers are in an ideal position to make their selections because they can evaluate the quality of the products and maybe handle the fruits and vegetables to make sure they are not too soft or bruised. The sellers may not like that, but if they are selling enough, they can't watch everyone who is handling their products. Sellers have signs indicating prices for their products. Buyers can choose to come early to get the best produce or come toward the end of the time the market is held and get good deals because the sellers are more willing to reduce their prices so they can pack up and go home.

Sellers are very much aware of each other's products. It does not take much effort to walk around and see what everyone else is selling and at what price. Sellers know that they must adjust their prices in reaction to the prices other sellers are charging for comparable products to be competitive. They do not have to be told to be responsive to buyers' preferences. Everyone who participates in the market knows that the sellers are interested in making a profit. Selling produce is a commercial enterprise. It is not a charitable, nonprofit activity. Everyone understands that sellers can and do set a higher price for produce that is especially attractive, appealing, or special in some other way because buyers who want those products are willing to pay the asking price. Everyone is also aware of the fact that other sellers are quick to recognize that one of their competitors is offering products that buyers are especially interested in buying. That encourages sellers to make every attempt to bring more of the highly desirable but scarce products to the market. Increased production of those desirable products may not occur overnight, but there is little doubt that it will happen as soon as sellers can arrange it. In short, the supply of popular fruits and vegetables increases to meet demand, which in turn has a powerful effect on price. Sellers reduce prices when there is an oversupply, in the hope of attracting more buyers. This is, of course, the essence of competition among sellers, which stands at the core of the free-market model. The way the farmers' market operates exemplifies the functionality of the *supply/ demand curve* in meeting society's needs.

Another important characteristic of the farmers' market is the *ease of entry and exit* on the part of both parties to the exchange. Buyers enter the market and buy as little or as much as they wish based on price and quality and leave when they have bought what they want.

Sellers don't have onerous barriers to entry. They may have to get a permit from the city agency in charge, pay a fee, and not violate any of the most basic health standards to participate in the market. They do not have to complete any courses, take tests, pass licensure exams, and so on. And they do not have to make a major investment in building a structure or renting space. They can put up a tent-like covering and some folding tables. Sellers who do not make enough profit can just quit bringing their produce without sustaining an enormous loss. They can simply not show up anymore if they no longer wish to participate.

One feature of the farmers' market that makes it unique is that it is, in most cases, a summertime phenomenon. The market has a set start and end date. The fact that the period of time involved is short and there is an end point makes a significant difference. There are few signs of one seller attempting to buy out other sellers. Few sellers drop out over the short period of time the market lasts. This applies to sellers whose products are not selling very well but who seem to be willing to keep coming anyway because the market offers other benefits, such as sociability. It is unlikely that less than successful sellers would continue if the farmers' market became a more permanent arrangement. No one objects to the presence of one or two unproductive sellers. Many more would taint the market as a failing enterprise.

CLASSICAL FREE-MARKET THEORY: SELF-EVIDENT ASSUMPTIONS

There is more to the free-market theoretical model than a tour through a farmers' market can reveal. The model is grounded in a series of assumptions that are considered self-evident, including those identified in this section. The core principle, as already noted, is that *competition* is the basic mechanism responsible for the effective distribution of goods and services. *Self-interest* is the force responsible for success in achieving *efficiency*. A basic underlying proposition is the assumption of *rationality* on the part of participants in the exchange.

Efficiency is achieved when sellers set a *price* that consumers are willing to pay for the goods and services on offer. The manifestation of rationality on the part of *sellers* is expressed in intent to maximize *profit*. Rationality on the part of *buyers* is expressed in intent to maximize *utility* in purchasing what best suits their needs and preferences. A price that is higher than what buyers are willing to pay results in reduced *demand* for those products. Buyers benefit when more sellers are willing to increase the *supply* of goods that consumers want to buy and reduce the *price* of goods in response to lower demand. In short, self-interest is the force that produces a balance in the *supply of and demand for* the products on offer. Competition is the mechanism that reifies self-interest. The exchange between buyers and sellers that results in the balance achieved in the supply-demand curve exemplifies the workings of what Smith called the "invisible hand."

The assumption that the utility feature is being met has a prerequisite that is considered so self-evident that it does not garner a lot of attention, namely, that price is what matters most. The idea is that buyers are prepared to pay a *higher price* for what they perceive to be *higher quality*. But they are also willing to accept *lower quality* if it carries a *lower price*. The ability to balance price and quality in making a *choice* reflects the assumption of rationality underlying the evaluation of utility on the part of the buyer. Rational choice is based on the assumption that buyers are entering into market transactions with full *knowledge of the price and quality* of the goods and services they seek to purchase. This feature deserves far more attention in the case of the health care goods and services market.

Buyers in a farmers' market generally don't have to ask about prices. They are typically clearly posted. It is worth noting that the lack of clear price information in other markets is generally considered responsible for *inefficiency* associated with *transaction costs*. Transaction costs include the time and effort that buyers must invest in searching for information on prices. If prices are not clearly stated and can change at any time, consumers must repeatedly check for changes in price. Price uncertainty detracts from the clear and simple elegance of the free-market model.

It is also true that the theoretical free-market model is characterized by several self-correcting features. Built into the model is the notion that economic considerations are functional and/or advantageous to society because self-interest reflected in profit is what motivates producers to provide a sufficient supply of products that consumers are ready to buy.

The ease of market entry and exit is highly functional because producers who offer goods and services in which buyers have little interest don't have much incentive to participate in the market. This self-correcting feature is more beneficial to society than it may at first appear to be. It is not only a matter of eliminating market clutter; it operates to encourage innovation in light of evidence regarding which goods and services result in profit and which do not.

Proponents of the free market are opposed to obstacles imposed by third parties to the entry of sellers. They are opposed to many of the rules and regulations society imposes in the effort to set standards for the production and sale of various goods and services. These include specification of years of education required before certification or licensure, fees that allow individuals and organizations that represent categories of providers to offer goods and services, standards and conditions that must be observed in the production of certain products, ingredients that may not be used in the production of some goods, and so on.

Free-market proponents are not eager to expose disagreement in their ranks, but they do not always agree about the controls the market can tolerate and still be efficient. They disagree about the extent to which the caveat emptor—that is, the "buyer beware"—concept should apply when a buyer purchases damaged or dangerous goods that result in injury. The question is, Can buyers who sustain an injury be viewed as deserving their fate, as some eminent proponents of this model have suggested?

A NOTE ON SELF-INTEREST

Self-interest, according to market-based health care proponents, serves a valuable purpose. Its theoretical function is to allow buyers and sellers to arrive at a set of marketplace offerings that satisfy both parties. The existence of self-interest on the part of sellers is unquestionable. For a closer look at how it operates, I recommend Elisabeth Rosenthal's 2017 book, *An American Sickness*. Her take on the health system strips away any illusions one might have about sellers of health care goods and services being motivated by something other than financial self-interest. While she does recount the heroic efforts of isolated individuals who have struggled to work on their patients' behalf against powerful forces primarily motivated by financial gain, she makes clear that their efforts generally meet with limited success. The picture she paints of the way self-interest works in this market shows that it invariably fosters more spending and higher prices. Her point is that self-interest on the part of sellers is relatively easy to fulfill but that self-interest on the part of buyers is very hard to fulfill.

Rosenthal begins her book by listing ten "economic rules of the dysfunctional market." The book includes one example after another of the rules in action.

1. More treatment is always better. Default to the most expensive option.
2. A lifetime of treatment is preferable to cure.
3. Amenities and marketing matter more than good care.
4. As technologies age, prices can rise rather than fall.
5. There is no free choice. Patients are stuck. And they are stuck buying American.
6. More competitors vying for business doesn't mean better prices; it can drive prices up, not down.
7. Economies of scale don't translate to lower prices. With their market power, big providers can simply demand more.
8. There is no such thing as a fixed price for a procedure or test. And the uninsured pay the highest prices of all.
9. There are no standards for billing. There's money to be made in billing for anything and everything.
10. Prices will rise to whatever the market will bear.[4]

She advocates far greater self-interest on the part of the consumer and provides lists of resources to help consumers achieve that.

What troubles me is that the market-based theoretical stance assumes that self-interest as a basis is obvious and is shared. I would argue that consumers of health care are motivated by something other than what motivates sellers. Consumers of health care are primarily interested in improving their health and not in getting health care bargains. If the basis of self-interest is not the same, then it is difficult to see how a balance of interests can happen between buyers and sellers.

GOODS VERSUS SERVICES

The farmers' market portrayal of the free-market model is obviously over-simplified and limited. But it should suffice to permit us to consider how closely the health sector comes in matching the free-market model. Before proceeding with this exercise, I would like to focus on a distinctive characteristic of the farmers' market.

The farmers' market illustration makes clear that markets work, just as free-market theory says they work, to distribute goods that consumers find easy to evaluate. There is no comparable example of a market that deals in distribution of services. In short, I would argue that the free-market model is far more accurate in describing the process through which goods are distributed in contrast to services in general and health care services in particular. I offer the observation made by Victor Fuchs, whom colleagues refer to as the "dean of health economics," to make this point. He says, "Medical care is, in many respects, the quintessential service industry."[5] He makes another provocative observation, namely, that "by 1957, the United States had become the world's first 'service economy'—that is, the first nation in which more than half of the labor force was engaged in producing services rather than products."[6] The question this brings to my mind is, Does the model that supports the picture of free market in which goods (some much like those available in Adam Smith's time and others not) are exchanged really work as well to support the exchange of services? Maybe the question is unreasonable and inappropriate, but it is one that overshadows the discussion to follow.

Two examples of simple services that any of us may have occasion to use will serve to highlight the contrast between the market for goods as opposed to services. Consider the matter of getting a haircut. How does one choose a good barber or beautician? Shopping behavior that is so easy in the farmers' market is so much more burdensome in this case. Making comparisons on the basis of price of haircuts is time-consuming. Obtaining information about quality is not only time-consuming but is also far less certain. One can ask friends. Internet sites have appeared that report the comments made by other people, in some cases many people and in some cases only a few. However, learning that others were satisfied with their haircuts does not ensure that things will go the same way in one's own case. We know that barbers and beauticians must be licensed; their shops undergo inspections by consumer protection agencies to ensure cleanliness. We can have some confidence regarding certification and cleanliness, which tells one nothing about how one's own haircut will turn out.

The good thing here is that a person does not risk that much in getting a haircut. If it is a bad haircut, we may be displeased, but hair grows out and not that much damage has been done. Let's contrast that to getting a new pair of pants shortened. If the tailor makes them too short, the pants will not grow back. That may or may not be more frustrating than getting a bad haircut. The point is that the outcome in both cases is unpredictable.

Putting this in perspective, the market for services includes a measure of uncertainty or lack of predictability that can only be fully satisfied after the service is experienced. Thus, if full knowledge of price and quality are basic to the free-market model, the distribution of services does not provide as good a fit to the model as the distribution of goods.

How serious the consequences of poor service due to lack of full information on price and quality turn out to be depends on the sector of services we are talking about. It matters whether the consumer is in the market for a haircut, the services of a tailor, a good restaurant, or the services of a neurosurgeon. Clearly there is an enormous range in the impact that the consequences of first-rate service versus third-rate service will have, and it becomes apparent only after one has received the service.

Something similar can, of course, be said of buying some goods, goods that are so complex that one is unable to judge quality. Just as is true in purchasing services, the level of risk associated with buying goods varies with the sector of the market. Buying a new electronic product—a computer, cell phone, or plasma TV—can be costly if it has problems. Buying a cell phone that suddenly ignites is the example that made news in recent years. Buying a car that has faulty brakes or defective airbags (also newsworthy in the recent past), poses an even greater risk. Even the most adamant proponents of the free market have not been heard arguing that buying a car is a matter of "buyer beware" in reaction to such stories. Nor are the most adamant advocates of the free market ready to oppose government stepping in to institute some sort of regulatory intervention. Nevertheless, the role of government is a source of continuing dispute.

In the meantime, organizations dedicated to evaluating products have come into existence; one is the Consumers Union, which employs engineers and other experts to test products and publishes *Consumer Reports*. This works well because the products tested are standardized. The reports identify products using production code numbers to distinguish them from similar products made by other companies, even the same company. Prices are reported as well. The "best buys" are identified.

Services don't come packaged that way. Yelp is a good example of a popular online service-rating site. The public does the rating based on personal experience with the service provider. In some instances, one can find comments and ratings offered by a few people; in other cases, by many people. It is interesting to see the range of reactions. Even when the majority of raters express satisfaction, there are some who have major complaints. In the end, one may be better informed, but this is not to say that one can be sure that one will be satisfied with whatever service is at issue.

It is hard to overlook the fact that the difficulty obtaining accurate information regarding quality of services as well as complex products violates one of the basic tenets of the ideal type of free-market model. Is it reasonable to assume that *cost-benefit analysis* is really the most effective mechanism for making a choice when products carry risk? How many people would willingly choose to buy an unsafe car even at a very low price or choose to have brain surgery performed at a cut-rate price? Quality is obviously far more important than price as a consideration in such cases. But the quality of services is considerably more difficult to establish than the price of services.

One can argue that this does not disprove the validity of the free-market model. Ultimately the market does work to eliminate goods and services that are inferior and that consumers do not choose to buy. It is just that in many cases, buyers are not able to evaluate quality of highly technically sophisticated products until there is a record indicating the performance of those products. This is harder to arrange in the case of services. An added complication is that self-interest discourages sellers from making negative information public about the goods and services they are interested in selling. How long it takes and how much damage must occur before negative information becomes available varies. Although none of this poses a significant threat to the free-market rationale at the theoretical level, it does not look especially advisable as a paradigm for consumer-driven health care.

SUMMING UP

Based on the discussion presented in this chapter, my conclusion is that the market-based model that appears to work so well in the farmers' market context, as I describe it here, cannot work if the conditions stipulated by the theoretical model and illustrated so well in the operations of the farmers' market are not observed. (Okay, this is a superficial overview. What about the markets the farmers' market sellers have to deal with—the gas to get there, the price of seeds and pesticides, even the price of the land, managing the quality of the soil, and so on? The picture gets more complicated the closer one gets to the story, but greater clarity would distract from the elegance of the model.)

I intend to employ three core elements of the market-based approach in examining parts of the health care system. The three are: (1) many buyers and many sellers, (2) easy entry and easy exit, and (3) consumer choice. The latter revolves around the availability to consumers of information on quality and price of health care goods and services. My objective is to assess the fit between theory, as represented by the market-based health care model, and reality, or how the health sector operates in practice. I propose to begin by assessing the fit between theory and practice in the health insurance industry.

NOTES

1. Seema Verma, "Empowered Patients Are the Future of Health Care," RealClear Health, May 3, 2018, https://www.realclearhealth.com/articles/2018/05/03/em powered_patients_are_the_future_of_health_care_110784.html.

2. Alex Azar, "Remarks on Value-Based Transformation to the Federation of American Hospitals," HHS.gov, March 5. 2018, https://www.hhs.gov/about/leadership/secretary/speeches/2018-speeches/remarks-on-value-based-transformation-to-the-federation-of-american-hospitals.html.

3. Robert Field, *Mother of Invention: How Government Created Free-Market Health Care* (New York: Oxford University Press, 2014), 207.

4. Elisabeth Rosenthal, *An American Sickness* (New York: Penguin Press, 2017).

5. Victor Fuchs, *Health Economics and Policy* (New Jersey: World Scientific, 2018), 13.

6. Fuchs, *Health Economics*, 472.

3

The Market for
Health Insurance

This chapter begins with a very brief outline of the development of health insurance in the United States. It goes on to describe the state of health insurance after the passage of the Affordable Care Act (ACA), or Obamacare, in 2010. Reference to the ACA is occasioned by the need to address the impact of the changes in the health insurance market that were introduced by the law. The discussion outlines the efforts both buyers and sellers of health insurance have made to adjust to those changes. It looks at the turmoil associated with efforts to overturn the law following the Republican takeover of two branches of government in 2017. I do not propose to critique or praise the ACA. My objective is far more limited: I aim to examine the extent to which the market-based health insurance approach matches the requirements inherent in the free-market model. I will do so by posing questions stemming from the assertions and expectations built into the model as we move along in the discussion.

I use three basic features of the free-market model that were identified in the previous chapter to review the workings of the health insurance sector: (1) many buyers and many sellers, (2) consumers' ability to choose, (3) ease of market entry and exit. The three characteristics serve as the foundation for fulfilling the promise of lower prices and high quality that advocates of the market-based health care model say it will deliver. Advocates maintain that competition among sellers is the basic mechanism to achieve this objective.

They say that obviously, buyers will buy the health care goods and services that best meet their needs in terms of price and quality, which will result in a balance between supply of and demand for health insurance products. The basic question I aim to address in this chapter is, How accurate is this portrayal of the health insurance market?

Before launching into this discussion, I want to make the following point: health insurance is generally referred to as a product. However, the product in this case is in fact a bundle of services. That makes a difference because, as I argued in the preceding chapter, the utility of services is not as easy to assess as the utility of goods. The services include collecting fees from enrollees and reimbursing providers based on negotiations between the insurance company and providers as to how much the insurance company will pay for the providers' goods and services. As such, the service health insurance companies provide is far more complicated than it sounds, in large part because so many health care goods and services continually change due to upgrades or other alterations. Insurance companies do not publish rates of coverage for specific forms of medical care or the rules outlining that coverage. The lack of transparency is a source of constant frustration to providers of health care services because they regularly must ask for the information before proceeding to deliver health care services and products. As to the consumers of insurance products, the reality is that they are in the position of shopping for a health insurance policy without complete information on the scope of the coverage in the policy.

THE GROWTH OF HEALTH INSURANCE

The origins of market-based health insurance in this country can be traced to Baylor University Hospital's difficulty collecting on its bills during the Great Depression era. In reviewing its records, it found schoolteachers to be an identifiable category of persons defaulting on their bills. The hospital came up with the idea of offering the Dallas Board of Education insurance, covering twenty-one days of hospital care for fifty cents a month. The plan was designed to be self-supporting rather than profit-making. The year was 1929. The plan was called Blue Cross. The rest is history.

The Blue Cross plan began to spread during the decade of the 1930s. But it took World War II to make employer-based health insurance a common phenomenon. The explanation is pretty simple: Men went to war, and women went into the workforce to take their place. Because employers could not, by law, increase wages during the war, they began offering benefits—most notably health insurance—to attract employees, especially the limited number of male employees.

The emergence of another pioneering health plan, Kaiser Permanente, in 1938, a few years after Blue Cross, is also interesting to consider. It reads like an action story. It is an account of a creative solution to a practical problem, namely, that men were doing a dangerous job, building an aqueduct in unsettled territory in California, with no medical care within a reasonable distance. A doctor willing to go to the area would be setting up a practice with no assurance of income to support opening an office. The construction company came up with a solution: the company itself provided an office and a secure income. The income came from the five cents per day charged to the workers to ensure access to care. Once World War II ended, the Kaiser Permanente plan was opened to anyone who wanted to join. It continued as a prepaid plan, paying physicians on a salaried basis. The medical establishment was aggressive in its opposition to the arrangement. Hospitals were pressured to deny privileges to Kaiser doctors and reject their patients. The upshot of that was that Kaiser built its own hospitals.

In the Kaiser Permanente model, staff consists largely of primary care physicians who coordinate care with specialists and with the hospital. It has grown and flourished largely in West Coast states. We will see this plan again in chapter 4.

It is noteworthy that both the Kaiser plan and the Blue Cross plan were private sector, nonprofit organizations. This means that the earliest insurance arrangements were established as something other than for-profit, market-based arrangements. Blue Cross plans went through considerable change, coming closer to a market-based model. Kaiser Permanente did not.

Employers received an additional incentive to offer health insurance to their employees after the war ended when legislation giving employers a tax subsidy for providing health insurance was passed. Health insurance continued to spread as employees began to expect it. It is not clear, though, how many people gained health insurance over the two decades following the war. A 2009 National Health Statistics Report indicates that by 1968, 79 percent of the entire population had health insurance. By 2000, the percentage under age 65 had fallen to 67 percent, and by 2010 it was down to 62 percent.[1] This includes both private and public insurance coverage.

Coverage provided to the majority of Americans has always been employer-based, that is, insurance offered by private sector insurance companies. The number of people covered by employer-sponsored health insurance peaked during the 1980s. The numbers started to decline during the 1980s as employers began to see it as too much of an economic burden. In 1984, the percentage of people covered by employer-sponsored health insurance was 69 percent, by 2000 it was 67 percent, and by 2010 it had fallen to less than 57 percent.[2]

Employees across the country have traditionally been expected to share the cost of insurance with the employer. How much the employee is required to contribute has always been at the discretion of the employer. The money is simply deducted from the employee's paycheck. Many employers provide family insurance coverage if the employee is willing to pay the additional charge set by the insurance company. Employers typically present employees with a choice of a number of plans offered by different companies.

Health insurance purchased on an individual basis has been slow to evolve. Private sector insurance companies have not been interested in selling to individuals because risk assessment is so uncertain. In other words, setting a price on a health insurance policy for an individual meant the insurer had to project the risk of that particular person needing medical care services. The concept economists employ to explain the problem is *adverse selection*. In order to overcome the problem of having inadequate information about the risks of insuring any one individual, the insurance company compensated for the risk of financial loss by increasing the price of the policy by a significant amount.

Projecting risk for large groups of people—employees—is more conclusive. Administering a plan on an individual basis is also time-consuming and therefore costly to the insurer. Insurance companies used two mechanisms as a hedge against financial risk and costs associated with insuring individuals. One was refusal to cover preexisting conditions. The definition of a preexisting condition was at the discretion of the insurance company. The other was setting a sufficiently high premium to minimize risk, which, of course, discouraged prospective buyers from buying the insurance.

The two measures meant that consumers were not buying a product that they determined had far too little utility—that is, it was too costly for what was being offered. The numbers of people enrolled in individual plans remained small.

PUBLIC HEALTH INSURANCE

Government-sponsored health insurance includes the following: Medicare and Medicaid, established in 1965, and the Children's Health Insurance Program (CHIP), established in 1997. CHIP is combined with Medicaid in some states. Federal employees, veterans, active military personnel, and Native Americans are covered by other government-sponsored plans.

Medicare

Persons over age 65 who have worked for ten years or more and contributed to the program through 1.45 percent payroll deductions are eligible. Employers contribute another 1.45 percent. Some disabled persons are also eligible. The program consists of four parts. Part A provides hospital coverage. Enrollment is automatic for all who are eligible. Part B, which covers care by health providers, requires the individual to enroll. Enrollees pay for Part B through a monthly deduction that comes out of their Social Security check. The amount increases with higher income. Part C is Medicare Advantage, which we will discuss in chapter 4. Part D is the pharmaceutical coverage, which we will discuss in chapter 7.

Persons who sign up for traditional Medicare, that is, Parts A and B, may choose to purchase supplementary insurance, often referred to as Medigap, to cover out-of-pocket costs. Medigap policies are sold by private companies. There are ten plans, labeled A through N (E, H, I, and J are no longer sold). What is included in the plans is outlined in Medicare Administration publications. Insurance companies may choose which to sell and how much to charge but may not alter what is covered in the plans. We will get back to discussion of Medigap plans later in this chapter when we address the topic of efficiency.

Medicaid

Medicaid is a public health insurance plan operated by states and funded by the federal government at a rate of 50 percent, more in some states. States are permitted to set the rules regarding economic eligibility, a percentage that may be well above or far below the annual poverty level guidelines. The state is required to abide by federal guidelines regarding categories of service that must be covered. The original version of Medicaid covered only children and pregnant women. It underwent continuous expansion and is now the largest public health insurance program in the country.

HEALTH INSURANCE AFTER PASSAGE OF THE ACA

The momentous change in US health insurance arrangements brought about by the ACA was the requirement that everyone in the country obtain health insurance. In 2010, the year the ACA was passed, more than 18 percent of the population had no health insurance.[3] By 2016 that figure had dropped to 10 percent.[4]

The legislation was set down in about 2,300 pages. Over the ensuing years, thousands more pages of regulations were added. (As of 2019, the Republican head of the Senate claims that 20,000 pages were added.) The following addresses the most basic changes.

It is important to remember that prior to passage of the ACA, employers were not required to offer health insurance to their employees. Many of those who offered it did so because it became something employees seeking work in large companies expected. Small employers were not as likely to provide health insurance. As of 2016, less than half of all firms across the country, 45 percent, offered health insurance coverage to their employees; of those, 97 percent had fifty or more employees and 29 percent had fewer than fifty employees.[5] Hawaii is an outlier. More than 70 percent of firms with fewer than fifty employees offer health insurance in Hawaii, compared to an average of 20 to 25 percent of firms in the majority of other states. The reasons for that are worth exploring. Unfortunately, we can't explore all the interesting facts we come up with. However, I do have a hypothesis to propose, which is that Hawaiians are readier to see themselves as members of the same group or society than people in other states. They are more likely to see fellow Hawaiians as *deserving* rather than *undeserving*—in this instance, deserving of health care. I suggest that this is a point to keep in mind in considering debates about universal insurance coverage.

According to the National Center for Health Statistics, as of early 2018, the uninsured rate among working-age adults was 12.5 percent.[6] A survey conducted by the Commonwealth Fund over the same period estimated the rate at 15.5 percent.[7] This indicates that since 2016, there has been a reversal of the gains in health care coverage associated with passage of the ACA. The significance of the increase in uninsurance that is worth stopping to consider is its relationship to the increased risk of death. It is estimated that for every eight hundred thousand persons who are uninsured, one thousand will die.[8]

Three routes to coverage were outlined by the ACA: the employer mandate, the individual mandate, and Medicaid coverage. Coverage of persons over age 65 through Medicare was largely unaffected. As of 2017, the National Health Interview Survey of working-age adults covered by health insurance reported that 69 percent had private insurance and 19 percent had government-sponsored health insurance.[9]

Employer Mandate

The employer mandate requiring employers to provide health insurance to all full-time employees had little impact on most large employers who had been providing health insurance all along. Small employers, some of whom were providing it and others who were not, said that they had less leverage than large employers in negotiating with large insurance companies and therefore ended up being charged higher rates. Some revisions in the law were introduced to assist employers with fewer than fifty employees, including the creation of a special market called Small Business Options Program. For those with one hundred or fewer employees, the deadline for compliance was extended twice, to January 2016. Failure to provide employer-based insurance would result in a per-person penalty to be paid by employers, and the penalty would rise on a yearly basis.

The proportion employees pay for insurance premiums has been increasing at a faster rate than their wages. "For Americans whose incomes fall in the midrange of the income distribution, total spending on employer plan premiums and potential out-of-pocket costs to meet deductibles amounted to 11.7 percent of income last year, up from 7.8 percent a decade earlier."[10] The average annual, employer-based insurance premium in 2018 was $6,896 for single coverage and $19,616 for family coverage.[11]

Individual Mandate

The ACA mandated that individuals were to have health insurance as of 2012. Failure to do so would result in a penalty that would rise on a yearly basis. Congress repealed the penalty in 2017, scheduling the ruling to go into effect in 2019.

The ACA caused the individual health insurance market to undergo significant restructuring. States were required to create state health insurance markets. The federal government stepped in to create the markets in states that refused or could not manage to do so. Insurance companies were under no obligation to participate in state markets, and state insurance regulators were under no obligation to accept applications from insurance companies interested in entering markets. The result is that the markets are not the same from state to state.

The law created four "metal" plan levels that differ by the percentage of charges that enrollees would be responsible for paying for health care before insurance coverage kicks in. That is the *deductible*. *Co-payment* is the out-of-pocket cost to the consumer of health care. The following is based on 2018 costs:

Platinum: no deductible; 10 percent co-payment for services

Gold: no deductible; 20 percent co-payment for services

Silver: $2,250 deductible; 30 percent co-payment for services

Bronze: $6,000 deductible; 40 percent co-payment for services

The premium insurance companies can charge for insurance policies or "products" is not regulated. The thinking behind this arrangement was that the price differences between the policies available in the health insurance market would be clear to consumers. All plans were required to cover a list of basic services. The deductibles were fixed for each level of plan. Sellers were expected to compete over price of premiums and other amenities the insurer was willing to offer to attract buyers. The stated intent was to ensure that consumers would be able to choose the plan that best met their needs and preferences.

The law includes a number of provisions that have had a significant impact on the individual market. The prohibition against denial of coverage for a preexisting condition is the one that presented the greatest challenge to insurance sellers. Other provisions that pose less of a problem include coverage of an annual physical and coverage of persons under age 26 under their parents' policies. In order to ease the financial burden on individuals, two government-sponsored subsidies were introduced. One is *tax credit subsidies*, which can be taken at the time of purchase, when taxes are filed, or in some combination of timing, were made available to persons whose income fell between 100 and 400 percent of poverty. (The 2019 100 percent poverty line for individuals is $12,140 and $25,100 for a family of four; the 400 percent for an individual is $48,560 and $100,400 for a family of four.) The other is *cost-sharing subsidies*, limited to the Silver plan and made available to persons whose income fell between 100 and 250 percent of poverty. More about this in the next chapter.

The penalty for not observing the individual mandate was repealed in 2017 to go into effect as of 2019.

Medicaid and Medicare

The ACA required states to expand Medicaid coverage to all persons under 138 percent of poverty or lose Medicaid funding altogether. The Supreme Court held this section of the law to be unconstitutional, which allowed twenty-six states to refuse to extend Medicaid coverage. The law provided 100 percent reimbursement to states for every new Medicaid enrollee during 2014–2016 and 90 percent reimbursement through 2020. A number of governors have had a change of heart since the law was passed. As of 2017, thirty-six states had expanded Medicaid.

The ACA left basic Medicare coverage intact.

ASSESSING MARKET-BASED HEALTH INSURANCE AFTER THE ACA

After years of failed effort, the ACA was passed largely because the Democrats, who had been advocating universal coverage for most of the twentieth century, had gained control over the two branches of government involved in legislation. However, passage was not a sure thing. It required a range of compromises.

The framers of the ACA legislation succeeded by constructing a framework combining a liberal goal, health insurance coverage for everyone, with a conservative approach, private sector health care insurance. Requiring those individuals without employer-based or public insurance to buy their own health insurance in the state-based health marketplace allowed the individual mandate to go forward. The employer mandate had little effect on large employers who were providing health insurance coverage already. The employer mandate had the greatest impact on small employers. The fact that they would be shopping for private sector health care coverage, with some support from the government, helped to justify the mandate. While the law did introduce new government regulations, it left control over provision of the country's health insurance arrangements largely in the hands of the private sector. In short, the ACA legislation, produced by the government, is grounded in a market-based approach to health insurance coverage.

Attempting to assess how well market-based health insurance is working in the wake of passage of the ACA is not easy. Interpretation varies depending on the indicator one chooses to use, whether it is at the national level or by state, health insurance costs, or proportion of the population that has gained coverage. The time span used to evaluate change is important. The question of whether the ACA has had a beneficial effect on the health status of Americans—a question of some importance, one would think—is something that will take a few years to answer. Most people suffer from and die of chronic illnesses that develop over time, so rates of change in health status do not occur over a year or two. But the evidence is mounting.

At certain moments I fall back on believing that the analytical perspective that captures the workings of the health insurance market best involves the imagery of the staircases in Harry Potter movies. The staircases shift while the person is climbing them, they end in open space, and some are there one moment and gone the next. Fixing those staircases in place requires that we agree on the measures we want to use to evaluate success. Of course, before we can do that, we have to agree on the objectives we want to achieve: Better health status in the population is only one option. Proving the validity of the market-based model of health care stands as another option.

At a more conventional analytical level, I would like to return to the basic question posed at the beginning of this chapter: How well does private sector health insurance conform to basic tenets of the free-market theoretical model? I begin with the first of the three basic features of the model I identified previously: many buyers and many sellers.

MANY BUYERS AND MANY SELLERS

The market-based health care model does not specify an ideal seller-to-buyer ratio. It asserts that the presence of large numbers of both buyers and sellers is necessary for establishing a balance between the supply of and demand for goods and services. The mix of buyers and sellers in the employer-based market is very different than it is in the individual market. Let's start with the employer-based market.

The Employer-Based Market

Identifying the participants poses the first hurdle. Who the sellers are is perfectly clear. Who the buyers are is not nearly as clear. Employees are buyers only in the sense that they pay a portion of the premium for the plan in which they are enrolled. Employers decide the proportion of the cost of the plan employees must assume. Employees' choice of plans is restricted by the employers' decisions regarding the plan or plans they make available to employees. It seems to me that it would be more accurate to call employees "payers" rather than "buyers."

The employer-based market operates at the national level. There is no count of the number of insurance companies that have come and gone since the employer-based health insurance market took off during the middle of the twentieth century. What is readily apparent is that competition worked to weed out a lengthy list of health insurance companies just as the free-market model would predict. A number of smaller companies survived and continue to operate in regional markets. As of 2018, five major health insurance companies remain in the national market: Cigna, UnitedHealth Group, Aetna, Humana, and the Blue Cross network. (The for-profit Anthem Corporation owns and operates Blue Cross organizations in fourteen states.)

The imbalance between the small number of sellers and the large number of buyers in this market attracted some comment as the number of insurance companies continued to decline. However, the trend did not result in business media headlines until 2015. This is when two sets of mergers were announced: a merger between Anthem and Cigna and another between Aetna and Humana.

Business-page editorial writers and others called upon to comment on the matter argued that reducing the number of insurance companies to three meant that the market would be less competitive and that start-ups, which were already having a very hard time entering the market, would have an even harder time competing with the well-capitalized behemoths. These assessments were accompanied by what appeared to be a unanimously called-for solution, namely, government stepping in to enforce antitrust regulations.

> Anthem, which operates for-profit Blue Cross plans in 14 states, merging with Cigna, another large for-profit carrier, along with the planned deal for Aetna to

join Humana, a smaller rival known for its private Medicare plans, would create two behemoths.

Along with the already enormous UnitedHealth Group, these companies would control nearly half of the American commercial health insurance market.[12]

A federal judge blocked the proposed $37 billion Aetna-Humana merger in January 2017. The Cigna-Anthem merger was blocked by another federal judge in May 2017. The latter merger was complicated by the fact that Cigna rejected the $48 billion acquisition offer. Cigna went on to file a complaint against Anthem, seeking $1.85 billion in a termination fee and additional damages of $13 billion.

The Rationale for Seeking to Merge

The reasons offered by the companies to explain the planned mergers deserve consideration. Company representatives said that they were seeking to benefit from "economies of scale." They said they wished to reduce costs incurred by the need to compete with other companies. They argued that many functions carried out by competing companies are duplicative and that merging office operations would eliminate administrative waste. Furthermore, they pointed out that becoming larger would provide them with a better bargaining position in interactions with providers of health care goods and services, which would result in lower costs, better quality, greater opportunities for diversification—that is, new business ventures—and, of course, higher stock prices, not to mention increased profits. In reaction to the court ruling against the Anthem-Cigna merger, Anthem representatives stated that consumers would be negatively affected. They would be denied improvements in access to high-quality care and denied more than $2 billion in medical cost savings.

The claim that insurers in markets where there are many sellers have the power to reduce the price of health care goods and services is often cited. True. (The competition among hospitals in California suggests that it has the opposite result, but we will have to get back to that in chapter 8.) But a finding that is repeated less often is more revealing: "There is little evidence that these savings will be passed on to consumers through lower premiums."[13]

The effects of the proposed health insurance company mergers and acquisitions on competition are continually and extensively debated in the business press. However, I believe that the points made by the companies in arguing for the benefits of merging their operations have not received as much attention as they deserve. Why have they not? That question brings me to some other whopping big questions related to the assumptions underlying the market-based health care model.

To begin with, one fundamental question revolves around what competition is supposed to achieve. Competition, based on dictionary definitions, is a contest for a prize; rivalry for supremacy; rivalry between two or more persons or groups for an object desired in common, usually resulting in a victor and a loser. The reduction from five remaining competitors, in this case five health insurance companies, to three is the logical progression of competition. Reduction to one winner is not conceivable, given the objections, by anyone with any say, to monopolization of the health insurance market.

Assuming there is little disagreement about the need to prevent the emergence of a single winner, ongoing talk about the value of competition in the health insurance market provokes the following questions:

- Aren't all competitive matches set up to produce a winner? Doesn't that mean that competitors would, under normal circumstances, continue to drop out until there is a single winner? Isn't that the whole point of all competitive pursuits? Isn't a reduction in the number of competitors predictable?
- Why was a field of five remaining competitors not nearly as objectionable as the prospect of three remaining competitors? Is there some sort of unstated understanding that competition is successful when five competitors are in the field? What makes five competitors left in the race acceptable and three competitors objectionable? Is there really that much difference?
- Isn't the demand that the government step in to prevent the competition from continuing to reduce the number of competitors in the race inconsistent with free-market principles? Isn't the demand that the government intervene by imposing antitrust legislation, to stop mergers between insurance companies, a violation of the antigovernment doctrine that is central to free-market theory?
- How do advocates of the free-market canon deal with the reasons the companies seeking to merge explain why they wish to do that? How do free-market advocates respond to the argument presented by competitors who say competition requires that they engage in costly, wasteful practices? And in arguing that reducing duplication of administrative processes is the

solution, aren't they charging that competition creates inefficiencies? And doesn't this mean that competition is itself an obstacle to lowering prices?

Market-Based Health Care and the Individual Market

The ACA requires states to establish health insurance markets to let private insurers sell health insurance policies on an individual basis. Many states have created their own state-based markets; others have left the task to the federal government. Insurance companies are under no obligation to participate in state-based markets. They can choose to participate in the markets in some states but not in others. If the insurance company does decide to participate, it must be licensed by the state to sell insurance policies in that state. States have different regulations governing the rules under which health insurance companies can do business in the state. Some states have chosen to limit the number of companies allowed to participate in state markets; others have not.

As sellers, insurance companies may not "bother" to enter state markets where the number of potential buyers is small. Not surprisingly, insurance sellers are readier to participate in urban areas where markets offer larger populations of potential buyers. That is where they can expect to find greater demand. They may choose not to participate in state markets in states populated by larger numbers of persons who qualify for Medicare or Medicaid; those populations reduce the number of potential buyers of market-based insurance. The result is that there are fewer sellers in some regions of the country than in other regions—not because buyers have not been willing to buy insurance, since they have been required to do so by law, but because insurance companies are not willing to sell it. It turns out that potential customers aren't all equally desirable. The effect is that there is a considerable amount of competition in some areas and little competition in other areas where there are only a few sellers, a single seller, or even no sellers. (Reports indicate that the situation may have stabilized between 2017 and 2018, meaning that there are no communities without sellers. This is explained by the fact that insurance companies raised their rates enough to ensure profitability over the last year.)

One interpretation for the decline in number of sellers willing to participate in state insurance markets in the recent past is related to the mergers and acquisitions phenomenon. According to some pundits, mergers and acquisitions occur when CEOs are confident that the economy is growing. As one CEO puts it, you want "a tail wind not a head wind."[14] He goes on to say that if mergers serve as a good indicator of a strong economy, the lack of mergers and acquisitions is a sign of negative economic trends: falling stock market prices, for a start, and eventually a rising level of anxiety about job security in the public sphere. That in turn affects consumers' views about being able to afford health insurance (among other things) and increases their readiness to buy the cheapest policy. The concatenation effect looks like this: fewer consumers buying higher-priced policies, which causes sellers to reduce the number of offerings, which leads to lower profits, which leads to sellers leaving markets that are less profitable than initially projected. There appears to be some inconsistency in the assessment of the impact of market concentration. From the business executive perspective, market concentration is a sign of a strong economy. That may be a good thing for the country as a whole but not necessarily a good thing when it involves the specific sector we are discussing.

Research conducted by the Government Accountability Office, at the request of Congress, on the concentration of the health insurance market in the four years following passage of the ACA found that markets were concentrated among a small number of insurers in most states. A 2016 Kaiser Family Foundation analysis found a great deal of variation by state. The market share controlled by the largest insurer ranged from 21 percent in Wisconsin to 96 percent in Wyoming with an average of 57 percent across all states. In five states, the largest insurer had more than 90 percent of the market.

In summing up the situation, it appears that state-based health insurance markets function the way the market-based health care model says they should function in some parts of the country but not in others. Regions of the country that are sparsely populated do not have the number of potential consumers to make it worthwhile for sellers to enter those markets. This leads to a number of observations and related questions such as the following:

- If sellers are readier to participate in markets in which they can expect profit and stay out of markets where the prospects of profit are low, what are the consequences for buyers of health insurance? For sellers?
- Doesn't this mean that there is not only little competition in some areas of the country but that there might be no sellers and therefore . . . no market?
- Is having market-based health care operating in some parts of the country but not in others understandable and perfectly acceptable according to market-based health insurance advocates?

- If rising prices are what assure participation, what happens to the idea that competition would lower prices?

CONSUMER CHOICE

In focusing on consumer choice of health insurance, it is good to keep in mind, as mentioned earlier, that consumers of employer-based insurance are not the primary decision-makers in this exchange. Small numbers of employers make the choice for large numbers of employees. One can argue, however, that employer-based insurance fits the market-based health care model because the number of health insurance sellers and the number of employers are less imbalanced than is true of the vast number of employees—that is buyers, who are the ultimate consumers of the health insurance products—compared to the number of health insurance sellers. The idea of numbers of buyers and sellers being more evenly matched fulfills one of the basic tenets of free-market theory.

"[Employer-based] plans were historically far more comprehensive and cost-protective than individual market coverage. However, over the past decade, premium cost pressures have led companies to share increasing amounts of health costs with workers, particularly in the form of higher deductibles."[15]

That does make one wonder,

- Why is the price of health insurance not falling in response to this basic free-market theoretical proposition regarding how the interaction between supply and demand affects price?

Turning to the individual health insurance market and consumer choice, this is where individuals do choose the product they buy. The fact that this market is characterized by vast numbers of buyers and very few sellers means that it does not conform to the market-based health care model precepts we have been considering.

- Does that lack of conformity to the market-based model help to explain why the price of health insurance is not falling?

Persons covered by both individual or employer-based insurance are increasingly facing rising out-of-pocket costs, which carries the risk of turning into underinsurance. "This is occurring at a time when wages have been largely stagnant, and even seemingly modest out-of-pocket expenses can be difficult for people with little in savings."[16] In short, because of high out-of-pocket costs, people are having problems paying medical bills and/or are failing to seek care because of cost. Consumers are obviously not choosing to be in this situation. That raises very basic questions:

- Are rising out-of-pocket costs having an effect on the quality and/or price of the product health insurance sellers are offering? Are the policies that consumers can afford (that is, the Bronze plan with a 40 percent deductible) leaving consumers "underinsured"?
- To what extent is the introduction of the newest version of much cheaper, scaled-down plans that offer far less coverage (e.g., Association Plans) a reflection of consumer preference? Or of something else?

While these criticisms and concerns are certainly worth attending to, the underlying assumption that consumers are fully equipped to choose—that they have sufficient information on price and quality to determine utility—is especially troubling. Remember, buyers are expected to shop for the health insurance policy that, as proponents of the market-based approach always say, "best serves their needs and preferences." That brings us to the topic of health insurance literacy.

Health Insurance Literacy

In entering the marketplace and deciding which policy to buy, consumers must understand the information on quality and price they are presented with. The four metal tiers were created to address this problem, to clarify the basic differences. It did not take long to find that consumers did not fully understand the insurance products on offer in the state-based health insurance markets. Comprehension of the terminology used to identify differences across the four metal levels of plans is a basic requirement. Understanding what is meant by *premium, deductible,* and *out-of-pocket costs* is only the first step. Knowing how the terms interact with each other to add up to what the enrollee will end up paying is far more complicated. Beyond that, awareness of the dates that enrollment periods begin and end and of the consequences of not enrolling is essential. Discerning what the plan covers is a far bigger challenge for obvious reasons. The list of health problems with which the consumer is afflicted or may be concerned about having covered is endless. There is no way they could all be listed. If one does not come to the market concerned about a specific diagnosis, then what is and is not covered may come as a surprise when a person receives a diagnosis and finds that the recommended treatment is not covered. Enrollees may also be surprised to find that the kinds of tests and treatments that they expected to be covered are not covered. In some instances, coverage requires the doctor to spend time convincing the insurance company that the treatment should be covered. Coverage may depend on whether the person inputting the information on the diagnosis knows which iteration or electronic code for the diagnosis will result in coverage. Is it any wonder that buying health insurance is perplexing?

Buying health insurance through state markets is done online. Buyers are expected to be computer literate in addition to being health insurance literate. When it became clear that buyers were having difficulties evaluating the "product" they were required to purchase, the solution came in the form of a person who would help. This occurred in 2014 in the wake of the first enrollment period. The federal government created a new occupational category—"assisters"—charged with helping consumers shop for health insurance. They were renamed sometime later and became known as "navigators." In short, it became clear that interactions between buyers and sellers in the health insurance market required an intermediary who could explain the products to buyers. By the end of 2016, more than 4,600 navigator programs were in existence, staffed by an untold number of navigators.[17]

In an effort to further assist consumers in making buying decisions and evaluating the utility of the product, health policy makers created a decision-making tool, a "cost estimator." It was designed to help consumers compute total costs of the combination of premiums, deductibles, and out-of-pocket costs. Cost estimators were available in most states by 2016, the fourth enrollment period. As health policy analysts point out, cost estimators stand as yet another attempt to address consumers' inability to act as informed buyers:

> Health insurance is complicated: many people have difficulty understanding and applying key insurance concepts. The complexities are compounded when individuals must weigh the features of competing plans—a task most people

dread and do not do well. Consumers who are confused or overwhelmed by their options may be discouraged from enrolling, while those who choose poorly are likely to face higher costs or be unhappy with their plans. . . .

People may understand differences in plan premiums, but evidence shows many have a hard time evaluating out-of-pocket spending, a calculation that requires consumers to understand plans' cost-sharing structures and predict the amount and kind of care their household is likely to use.[18]

The tool did not turn out to be a perfect solution because some navigators had reservations about using it. The reasons navigators gave for not using it include "time pressure, insufficient training, reluctance to change ways of providing assistance, and concerns about accuracy." And, it did little to overcome the challenge inherent in predicting how much health care the household could expect to use.

New and improved cost estimator tools have been introduced since then. For example, the Kaiser Family Foundation offers one that is simple to use: https://www.kff.org/interactive/subsidy-calculator/.

Government officials have taken a different direction in the wake of the 2016 elections. Funding for navigators was cut in 2017 by 41 percent. In 2018, funding was cut again, meaning that funding has fallen by 84 percent over the last two years. While presented as an effort to reduce government expenditures, it has the effect of reducing access to health insurance and by extension to health care. The reason the navigator program was created in the first place was to assist people in shopping for health insurance. The reduction in funding is a reversal of that objective. People did not suddenly become more competent shoppers, and the market-based approach did not suddenly make it easier for consumers to understand health insurance products.

Shopping

Learning how to interpret the cost and coverage of a health insurance plan is just the beginning of the shopping experience. Next is the matter of comparing plans. The Consumers Union, which collects information and uses the *Consumer Reports* publication and website to report reviews of the products it evaluates, explains what makes this task so challenging.[19] It makes the following observation: "Consumers . . . can face between 20 and 40 options. A key question that policymakers must consider: is more choice better?"

Look at the options that confront consumers in the individual market. In addition to considering the features of the four metal tiers, buyers may be forced to choose among additional options that govern the selection of health care providers, that is, EPO, POS, PPO, and HMO managed care arrangements:

- POS, Point of Service. The enrollee must get a referral from a primary doctor to see a specialist.
- PPO, Preferred Provider Organization. The enrollee may seek care from providers outside of the network but is charged more for such care.
- HMO, Health Maintenance Organization. The enrollee is limited to seeking care from network doctors, a "gatekeeper" who is a primary care provider is generally expected to oversee care, and services provided outside of the network are covered only in cases of an emergency. Enrollees pay a fixed annual fee. Physicians are generally paid per enrollee, that is, on a capitation basis.
- EPO, Exclusive Provider Organization. The enrollee is limited to seeking care from a narrow list of network providers, which includes many but not necessarily all specialists; enrollees may self-refer to specialists; services provided outside of the network are generally not covered even in cases of an emergency. Physicians are paid on a fee-for-service basis.

Insurers are under no obligation to offer all four alternatives. However, buyers still face the complicated task of figuring out who the providers are, associated with whatever managed care arrangements the seller chooses to offer, known as "networks." Patients who wish to have a continuing relationship with a doctor of long standing may have difficulty determining whether the doctor belongs to a particular network, and they may at some point find that the doctor is suddenly out of the network. (A lot more on networks is covered in chapter 5, "Doctors.")

Based on a review of the literature on choice, the Consumers Union states that "a little bit of choice is good" but that "too many choices undermine consumer decision making":

> People have cognitive limits on what they can absorb and analyze. When the amount of information exceeds a person's ability to assess it, the cognitive costs impair their decision making abilities.

Cognitive costs can be broken down into three types: time, error and psychic costs. The time cost of choice is, literally, the increased amount of time required to make a decision. The larger or more complex the choice set, the larger the likelihood of errors in the decision making process. The psychic costs of choice involve the emotional effort that has to be expended to make the choice.[20]

Choosing a health insurance policy is made more consequential by the financial commitment that it requires. The high stakes involved increase the cognitive costs. This, in turn, increases the chances of undesirable effects such as delaying or avoiding the decision, delegating the decision, and experiencing loss of confidence or regret regarding the choice.[21]

As if going through the decision-making process once is not enough of a burden, consumers in both the individual and employer-based markets are expected to repeat the process again and again. Policy makers committed to making the market-based arrangement work say that it is important to review one's decision about the policy on an annual basis during the open enrollment period because, they say, competition will produce plans that are better and cheaper. In actuality, advocating choice is an "underhanded way to segment the market." (I am indebted to Michael Ash for that observation.) Buyers are regularly scolded for failing to fulfill the role they have been assigned: that of shoppers who will make the effort to inform themselves and select the best buy. It is more common for consumers to just re-up without checking to see if there are cheaper plans available to them. In doing this, they are refusing to act in accordance with the theoretical model, refusing to fulfill the expectations it holds forth.

Consumer behavior is at the heart of the claim that we have entered the era of "consumer-driven" health care. Advocates of market-based health care maintain that the choices consumers make in the health insurance market is a determining factor governing price and quality of this product. That raises a whole series of questions:

- How convincing is the portrayal of the role consumers are expected to play in this market?
- If consumers have difficulty determining the costs involved and other features of the product they are shopping for, isn't this a clear sign that the

market-based health care arrangement is not meeting the promise of providing consumers with a real choice?

- Isn't the purpose of insurance to cover unanticipated costs? Doesn't that sound inconsistent with saying that consumers should estimate the need for health care over the next year in evaluating which policy to purchase? Isn't that exactly what health insurance is supposed to do—deal with unanticipated health care costs?

- Don't all the problems associated with choosing a health insurance plan outlined above make it a burdensome ordeal rather than the gratifying experience that results in a product that serves a person's needs and preferences?

- How much does the reluctance to spend time studying health insurance offerings have to do with the fact that shopping for health insurance is not something anyone looks forward to doing? That it is unlike shopping for products that the buyer is eager to purchase and willing to spend time and energy getting information on before making a choice, because the shopping experience itself in those cases brings satisfaction?

- Doesn't the introduction of a new category of health care workers, assisters or navigators, confirm the fact that buyers are poorly qualified to evaluate health insurance products on their own?

EASE OF ENTRY AND EXIT

The fact that Amazon, Berkshire Hathaway, and JPMorgan Chase have joined together to craft a plan to cut health care costs for their employees has grabbed the attention of the business media in general and health insurance industry watchers in particular. The question that some are posing is, Can Amazon do for the health insurance market what it has done for books and bookstores plus a whole lot of other products? In combination, the three companies employ about one million people, which is actually a small proportion of employed Americans. However, what the leaders of these three companies come up with will be given careful consideration. We will have to wait and see how that turns out.

One of the most commonly voiced claims made by proponents of market-based health care is that it is efficient, that it eliminates the waste characteristic of public programs. I don't find that to be convincing. Indeed, I believe that there is something very different going on. Let's take a closer look at how the market-based approach aims to achieve greater efficiency. I would argue that the singularly most important mechanism employed by market-based health insurance companies in their quest for efficiency is based on reducing *access* to care. Prior to passage of the ACA, which prohibited exclusion on the basis of preexisting conditions, persons with preexisting health conditions or those whose health profile indicated potential risk of new health problems were simply cut out of the health insurance market. Not having the option to exclude applicants with preexisting health conditions meant that insurance companies had to face a steep learning curve to calculate risk in populations that include high-risk applicants—that is, to avoid "adverse selection" of consumers who have a greater chance of using more health care services and thereby negatively affect the company's bottom line.

Market-based health care proponents continued to laud the private sector for creating innovative mechanisms to achieve efficiency after they were prohibited from considering preexisting conditions. But a closer look at the variations on managed care, EPO, POS, PPO, and HMO arrangements reveals that the underlying mechanism amounts to reduction of access to care. The narrowing of networks limits access to more expensive care. Since quality is not a consideration, this is not a mechanism designed to limit access to low quality, expensive care. Thus the mechanisms may be innovative in design but not innovative in basic purpose.

Restricting access using the newly devised arrangements may appear to increase efficiency, but it is at the cost of increased complexity, which has a negative impact on administrative costs in the short term and the potential of higher health care costs in the long term. Incentives aimed at increasing efficiency employ annual-review accounting models and measures to determine provider reimbursement. This is a short-term time line that focuses largely on the delivery of acute care services. However, according to the Centers for Disease Control and Prevention (CDC), six out of ten Americans have a chronic disease and four out of ten have two chronic diseases, meaning that "90% of the nation's annual health care expenditures are for people with chronic and mental health conditions."[22]

Medigap insurance provides another vivid example of the relationship between efficiency and access. Consider the fact that consumers have

a one-time, 6-month open enrollment period that begins when they first enroll in Medicare Part B. . . . Only four states (CT, MA, ME, NY) require either continuous or annual guaranteed issue. . . . Guaranteed issue prohibits insurers from denying a Medigap policy to eligible applicants, including people with pre-existing conditions, such as diabetes and heart disease.[23]

In all other states, people seeking to buy a Medigap policy or to switch from a Medicare Advantage plan to traditional Medicare may be denied coverage due to a preexisting condition. This rather important piece of information is not well publicized, which makes delaying enrollment when it is initially offered or deciding to opt for Medicare Advantage more fateful than the consumer likely realizes. It certainly makes one wonder how many people know whether their state has passed legislation requiring private insurance companies to provide coverage for a preexisting condition.

The requirement that insurance companies cover preexisting conditions has been reversed at the national level with approval of Association Plans that are not required to provide such coverage. Associations are loose coalitions of organizations that have their own employees. Associations are not employers, so they are not covered by ACA regulations. Association plans are not in compliance with ACA regulations, which has led to court challenges.

From a big-picture perspective, there is good reason to expect that the rate of chronic illness will continue to rise as more acute illnesses become resistant to treatment and as the population continues to age. In the meantime, third-party incentive arrangements continue to focus on acute health care services. There is a disconnect. Indeed, current health insurance arrangements stand in opposition to the urgent need to create more efficient reimbursement arrangements to deal with the long-term health care issues of the chronically ill—issues that present as preexisting conditions.

UNDERINSURANCE

While the proportion of Americans who are uninsured has dropped significantly with the introduction of the individual and employer mandates, there is growing recognition that the number of people who are underinsured is rising. Underinsurance is defined by the percentage of income people spend on health care. In the case of lower-income families, this means spending 5 percent or more of income, and for higher-income families it means spending 10 percent or more.[24] It is estimated that 28 percent of working-age adults who have health insurance were underinsured in 2016. "People who are underinsured have high deductibles and out-of-pocket expenses relative to income. . . . More than half of the 41 million people estimated to be uninsured have coverage through an employer."[25]

> Among nonelderly households, the median level of liquid assets in 2016 was about $2,500 for single-person households and $5,000 for households with more than one person. This means that one-half of single-person households could only contribute $2,500 from their liquid assets to pay for cost sharing, and that one-half of multi-person households could contribute $5,000. These amounts were below the cost sharing requirements in many plans.[26]

Concern about affordability of insurance in the individual market has been attracting the most attention over the last few years. But there is also growing concern about underinsurance among persons covered by employer-based health insurance. According to the Commonwealth Fund, nearly a quarter of working-age adults with employer-based health insurance were underinsured. "The share of people covered by job-based insurance with deductibles exceeding 5 percent of household income grew sixfold, from 2 percent to 13 percent between 2003 and 2016."[27]

The main reason behind the rise of underinsurance is the fact that health insurance premiums are rising faster than wages. Insurers have been raising premiums in the face of uncertainty about the extent to which the government will be willing to take steps to stabilize the health insurance market in the future.

SUMMING UP: SOME REFLECTIONS
ON CONSUMER-DRIVEN HEALTH CARE

Proponents of market-based health care hold forth an image of market transactions in which consumers play a defining role, claiming that we have entered an era of consumer-driven health care. It is not the right to choose one's doctor or the right to choose the kinds of tests and treatments or some combination of rights that is being lauded. It is the right of the consumer to make the choice of a health insurance policy based on "need and preference" that is at the center of the claim. Not only does the claim require that patients relinquish the role of patient and turn themselves into consumers of health care but it also requires that they turn themselves into dedicated shoppers.

Personally, I find the portrayal of shopping for health insurance to be unhinged from reality. Is there anyone out there who is ready to claim that people are eager to shop for health insurance, that they find satisfaction in scoring a great plan? Doesn't conversation about the experience amount to recounting how frustrating it is and how happy the person is to be done with it? Why are advocates of market-based health care surprised to find consumers who are forced to shop for health insurance expressing dissatisfaction about the process as much as the cost of the product? Critics regularly say that consumers could have purchased a more comprehensive policy at lower cost if they just shopped around, yet they don't.

In the end, as I noted earlier, it is easier to shop for products that one can see and evaluate as opposed to products that are intangible, including the bundle of services known as an insurance policy. And deciding which insurance policy to buy is just the first hurdle in gaining assurance that one can see the doctor one wants to see and receive the medical services one thinks are necessary. Most people would agree that shopping for doctors, hospitals, and medical care has more meaning to them than shopping for insurance.

NOTES

1. National Center for Health Statistics, "Table 102. Private Health Insurance Coverage among Persons under Age 65, by Selected Characteristics: United States, Selected Years 1984–2016," CDC/National Center for Health Statistics, 2017, https://www.cdc.gov/nchs/data/hus/2017/102.pdf.

2. National Center for Health Statistics, "Table 103. Private Health Insurance Obtained through the Workplace among Persons under Age 65, by Selected Characteristics: United States, Selected Years 1984–2015," CDC/National Center for Health Statistics, 2016, https://www.cdc.gov/nchs/data/hus/2016/103.pdf.

3. National Center for Health Statistics, "Table 105. No Health Insurance Coverage among Persons under Age 65, by Selected Characteristics: United States, Selected Years 1984–2016," CDC/National Center for Health Statistics, 2018, https://www.cdc.gov/nchs/data/hus/2017/105.pdf; "Key Facts about the Uninsured Population," Kaiser Family Foundation, December 7, 2018, https://www.kff.org/uninsured/fact-sheet/key-facts-about-the-uninsured-population/.

4. Robin Cohen, Michael Martinez, and Emily Zammitti, "Health Insurance Coverage: Early Release of Estimates from the National Health Interview Survey, January–March 2018," CDC/National Center for Health Statistics, August 2018, https://www.cdc.gov/nchs/data/nhis/earlyrelease/insur201808.pdf.

5. Sara Collins et al., "First Look at Health Insurance Coverage in 2018 Finds ACA Gains Beginning to Reverse," Commonwealth Fund, May 1, 2018, https://www.com monwealthfund.org/blog/2018/first-look-health-insurance-coverage-2018-finds-aca -gains-beginning-reverse; Edward R. Berchick, Emily Hood, and Jessica C. Barnett, "Health Insurance Coverage in the United States: 2017," United States Census Bureau, September 12, 2018, https://www.census.gov/library/publications/2018/ demo/p60-264.html.

6. Cohen, Martinez, and Zammitti, "Health Insurance Coverage."

7. Collins et al., "First Look at Health Insurance Coverage in 2018."

8. Philip Bump, "The Hard-to-Answer Question at the Core of the Health-Care Fight: How Many More People Might Die?" *Washington Post*, June 27, 2017.

9. Robin Cohen, Emily Zammitti, and Michael Martinez, "Health Insurance Coverage: Early Release of Estimates from the National Health Interview Survey, 2017," CDC/National Center for Health Statistics, May 2018, https://www.cdc.gov/ nchs/data/nhis/earlyrelease/insur201805.pdf; Michael Martinez, Emily Zammitti, and Robin Cohen, "Health Insurance Coverage: Early Release of Estimates from the National Health Interview Survey, January–September 2017," CDC/National Center for Health Statistics, February 2018, https://www.cdc.gov/nchs/data/nhis/ earlyrelease/insur201802.pdf.

10. "Americans Are Paying More for Employer Health Coverage," Commonwealth Fund, December 18, 2018, https://www.commonwealthfund.org/publications/news letter-article/2018/dec/americans-are-paying-more-employer-health-coverage.

11. "Premiums for Employer-Sponsored Family Health Coverage Rise 5% to Average $19,616; Single Premiums Rise 3% to $6,896," Kaiser Family Foundation, October 3, 2018, https://www.kff.org/health-costs/press-release/employer-sponsored-family -coverage-premiums-rise-5-percent-in-2018/.

12. Reed Abelson, "Bigger May Be Better for Health Insurers, but Doubts Remain for Consumers," *New York Times*, August 3, 2015, 1 (Business).

13. Richard Scheffer and David Arnold, "Insurers Market Power Lowers Prices in Numerous Concentrated Provider Markets," *Health Affairs* 36, no. 9 (September 2017): 1539–46.

14. Andrew Ross Sorkin, "C.E.O.s Voice Confidence, but Deals Say Otherwise," *New York Times*, June 13, 2017.

15. Sara Collins, Munira Gunja, and Michelle Doty, "How Well Does Insurance Coverage Protect Consumers from Health Care Costs?" Commonwealth Fund, October 18, 2017, https://www.commonwealthfund.org/publications/issue-briefs/2017/oct/how-well-does-insurance-coverage-protect-consumers-health-care.

16. Bradley Sawyer, Cynthia Cox, and Gary Claxton, "An Analysis of Who Is Most at Risk for High Out-Of-Pocket Health Spending," Peterson-Kaiser Health System Tracker, https://www.healthsystemtracker.org/brief/who-is-most-at-risk-for-high-out-of-pocket-health-spending/.

17. Karen Pollitz, Jennifer Tolbert, and Rosa Ma, "2015 Survey of Health Insurance Marketplace Assister Programs and Brokers," Kaiser Family Foundation, August 6. 2015, https://www.kff.org/health-reform/report/2015-survey-of-health-insurance-marketplace-assister-programs-and-brokers/.

18. Justin Giovanelli and Emily Curran, "Efforts to Support Consumer Enrollment Decisions Using Total Cost Estimators: Lessons from the Affordable Care Act's Marketplaces," Commonwealth Fund, February 8, 2017, https://www.commonwealthfund.org/publications/issue-briefs/2017/feb/efforts-support-consumer-enrollment-decisions-using-total-cost.

19. Consumers Union, "The Evidence Is Clear: Too Many Health Insurance Choices Can Impair, Not Help, Consumer Decision Making," *Consumer Reports*, November 1, 2012, https://advocacy.consumerreports.org/research/report-the-evidence-is-clear-too-many-health-insurance-choices-can-impair-not-help-consumer-decision-making/.

20. Consumers Union, "The Evidence Is Clear."

21. George Loewenstein and Saurabh Bhargava, "The Simple Case against Health Insurance Complexity," NEJM Catalyst, August 23, 2016, https://catalyst.nejm.org/simple-case-health-insurance-complexity/.

22. National Center for Chronic Disease Prevention and Health Promotion (NCCDPHP), "Chronic Diseases in America," last reviewed March 18, 2019, https://www.cdc.gov/chronicdisease/resources/infographic/chronic-diseases.htm.

23. Cristina Boccuti et al., "Medigap Enrollment and Consumer Protections Vary across States," Kaiser Family Foundation, July 11, 2018, https://www.kff.org/medicare/issue-brief/medigap-enrollment-and-consumer-protections-vary-across-states/.

24. "Underinsured Rate Increased Sharply in 2016; More Than Two of Five Marketplace Enrollees and a Quarter of People with Employer Health Insurance

Plans Are Now Underinsured," Commonwealth Fund, October 18, 2017, https:// www.commonwealthfund.org/press-release/2017/underinsured-rate-increased -sharply-2016-more-two-five-marketplace-enrollees-and.

25. "Number of Americans with Inadequate Health Insurance Coverage Rose Sharply in 2016," Commonwealth Fund, October 30, 2017, https://www.common wealthfund.org/publications/newsletter-article/2017/oct/number-americans -inadequate-health-insurance-coverage-rose.

26. Matthew Rae, Gary Claxton, and Larry Levitt, "Do Health Plan Enrollees Have Enough Money to Pay Cost Sharing?" Kaiser Family Foundation, November 3, 2017, https://www.kff.org/health-costs/issue-brief/do-health-plan-enrollees-have-enough -money-to-pay-cost-sharing/.

27. David Blumenthal, "The Decline of Employer-Sponsored Health Insurance," Commonwealth Fund, December 7, 2017, https://www.commonwealthfund.org/ blog/2017/decline-employer-sponsored-health-insurance.

4

Government Intervention and Health Insurance

While my students' recommendation—that the government get out of the way—seems on the surface to be a fairly clear policy statement, it is anything but that. Most of the students are not of the age to appreciate the call for government to "get its paws off my Medicare" that was prominently voiced prior to passage of the Affordable Care Act (ACA). I mention this call for getting government out of the way to suggest, once again, that the public's level of understanding of government involvement in health care leaves a lot to be desired.

It is interesting to see that, upon closer examination, one finds that in some cases proponents of market-based health care, as the political pundits would put it, "talk the talk but don't walk the walk." They say they want the government out of the way. In the meantime, the same proponents are actively engaged in arguing that mechanisms be put in place—by the government—that are designed to protect private health sector organizations. This doesn't always work out so well largely because the relationship between the government and the health care sector is not a steady one. It changes with the party in office.

Discussing government intervention becomes more problematic the closer we get to identifying how getting it out of the way could happen. The government is not a single entity. The federal government consists of three branches: the executive branch, Congress, and the Supreme Court. Within the federal government is a whole host of agencies, some with a great deal more power than others, and their power may always be diminished or expanded by one of the branches. Then there are state governments and even local governments all playing a sizable role. What really matters has to do with the values and beliefs of the political party in office. They affect who wins and who loses when laws and regulations are legislated. We return to consider the values underlying the government's role in health care more closely in the final chapters of the book.

This chapter documents six cases of government involvement in health insurance coverage arrangements. The lesson it holds is that government is inextricably intertwined with those arrangements. The cases include the following: (1) government subsidies introduced to help consumers afford health insurance in the individual market; (2) mechanisms established to minimize the risk of financial loss for insurers in individual market transactions; (3) government incentives provided to the private sector to foster competition with a major public insurance program, that is, Medicare; (4) Medicaid waivers and state Medicaid programs; (5) accountable care organizations (ACOs); and (6) Medicare Part D.

In looking at these examples I cannot help but see a scene in which the original intent of the legislation becomes obscured as soon as it appears on the health policy stage. It would do well to remember that we will witness what happens when concerted efforts to do what my students said they wanted to see happen—to get the government out of the way—are actively pursued by some politicians. There is turmoil.

One should expect that the particulars presented in this chapter constitute what amounts to a single still shot in a fast-moving video. In other words, the matters we discuss here can be expected to continue to undergo change. But there is good reason to believe that the lessons learned about how this happens should be (and are) remembered. It is in this spirit that I would like to begin by considering government subsidies legislated by the ACA to help consumers buy health insurance in state-based markets in the wake of the failure of the "repeal and replace" Obamacare effort.

CASE 1: GOVERNMENT SUBSIDIES AND THE INDIVIDUAL MARKET

Republicans began aggressively championing repeal as soon as the ACA was passed. They had no chance of achieving their objective until 2017, when they gained control of both Congress and the executive branch of government. The legislation Republicans introduced that was aimed at fulfilling their promise to repeal and replace Obamacare failed. The effort had an interesting effect—it made this government's role vis-à-vis the welfare of its citizens more transparent. The failure of repeal and replace morphed into a "stay with the law but chip away" effort or, as I like to think of it, messing around with the law. (I am afraid I don't see any other objective of the messing-around effort than getting more people off health insurance rolls. The effort is achieving results, as we saw in the last chapter.)

Political conservatives have long argued that people who had no health insurance were simply not interested in getting a job that would provide them with employer-based coverage. The onset of the Great Recession that befell the country in 2008 changed that. Stories in the media began to appear that challenged the idea that people were not willing to get a job. The stories often described the uninsured as hardworking small-business owners, employees of small businesses, and persons who had worked all their lives but had suddenly lost their jobs along with their health insurance. Nearly a fifth of the population had no health insurance in the years just prior to passage of the ACA. The stories revealed that the people who were not covered by employer-based insurance or public insurance plans wanted to buy health insurance but simply could not afford it. They wanted to work but could not find jobs.

Such stories did not deter Republicans, that is, the congressional majority and the president, from moving ahead to carry out their promise to repeal the ACA. They said that they were committed to cutting welfare to the undeserving. This took the form of eliminating the subsidies to persons who were enrolling in insurance through state markets. It seems that the Republicans were not prepared for the reaction of health insurance companies, which made it clear that the government dropping health insurance subsidies would force them to raise the price of insurance policies. The effect of talk about cutting subsidies that took place when the repeal and replace effort failed was to lift the veil on who really benefits from government-subsidized health insurance. The conservative ranks fell into disarray, with some dropping claims about welfare to the undeserving and others taking up the claim that the subsidies constitute corporate welfare.

Leaving welfare rhetoric aside, it became apparent that unsubsidized health insurance in state-based markets would become unaffordable for many consumers. In the absence of the subsidies, some people would be forced to drop out of the state-based health insurance markets. Insurance companies were certain to lose customers. The threat of eliminating the subsidies created market uncertainty. Insurers could not predict how many consumers would be in the market for health insurance. They announced that they would have to raise the price of premiums without saying by how much. And some said they were considering dropping out of state-based insurance markets altogether. While it was not clear at that time how well the markets would fare in the future, the immediate effects were interesting.

The role played by subsidies is central to understanding the effects. There are two kinds, as you may recall from the preceding chapter: *Cost-sharing reductions*, direct subsidies to assist those with incomes below 250 percent of poverty, were received by 53 percent of marketplace enrollees in 2018. *Premium tax credits*, available either at the end of the year or at the time of purchase of the insurance policy for everyone under 400 percent of poverty, benefited 87 percent of enrollees in 2018.[1]

The cut in cost-sharing subsidies going to persons with incomes under 250 percent of poverty was predicted for months but was made just weeks before state-based annual insurance enrollment was to begin in 2017. The subsidy was eliminated by executive order without the participation of Congress. In other words, there was no public debate about it in Congress. Although the congressional majority would have probably agreed to do the same thing, it did not get the chance. The point that is worth noting is that the elimination of cost-sharing funding was the act of one branch of government, the executive branch. That is not the same as saying the government did it. Americans might not make the distinction, because so much takes place in Washington, DC, that it is hard to follow it all. Tracking changes to health care law requires more attention than many people are willing to allot. Yet the question, What do you mean by government? is worth keeping in mind.

Insurance companies did what they said they would do. They responded to the turmoil and uncertainty taking place in 2016 by raising the price of 2017 premiums on the most popular plan, the Silver plan, and in some cases dropping out of the markets. Remember, the law did not change. It was not repealed, nor was it replaced. What changed is the withdrawal of government funding to support parts of the law. How much premiums increased varied by state. The premium in Arizona went from $207 to $507. That is a 145 percent increase, the highest of any state. While premiums rose in most states, they fell in a couple of states. The biggest drop occurred in Indiana, where the premium dropped from $298 to $286, a decline of 4 percent. Of course, there was enormous variation in the price of a health insurance policy before the increases took effect. In 2017, a forty-year-old nonsmoker could expect to pay $229 in Louisville or Cleveland and $904 in Anchorage.[2]

It is easy to see how the public would be confused about whether subsidies of any kind were still available. Because the law was not repealed, the cap on the amount consumers pay, "even if premiums go to the moon," as one pundit put it, remained intact.[3] That means that the increase in premiums was not hurting marketplace consumers eligible for subsidies, because the subsidies were not eliminated. But consumers whose income was higher than 400 percent of poverty did not receive subsidies before the insurance companies raised their rates. That group of consumers now faced paying considerably more because insurance companies increased the price of policies.

It is not likely that many Americans are fully aware of all the other changes affecting the workings of the ACA, that is, all those additional messing-around-with-the-law activities. This includes funding cuts, again by executive order, against navigators who were helping consumers understand health insurance options and changes in Medicaid regulations. Funding reductions to navigator programs ranging from 10 to 80 percent, depending on the state, were announced one day before enrollment for 2018 insurance coverage was to begin. There was no rationale provided for the differences in the amounts of decreases in funding, and there was no link to performance. The time allotted for enrollment was cut in half. Funds to allow for advertising the date that enrollment would start were eliminated.

In the meantime, insurance companies were cutting back on the commissions they paid to independent brokers who, operating outside of the state-based markets, typically sold policies to those who did not qualify for tax subsidies.[4] In short, shopping for health insurance in the individual health insurance markets became a lot more challenging largely as a result of the cuts in government funding and support.

There is more to this story. The government is not saving nearly as much as those who promoted cutting subsidies said it would. In fact, the tax credit subsidies now cost the government far more. Tax credit calculations are linked to the Silver plan. Because the Silver plan premiums increased but the government must, by law, continue to offer the tax credit subsidy, it is costing the government that much more. This has increased federal spending. The cost, projected to be $194 billion over the next ten years, was based on the anticipation of a 20 percent increase in Silver plan premiums. The cost has obviously become a lot higher because the increase in cost of health insurance became much higher than expected.

Any chance that consumers can get a break? Maybe. Consumers eligible for a tax credit subsidy could benefit if they choose to buy other metal plans because the amount of the tax subsidy that is calculated for the Silver Plan applies to all four plans. The tax credits made Gold plans a better buy and Bronze plans much cheaper.[5] The Bronze plan became so cheap that those who could not afford to buy insurance and were paying the penalty for not following the individual mandate could buy it for less than the penalty. As an aside, it is not clear why the Silver plan was treated differently from the other three plans other than the fact that it was the most popular.

A fact to keep in mind: "Cost-sharing reductions help only if you expect to pay out-of-pocket costs for docs and hospitals. If you don't—and if you do feel like gambling that you won't need care—a free or super-cheap bronze plan might be better."[6] If one does end up needing care, the costs could be huge. The pressure to shop for insurance is greater than ever.

To sum up, consumers whose income is below 250 percent of poverty still qualify for a *cost-sharing subsidy* if they buy a Silver plan—but only a Silver plan—in the marketplace. The subsidy is no longer covered by the government, but since the law did not change, insurance companies must continue to offer it. Consumers whose income is below 400 percent of poverty continue to qualify for *tax subsidies* regardless of the (metal) plan they buy, again because the law did not change. Persons whose income is higher than 400 percent of poverty pay the full price of the health insurance policy, which has become considerably more expensive.

The question that stands at the center of the debate concerns the role that private sector health insurance should play. It goes well beyond a simplified version of the question we started with, namely:

- Should the government get out of the way and let the market determine the supply and demand for individual health insurance without government subsidies?

A more informed version of the question is:

- Does it make sense to give private sector health insurance companies primary responsibility for making health insurance available with the understanding that affordability is linked to a complicated, but clearly not guaranteed, system of government subsidies to cover larger numbers of people?

Perhaps there is another question buried in here.

- Is there a reason that the government effort to mess around with the ACA produces greater complexity and confusion, increasing administrative costs?

Remember, what we have just reviewed is the 2017–2018 health subsidy snapshot. It makes clear that the increase in rates insurance companies were charging in 2017 produced market stability in 2018, equating to enough profit for insurance companies to continue participating in the state markets. The 2019 premiums are increasing but at a more moderate rate. It is hard to miss the fact that the market is not bringing the supply of insurance offerings into line with demand enough to lower prices. And there is no reason to think that will happen anytime soon.

CASE 2: PROTECTING INSURERS FROM RISK

The information presented in the second case is not at the center of the debate about the role that private sector health insurance should play, for a simple reason. I would bet that most people, including many proponents of market-based health care, are unaware of the mechanisms that were put in place—by the government—to protect health insurers from financial loss in the individual, state-based health insurance markets. What this case makes clear is that members of the government that legislated the ACA, together with insurers, were in agreement that the individual market for health insurance was so risky than market failure was a real possibility. For that reason, the government took steps to institute measures designed to protect health insurance companies from financial risk in order to encourage participation in the state-based markets.

How that works is, I would say, extremely complicated. By the time I finished examining the legislation involved, I concluded that a degree in accounting would be useful to attain full comprehension. But let's see if this explanation makes things somewhat more comprehensible. The story involves the "three Rs of health insurance," namely, risk adjustment, reinsurance, and risk corridors.

The ACA put the three Rs in place in recognition of the fact that it was requiring insurers to provide coverage for people with preexisting conditions and others previously deemed to be "uninsurable."[7] The provisions were "intended to promote insurer competition on the basis of quality and value and promote insurance market stability." The three mechanisms "were intended to protect against the negative effects of adverse selection and risk selection." *Adverse selection* occurs because persons who are most in need of health insurance, because they are sick or likely to become sick, are more likely to purchase it. The ACA made it difficult for people who are not in need of insurance, who are not sick, to wait until they need insurance to buy it. It did this by creating enrollment periods requiring people to buy insurance or pay a penalty. *Risk selection* occurs when insurers have an incentive to deny coverage to persons who are likely to run up high costs. They do so by trying to attract healthier people and discourage those who present higher risk. Risk selection makes the market less efficient when insurers compete "on the basis of attracting healthier people to enroll, as opposed to competing by providing the most value to consumers."[8]

Here is how each of the three Rs introduced by the ACA work:

1. *Risk adjustment* redistributes funds from plans with lower-risk enrollees to plans with higher-risk enrollees. Plans' average actuarial risk is based on enrollees' individual risk scores. (Time line: no expiration date)
2. *Reinsurance* provides payment to plans that enroll higher-cost individuals. If an enrollee's costs exceed a certain threshold (called an attachment point), the plan is eligible for payment (up to the reinsurance cap). (Time line: 2014–2016)
3. *Risk corridors* limit losses and gains beyond an allowable range. The Department of Health and Human Services (HHS) collects funds from plans with lower-than-expected claims and makes payments to plans with higher-than-expected claims. Plans with actual claims less than 97 percent of the target pay into the program and plans with claims greater than 103 percent of target amounts receive funds. (Time line: 2014–2016)

A "conference of leading actuaries, insurance company officials, and economists sponsored by The Commonwealth Fund" offers the following assessment. The risk adjustment feature redistributes monies collected by insurers. Additional taxpayer funds are not required. Reinsurance protects insurers against "bad luck in the form of relatively few customers who experience truly catastrophic illnesses that result in huge expenditures. . . . The plan is budget neutral: when the funds collected from insurers run out, the government stops paying. No taxpayer bailout here either."[9]

The Congressional Budget Office (CBO) projected that the net result of the risk corridor mechanism would result in a gain rather than a loss of government funds. This is based on the expectation that insurers would set premiums higher than necessary to make sure that they would not lose money on the state exchanges.

> To prevent this [loss of government funds], the federal government has created a program under which it will collect money from plans sold in the new marketplaces with unexpectedly high gains and redistribute them to plans with unexpectedly high losses. If plans make or lose up to 3 percent more than expected, they keep gains or eat the losses. However, if they make or lose 3 percent to 8 percent more than predicted, they give up 50 percent of the winnings or are compensated for 50 percent of their shortfalls above 3 percent. If losses or gains exceed 8 percent, the insurers give up or get back 80 percent of the gains or losses exceeding 8 percent of the predicted amount. If the government collects more from the winners than it has to pay out to losers, it keeps the balance. CBO thinks that's likely—thus, the predicted profit for the federal government.[10]

The three Rs case raises some basic questions:

- At the practical level, in the absence of government intervention, the assumption is that some insurers would fail. Does that mean that some individual health insurance markets would disappear? (As it turns out, that did happen in 2017.)
- Then there is the theoretical lens—assuming that the three Rs were put in place to prevent private health insurance companies from going bankrupt and going out of business—what does that say about the position taken by market-based health care proponents with regard to the value of competition and efficiency attributed to private sector insurers?

- Assuming that exiting markets that are not profitable enough is the core mechanism insurers can use to attain efficiency, what does that say about market-based health insurance as a plan for providing coverage for Americans?

Not surprisingly, the story does not end there; it is ongoing. In July 2018, the Centers for Medicare and Medicaid Services (CMS) announced that it would not be paying out the $10.4 billion in risk adjustment payments due to insurance companies for the 2017 enrollment year until a lawsuit finding that the agency had not justified part of the risk adjustment formula is settled. When that will happen is unclear.

CASE 3: MEDICARE ADVANTAGE

Medicare Advantage, or Medicare Part C, is an innovation in the organization of the delivery of Medicare services introduced in response to the familiar claim that the private sector is more efficient than the public sector. Part C was created with the expectation that the superiority of a market-based approach would be confirmed when contrasted with the performance of traditional Medicare.

The story of the evolution of a private sector alternative to traditional Medicare goes like this: Small-scale experiments started as far back as 1966. The private sector was given a more evident role with the passage of Medicare + Choice legislation in 1997. (The word *choice* is a big clue as to who promoted it—the folks who want to give us the freedom to choose based on need and preference.) The idea was that Medicare would reimburse private companies to provide Medicare Part A and Part B. Medicare was to pay a fixed fee to the companies based on whatever current Medicare expenditures were for Parts A and B.

By 1999, the number of Medicare+ Choice plans had grown to 407.[11] When analysts associated with the Medicare Trust Fund looked into who was choosing to leave traditional Medicare to enroll in Medicare + Choice plans, they discovered two things: (1) enrollees were generally younger and healthier than the general Medicare population, and (2) those who did become seriously ill proceeded to drop out of these plans and shift back to traditional Medicare. Given these findings, Medicare determined that it was overpaying the private insurers, because younger and healthier enrollees are less expensive to treat.

This is still the case. They also have lower levels of income.[12] The Medicare Trust Fund proceeded to reduce the rate that it was offering private insurance companies to provide the private alternative. That resulted in a drop in participating plans to 285 by 2003. More interesting is the finding that overpayment continued to edge up, averaging about 14 percent over traditional Medicare. Proponents of the market-based approach reacted by saying that the private alternative would succeed in saving money and only needed more time to prove it.

The Medicare + Choice plan was revised and renamed in 2003, becoming Medicare Advantage. The legislation changed how private insurance companies were paid. They were now required to submit bids to the Medicare Trust Fund for the right to sell plans.[13] The bids were based on the insurer's estimates of what it would cost to provide services, which were compared to benchmarks that varied by county. All bids that met requirements were accepted.

The ACA froze the benchmarks at the 2010 level. It instituted a formula designed to range from 95 percent of traditional Medicare in the top quartile of counties with high per capita costs to 115 percent in the bottom quartile of counties with low cost. It also allowed plans with higher-quality ratings to keep a larger share of the rebate. (Coming up with quality ratings is a huge problem to be discussed in more detail in later chapters.)

Recent research indicates that the "benchmark-and-bidding system to induce plans to provide benefits at lower costs" is not lowering costs; it "allows plans to bid higher than local input prices."[14] The explanation is that benchmarks are higher in areas where there is a concentration of Medicare Advantage plans. Rather than dropping their prices in response to competition, the plans seem to be better able to maintain high prices. The higher benchmarks provide all the plans in such areas with greater profit. That's kind of the opposite of what the presence of a large number of sellers in competition with each other is supposed to achieve, isn't it?

If the bidding process sounds complicated, you will be interested to know that it is also relatively easy to "game" the reimbursement formula. The game is called "upcoding," that is, making enrollees look sicker than they are.[15] Medicare pays plans more for sicker patients because they cost more. How sick patients are is established through medical records, which can be manipulated either through more aggressive diagnosing or creative electronic record keeping.

Government audits of 201 patient records from each of five health plans released last year found upcoding in 80 percent of cases. And an investigation
by the Center for Public Integrity found that upcoding accounted for nearly
$70 billion in additional payments to Medicare Advantage plans from 2008
through 2013.

"It amounts to $640 per Medicare Advantage enrollee per year."[16]

Medicare Advantage plans, unlike traditional Medicare, are based on managed care arrangements, that is, HMOs or PPOs. Insurers limit their costs by
managing access to health care goods and services. This is especially true in
the case of the HMO option, which involves keeping access to hospitals and
doctors within "narrow plan" networks, requiring prior approval to see a specialist, placing restrictions on drugs, and charging higher prices for specific
services such as home health care or medical equipment.

Medicare Advantage's popularity continues to grow largely because the
plans include drug coverage. As of 2017, about 33 percent of Medicare eligible
persons were enrolled. It is also true that some enrollees have had the choice
made for them by former employers whose retirement packages included
Medicare supplement coverage. Not all were happy about being forced to accept this alternative. Some big-city school districts and universities have made
this choice for their retirees.

Medicare Advantage premiums may be lower than the amount that enrollees
pay for the combined cost of Medicare Part B to the government plus Part D to
private insurance companies. However, the actual cost depends on the goods
and services the enrollee uses. Just as is true of the challenges involved in choosing any private sector insurance plan—whether it is a Medicare Advantage
plan, a plan in state-based markets, or an employer-based insurance plan—the
calculations depend on whether one uses health care services covered by the
insurance policy. Consumers who do not expect to be sick and don't expect to
need health care goods and services can save money by enrolling in a managed
care plan that has a lower premium but is more restrictive and requires higher
copayments when health care services are used.

In the name of efficiency, sellers work to introduce new ways to manage
costs mainly by changing the list of providers belonging to networks, revising
the drug list, and so on. Theoretically, both the insurance seller and buyer are
involved in calculating the risk of needing health care and deciding which

plan would deliver the greatest value. And everyone gets to do it every year. That is a lot of work.

That may explain why only 10 percent of Medicare Advantage enrollees switch plans over the year.[17] In order to do so, they would presumably need to calculate how much health care they will need and go on to weigh premium costs against potential out-of-pocket costs. How many Medicare Advantage enrollees do you think are doing that?

That raises a couple of other questions:

- Why ask people to go through this every year? Does anyone believe that all the effort it takes to enroll in a health insurance policy does anything to advance an individual's health? Isn't that the reason for buying health insurance: so one can afford health care when one needs it?
- Is the annual re-enrollment process doing anything to control rising health care costs?

CASE 4: MEDICAID — 1115 WAIVERS

Medicaid legislation passed in the 1960s gives the HHS authority to grant so-called 1115 waivers. The original intent of the waivers was to allow states to develop demonstration projects designed to provide Medicaid services more efficiently and effectively. The aim was to support innovation at the state level (rather than the federal level), which could then be adapted more widely. Most waivers were requested for the purpose of extending coverage. Changes introduced in 2017 largely through executive order reversed the original guidelines, meaning that states are now allowed to introduce measures restricting coverage.[18]

As of September 2018, forty-seven waivers across thirty-nine states had been approved; twenty were pending across nineteen states.[19] The waiver that has received most attention is the one approved for Kentucky in January 2018. The controversy largely revolves around its work requirement. Other notable features of the waiver include the requirement that Medicaid enrollees in the 100 to 138 percent of poverty range pay 4 percent of their income to stay enrolled. Another is a lockout of six months if the enrollee misses the renewal application deadline or does not report a change in family or economic status. The waiver includes an offer of extra benefits that kick in if the enrollee seeks less care over the year than what the state has established as the preset expenditure cutoff. The extra benefits include dental and vision care, which are not included in the basic coverage plan. The enrollee must keep track of the cost of services in order to apply for the extra benefits and report them online.

The work requirement is the feature that has attracted attention, because it was approved for the first time in the Medicaid program's history. It obliges all "able-bodied" persons to work in order to qualify for coverage. Exceptions are made for persons who are disabled, ill, acting as caretakers of other family members, or enrolled in school. Volunteering is also exempt. There is no count of how many people fall into that highly unlikely category. One has to ask, How are people in the latter category, who are poor enough to qualify for Medicaid, able to support themselves if they are unemployed but engaged in volunteering?

The work requirement is based on the argument that working benefits people's health. It turns out that the vast majority of Medicaid enrollees in Kentucky are either working or members of one of the exempt categories. How the work requirement would function is not entirely clear. Consider the matter of determining who is "able-bodied." What is the test? Is it to look at the person? Who will administer the sorting out of the able-bodied from those who are not? Will it be the state's Medicaid office staff or new personnel? What about able-bodied persons who face various practical barriers in finding a job? Lack of transportation comes to mind, as does an arrest record. Then there are individuals addicted to pain medications. (Kentucky has the fifth-highest opioid death rate in the country.) Are people who fall into that category to be considered able-bodied?

As if this story were not thorny enough, Kentucky was planning to allow persons who lost their Medicaid coverage to reactivate it by taking health and financial literacy courses and passing tests at the end of the courses. The courses were never developed, so it is not clear how difficult they would have been. Examples of potential questions focused on the relationship between symptoms and the need for particular tests. While no one would argue that offering more education is a bad thing, the Medicaid population may present a special challenge. Health literacy among Medicaid enrollees has been found to be low, with 60 percent having "basic" or "below basic" literacy. To illustrate:

> They could not recognize a medical appointment on a hospital appointment form (below basic) or would have trouble understanding why a specific test was

recommended for someone with certain symptoms, even when given a clearly written explanation (basic).[20]

Beyond that, keeping track of hours worked and taking health and financial literacy courses require the use of a computer. The majority of persons in this category do not own a computer and don't know how to use one.

I would guess that there are many people in the general population who might have trouble understanding why they might need a specific medical test to identify or monitor particular symptoms. Yet no one is suggesting that persons outside of the Medicaid population in Kentucky should be taking literacy tests to qualify for health insurance. That can't help but make one suspicious about the rationale behind the courses and tests. Here is my question:

- Why require Medicaid enrollees to complete health literacy courses—so the enrollee can question the doctor about the recommended diagnosis and treatment? So the enrollee can assume the role of consumer? Why else?

Kentucky's 1115 waiver application story encountered a serious roadblock. A lawsuit filed by sixteen Medicaid recipients, *Stewart v. Azar*, resulted in the finding that Kentucky's Section 1115 waiver was in violation of federal law. The court found that the HHS secretary's waiver approval was arbitrary and capricious. Furthermore, the court held that the secretary did not discuss how many people would lose coverage, contravening the primary purpose of Medicaid legislation, which is to extend coverage to those who need it. It was estimated that about 95,000 would lose coverage.[21] The Kentucky governor responded to the decision by announcing that the Medicaid program would no longer provide dental or optical coverage.

In the meantime, Kentucky hospitals registered concern about the fact that legislation, if it were reinstated, would cause large numbers of people to become uninsured. Those people would be forced to turn to the emergency room when things got really bad. As potential Medicaid recipients they could not be expected to have sufficient funds to pay for the care they receive, the most expensive form of health care. The hospitals would be stuck with increased uncompensated care costs. That would force some rural hospitals to close. Health sector jobs would disappear as hospitals cut back to compensate for lost income. The state would lose tax dollars. In short, once one begins to consider the effects of what appears to be a simple decision, to institute a work requirement, the implications just keep multiplying. It suggests that an analysis of the costs and benefits of the work requirement policy is in order.

The bigger question is this:

- Is this a reasonable use of tax dollars—spending money to pay staff to prevent Medicaid enrollees from accessing care if they do not do a good enough job in recording and reporting their efforts to find work and working enough hours to qualify?

Arkansas is the first state to have implemented the waiver. About 18,000 people were dropped from its Medicaid rolls due to noncompliance, that is, not fulfilling work-reporting requirements, during the first few months the waiver was in effect. The implications for all the parties involved have yet to be analyzed. However, it is clear that the administrative favors the 1115 work requirement feature and that additional waivers may be in the works. On the other hand, a federal judge in Washington, DC, rejected Kentucky's waiver for the second time and blocked "a similar rule" in Arkansas in March 2019.[22] Lawmakers in both states vowed to persist in their quest to require Medicaid recipients to work. Waivers granted to other states are being challenged in court as well.

CASE 5: ACCOUNTABLE CARE ORGANIZATIONS (ACOS)

ACO legislation, included in the ACA, was designed to support the development of an innovative approach that would result in greater coordination among health care providers. It is meant to establish a "medical home" for patients. Providers are being encouraged to create organizations that combine the delivery of primary, specialist, and hospital services with the expectation that sharing patient records will reduce costs and increase value. In order to participate in the Medicare incentive program, an ACO is required to cover the care of five thousand Medicare patients as a base plus any number of other patients. The incentive for providers is that they can earn more in Medicare reimbursements if they keep their patients healthy. Patients are not asked whether they wish to be part of an ACO and may not even know when they are part of one.

The first year of operation was 2011. By 2014, analysts reported that the 744 newly formed ACOs had generated savings of $411 million. But after paying out bonuses, the Medicare Trust Fund incurred a loss of $2.6 million, which turns out to be less than 1 percent of the Medicare budget.[23]

The difference in savings between 2016 and 2017 indicates that ACOs have gained experience and that 2017 may be a turning point in generating savings. Medicare lost $39 million after it paid out bonuses in 2016 but registered gains as of 2017.

"About 60% of the 472 ACOs generated a total of $1.1 billion in savings. . . . The CMS shared $780 million in savings with the ACOs, but the agency still scored a $313.7 million gain from the program."[24]

ACOs have begun to rely on management partners to provide assistance with data services (e.g., processing payer data, generating reports) as well as administrative services (e.g., writing the ACO contract, receiving and distributing savings), educational services (e.g., on new payment models and quality measures), and coordination services (e.g., operating a nurse call line).[25] In return, the management partners share financial rewards and risks. As can be expected, ACOs started by physicians are more dependent on managerial partners than ACOs started by hospitals and major third-party payer organizations, both of which already employ large numbers of managerial staff.

ACOs are expected to generate greater savings in the future as they gain more experience and are readier to enter into contracts that specify higher rewards for assuming a higher financial risk for not meeting quality targets. While the ACO experiment appears to be evolving in a promising direction with increased coordination of care, policy analysts have identified an unanticipated problem. It seems that the ACO incentive arrangements may have the effect of accelerating mergers.

> While ACOs are touted as a way to help fix an inefficient payment system that rewards more, not better, care, some economists warn that they could lead to greater consolidation in the health care industry, which could allow some providers to charge more if they're the only game in town.[26]

Whether this innovation turns out to deliver positive results, in increased quality and lower cost, remains to be seen. But it is also true that there may be something like the rediscovery of the wheel going on here, certainly a far more complicated wheel than earlier ones. As outlined at the beginning of the previous chapter, one can see that there are some similarities to what the Kaiser Permanente plan turned into after the aqueduct in California was built and World War II ended—that is, a health care arrangement in which primary care physicians in the Kaiser system play a major role in coordinating care with Kaiser specialists and Kaiser hospitals. Kaiser Permanente has had a lot of experience operating such a system. Each new ACO must learn do the same. While the basic idea is simple and elegant, the need for vastly expanded data and administrative services makes ACOs extremely complicated ventures. The need for managerial assistance to operate new ACOs in this day and age and its impact on costs are only beginning to be explored.

How this development and its apparent success in controlling costs fits into the market-based approach is not clear. What is clear is that consumer choice is playing no part.

CASE 6: MEDICARE PART D

Medicare Part D was passed in 2003 with the intent of showing that a private sector approach grounded in competition among sellers of drug plans to Medicare enrollees would lower drug costs. Its first year of operations was 2006. Although Medicare Part D is subsidized by the government, the plans are sold by private, for-profit health insurance companies. The legislation was passed based on the belief that competition would have a greater impact on drug pricing than Medicare could achieve through direct negotiation with pharmaceutical companies. In fact, the legislation specifically prohibits Medicare from negotiating with pharmaceutical companies.

The record shows that the idea that competition would keep prices from escalating was a fallacy. Drug prices continued to rise. They have not risen at the same rate for all payers. In 2006, the first year of operations, Medicare accounted for 18 percent of what was then a $224 billion bill in total US prescription drug spending. By 2015, the percentage had increased to 29 percent of a $325 billion total. By 2025, the percentage is projected to increase to 35 percent out of a $597 billion total bill. What is particularly noteworthy is finding that the percentage of the total attributable to Medicaid stayed about the same as did the percentage attributable to private insurers.[27]

An unintended experiment that has received virtually no attention allows us to compare what Medicare Part D enrollees pay, relying on competition to control prices, and the price that two government-run agencies, the Veterans Administration and the Department of Defense, pay for drugs by negotiating directly with manufacturers. The two agencies may negotiate separately or negotiate together. The result is that they are able to achieve prices "equal to 24 percent off of a drug's price or the lowest price paid by other (nonfederal) buyers."[28]

That Medicare Part D has been lucrative to private sector insurers who entered this market is not surprising. It is also interesting to note that competition in this corner of the health care sector has proceeded along a predictable path. "As of 2018, three Part D plan sponsors—UnitedHealth, Humana and CVS Health—account for more than half of the program's 43 million Part D enrollees."[29] In an effort to come closer to winning the competitive race, participants have proposed a couple of mergers between CVS Health and Aetna and between Cigna and Express Scripts. Business analysts predicted that the two mergers would cover 71 percent of all Part D enrollees and 86 percent of stand-alone drug plan enrollees. (More on this in chapter 7, where we see that the mergers happened.)

The explanation for skyrocketing Part D expenditures has been attributed in large part to the expanding "web of opaque financial arrangements" that mushroomed on the path that brings a medicine from the factory to the patient.

SUMMING UP WHAT THE SIX CASES CAN TELL US

Recognizing that the majority of people in the country are enrolled in market-based health insurance plans, the government's continuing challenge is determining how to encourage private sector insurers to provide health care coverage to as many people as possible at a price that people can afford. The fact that private sector insurers will participate in the market only if they make a profit is well understood. Thus the job of the government is to make sure that private sector insurers do make a profit—by protecting them from financial loss and, if necessary, by paying them. Government support comes through such mechanisms as subsidies, the three Rs, and opportunities to work around legislation via creative adaptations to the law. Exactly how consumer-driven health care fits into this picture requires some imagination.

The commitment to market-based health insurance is responsible for the overwhelmingly complicated health arrangements in this country. The arrangements have evolved in response to the theoretical proposition that the private sector is more efficient than the public sector. They allow the private sector to make significant profits and lower prices at the same time. Continuing to argue that the private sector is more efficient than the public sector in the face of overwhelming evidence that health care expenditures keep rising, with the government paying a good share of the bill, is disingenuous.

The Medicare Advantage option provides an excellent illustration of how market-based theory and health care system reality interact. Medicare Advantage, the private sector alternative to traditional Medicare, has long been based on the premise that it will be more efficient. Medicare Advantage has in fact achieved parity to the costs associated with Medicare in recent years. However, Medicare Advantage plans succeeded by employing a well-established mechanism: reduction of access via managed care. The insurers who offer the plans have also found a way to earn high profits by manipulating the reimbursement formula and selection of clients, making the costs involved look higher than they are. That is, the managed care mechanism, which is attaining cost savings by reducing access, is also being subverted for the purpose of increasing private sector profit.

The 1115 Medicaid waiver option, which was introduced by the federal government with the intention of supporting demonstration projects that would extend the original purpose of the Medicaid program, provides a clear example of messing with the law. We can see how the shift in values and beliefs of the political party noted at the beginning of the chapter is playing out in determining who gains and who loses on the Medicaid health care front. Government at both the federal and state level is involved in creating mechanisms aimed at restricting access to care. It is interesting to consider what getting government out of the way and increasing the role of market-based health care might mean in this context.

- Given that the Medicaid population cannot afford to buy health insurance, what role does the market-based health care model play absent potential consumers?
- What is the alternative to provision of government funding of health insurance coverage for the Medicaid population? No funding and no insurance?

Viewing ACOs, the last case of government intervention in health insurance arrangements, from the perspective of the market-based model is interesting because ACOs were designed to employ incentives aimed at providers rather than consumers. That brings about an obvious question:

- Is there reason to think that this approach could signal a shift in underlying assumptions in the market-based health care model? That it allows consumers to go back to being patients?

The lesson that the history of Medicare Part D offers is that health care markets require third parties to mediate between buyers and sellers of complicated products. The market for drug insurance plans offers the additional incentive of assurance that government subsidy will reduce the risk of market failure because the product is unaffordable. Accordingly, the Medicare Part D legislation created a market structure that brought in many sellers and many buyers. The size of the market and the complexity involved in selecting drugs to be included in formularies, that is, the drug plans, created the opportunity for intermediaries between buyers and sellers to get involved, and they have found ways to increase their share of the money Medicare Part D is putting on the table. In the meantime, competition is leading to the steadily decreasing number of Part D plan sellers left in the race.

What must be clear from the preceding discussion is that the government and the private sector are inextricably intertwined. Market-based health care arrangements are repeatedly introduced with the promise of increased efficiency through market mechanism, most notably competition. Government intervention aimed at making sure the market continues to operate is quick to follow. Government involvement is not stable. The form it takes changes in response to a shift in values on the part of the political party in office. This is not to say that the government's role is likely to be minimized when the political party that favors market-based solutions gains power. We will return to this observation in the final chapter.

NOTES

1. "Market Effectuated Enrollment and Financial Assistance," Kaiser Family Foundation, https://www.kff.org/other/state-indicator/effectuated-marketplace-enrollment-and-financial-assistance/?currentTimeframe=0&selectedRows=%7B%

22states%22:%7B%22all%22:%7B%7D%7D,%22wrapups%22:%7B%22united-states
%22:%7B%7D%7D%7D&sortModel=%7B%22colId%22:%22Location%22,%22sort%
22:%22asc%22%7D.

2. Cynthia Cox et al., "2017 Premium Changes and Insurer Participation in the Affordable Care Act's Health Insurance Marketplaces," Kaiser Family Foundation, November 1, 2016, https://www.kff.org/health-reform/issue-brief/2017-premium -changes-and-insurer-participation-in-the-affordable-care-acts-health-insurance -marketplaces/.

3. Jay Hancock, "Obamacare Shopping Is Trickier than Ever. Here's a Cheat Sheet," Kaiser Health News, November 10, 2017, https://khn.org/news/obamacare-shopping -is-trickier-than-ever-heres-a-cheat-sheet/.

4. Julie Appleby, "Brokers Are Reluctant Players in a Most Challenging ACA Open-Enrollment Season," Kaiser Health News, November 13, 2017, https://khn.org/news/ brokers-are-reluctant-players-in-a-most-challenging-aca-open-enrollment-season/.

5. Ashley Semanskee, Gary Claxton, and Larry Levitt, "How Premiums Are Changing in 2018," Kaiser Family Foundation, November 29, 2017, https://www.kff .org/health-costs/issue-brief/how-premiums-are-changing-in-2018/.

6. Hancock, "Obamacare Shopping Is Trickier Than Ever."

7. Cynthia Cox, Gary Claxton, and Larry Levitt, "Explaining Health Care Reform: Risk Adjustment, Reinsurance, and Risk Corridors," Kaiser Family Foundation, August 17, 2016, https://www.kff.org/health-reform/issue-brief/explaining-health -care-reform-risk-adjustment-reinsurance-and-risk-corridors/.

8. Cox et al., "2017 Premium Changes and Insurer Participation."

9. David Blumenthal, "The Three R's of Health Insurance," Commonwealth Fund, March 5, 2014, https://www.commonwealthfund.org/blog/2014/three-rs-health -insurance.

10. Gretchen Jacobson et al., "Medicare Advantage 2016 Spotlight: Enrollment, Market Update," Kaiser Family Foundation, May 11, 2016, https://www.kff.org/ medicare/issue-brief/medicare-advantage-2016-spotlight-enrollment-market -update/.

11. Yash Patel and Stuart Guterman, "The Evolution of Private Plans in Medicare," Commonwealth Fund, December 8, 2017, https://www.commonwealthfund.org/ publications/issue-briefs/2017/dec/evolution-private-plans-medicare.

12. Patricia Newman and Gretchen Jacobson, "Medicare Advantage Checkup," *New England Journal of Medicine*, November 14, 2018, https://www.nejm.org/doi/full/10.1056/NEJMhpr1804089.

13. Patel and Guterman, "Evolution of Private Plans."

14. Stephen Zuckerman, Laura Skopee, and Stuart Guterman, "Do Medicare Advantage Plans Minimize Costs? Investigating the Relationship Between Benchmarks, Costs, and Rebates," Commonwealth Fund, December 21, 2017, https://www.commonwealthfund.org/publications/issue-briefs/2017/dec/do-medicare-advantage-plans-minimize-costs-investigating.

15. Austin Frakt, "Missing from Medicare Advantage: True Competition," *New York Times*, May 2, 2016, https://www.nytimes.com/2016/05/03/upshot/missing-from-medicare-advantage-true-competition.html.

16. Frakt, "Missing from Medicare Advantage."

17. Newman and Jacobson, "Medicare Advantage Checkup."

18. For a thorough discussion, see "Web Briefing for Journalists: A Closer Look at the Evolving Landscape of Medicaid Waivers," Kaiser Family Foundation, February 2, 2018, https://www.kff.org/medicaid/event/web-briefing-for-journalists-evolving-landscape-medicaid-waivers/.

19. "Medicaid Waiver Tracker: Which States Have Approved and Pending Section 1115 Medicaid Waivers?" Kaiser Family Foundation, March 15, 2019, https://www.kff.org/medicaid/issue-brief/medicaid-waiver-tracker-approved-and-pending-section-1115-waivers-by-state/.

20. Austin Frakt, "A Twist to Get Medicaid in Kentucky: Pass a Course," *New York Times*, January 23, 2018, A12.

21. Amy Goldstein, "Trump Administration Again Permits Kentucky to Impose Work Requirements for Medicaid Recipients," *Washington Post*, November 20, 2018, https://www.washingtonpost.com/national/health-science/trump-administration-again-permits-kentucky-to-impose-work-requirement-for-medicaid/2018/11/20/04a097c0-ed2b-11e8-96d4-0d23f2aaad09_story.html?noredirect=on&utm_term=.6df1f4874420.

22. Abby Goodnough, "Judge Blocks Medicaid Work Requirements in Two States," *New York Times*, March 28, 2019, A18.

23. Jenny Gold, "Accountable Care Organizations, Explained," Kaiser Health News, September 14, 2015, https://khn.org/news/aco-accountable-care-organization-faq/.

24. Maria Castellucci and Virgil Dickson, "Medicare ACOs Saved CMS $314 Million in 2017," *Modern Healthcare*, August 30, 2018, https://www.modernhealthcare.com/article/20180830/NEWS/180839987.

25. Valerie Lewis et al., "The Hidden Roles That Management Partners Play in Accountable Care Organizations," *Health Affairs* 37, no. 2 (February 2018): 292–98.

26. Gold, "Accountable Care Organizations."

27. "10 Essential Facts about Medicare and Prescription Drug Spending," Kaiser Family Foundation, November 9, 2017, https://www.slideshare.net/KaiserFamily Foundation/10-essential-facts-about-medicare-and-prescription-drug-spending.

28. David Blumenthal and David Squires, "Drug Price Control: How Some Government Programs Do It," Commonwealth Fund, May 10, 2016, https://www.commonwealthfund.org/blog/2016/drug-price-control-how-some-government-programs-do-it.

29. "Three Firms Account for Over Half of All Medicare Part D Enrollees in 2018, and Pending Mergers Would Further Consolidate the Marketplace," Kaiser Family Foundation, May 17, 2018, https://www.kff.org/medicare/press-release/three-firms-account-for-over-half-of-all-medicare-part-d-enrollees-in-2018-and-pending-mergers-would-further-consolidate-the-marketplace/.

5

Doctors

This chapter looks at what the market-based health care approach says about doctors. It begins with some history on the structure of medical practice and how that has changed. The body of the chapter addresses the question of how well the organization of medical practice fits the features of the market-based health care model. It focuses on the three basic characteristics of free market arrangements identified in chapter 2: many buyers and many sellers; ease of entry and exit, on the part of sellers of medical care services; and consumers' freedom to choose based on need and preference.

MANY BUYERS AND MANY SELLERS

Setting the scene for considering the relationship between the supply and demand for doctors and the services they provide, we begin with the fact that in 1975, by which time a majority of Americans had gained health insurance coverage, there were 13.5 doctors for every 1,000 Americans and the total health care bill was $118.5 billion. In 2015, Americans spent $3.2 trillion on health care goods and service; 23.4 percent of that, $634.9 billion, was for medical care. The ratio of doctors engaged in patient care in 2016 was 29.5 for every 1,000 Americans.[1]

The steady increase in both national expenditures on health care and numbers of doctors is impressive. The two trends are not unexpectedly related. The parallel trends raise a basic question about what the market-based health care model says about supply/demand curves. If the supply of doctors is increasing, it must be in response to increased demand for medical care on the part of consumers. What else could it be?

- Then why isn't increased supply causing medical care prices to drop?

The need to explain why the supply/demand curve is not working to reduce prices as the market model predicts has become more urgent as costs continue to rise with no end in sight. A commonly heard explanation offered by advocates of market-based health is that it's the consumers' fault. They say that prices would fall if consumers just did what they are supposed to do: shop. Some go on to say that consumers don't do so because health insurance picks up most of the cost, making consumers insensitive to price. The concept covering that behavior is "moral hazard." The solution, according to these folks, is to make sure that consumers "have skin in the game," that is, pay a higher proportion of the cost of care, ensuring that consumers will not seek health care services that they do not really need.

The focus on buyer behavior comes and goes, as does focus on seller behavior. In the latter case, the favored concept used to explain the continuing rise in the cost of medical care is "supplier-induced demand." In other words, doctors are in the ideal position to convince patients that they need more medical tests and treatments, which doctors prescribe to benefit their pocketbooks. Accordingly, policy designed to change that scenario is built on the assumption that reordering financial incentives will change doctors' behavior. That involves removing the financial incentive built into "fee-for-service" reimbursement arrangements. Policy experts say fee-for-service payment means that doctors make more money if they do more. It rewards quantity, not quality.

The shift in policy requiring consumers to pay a higher portion of the bill would correct for the fact that people are currently getting too many tests, too many drugs, and too many procedures.

- What is too much?
- And who should decide what is too much or too little: consumers, doctors, the third-party payers, politicians, or some other group?

Another reason that explains why there is too much medical care has to do with the threat of a malpractice lawsuit. Doctors say that they must practice "defensive medicine" in order to avoid the risk of being charged with doing too little to identify the existence of a serious health problem. They engage in practices to establish a record of doing everything possible to identify the problem. No one is willing to venture an assessment on how big a role this plays. There is, however, continuing discussion about malpractice insurance rates.

The good news is that malpractice premiums have been dropping. A 2014 report indicated that premiums had been dropping for seven years.[2] The rates fell by 13 percent between 2008 and 2013. Of course, it is also true that the rates had increased by 20 percent per year in 2003 and 2004. In real dollars, the result is that the obstetrics-gynecology annual premium in New York dropped from $227,899 per year in 2013 to $214,999 in 2014. What is important to understand about that figure is that it is the highest in the country. Premiums vary tremendously by specialty and by area of the country. It is, however, not hard to understand why the threat of a lawsuit and the damage it does to the doctor's reputation, plus the resulting increase in premium, convince some doctors to practice defensive medicine.

There is also continuing discussion about state efforts to institute caps on awards for pain-and-suffering malpractice awards in an effort to contain health care costs. Awards for physical loss of function, loss of income, and so on are calculated without much controversy. The pain and suffering that goes along with the malpractice event is much more difficult to assess. Accordingly, some states, starting with California in 1975, have instituted a $250,000 cap on pain-and-suffering awards. Other states have instituted higher caps. That has not stopped individual plaintiffs from suing to have the cap overturned.

I do not propose to answer the highly controversial question that I posed here, that involves determining how much is too much or too little health care. My objective is far more limited. It is to look more closely at how reliance on market-based arrangements aimed at addressing consumer demand without raising cost of care is working out currently.

EASE OF ENTRY AND EXIT

There is no question that it takes long years of education, training, and licensure to become a practicing physician. In other words, entry on the part of sellers is highly regimented. The content of medical school courses is determined by medical school faculty, and on-the-job residency training is established by medical specialty groups. Three years of residency is required of all medical practitioners, as are many more years in more specific areas of specialization. Hospital committees composed of doctors decide which doctors will be permitted to admit patients to the hospital and what the extent of their hospital "privileges"—that is, the procedures the doctors will be permitted to perform—will be.

There has been relatively little enthusiasm for reducing the barriers to entry into medical practice on anyone's part—not policy makers, not the public, certainly not the medical profession. There is some enthusiasm and a great deal of debate about the value of allowing persons not trained as physicians to enter the health care field. Each state issues licenses to practice medicine in the state. States that have a shortage of doctors accept licensure obtained in other states. The state controls prescription-writing privileges, which it can extend to anyone it chooses. Thus a range of other practitioners are permitted to write prescriptions in some states but not in others. For example, psychologists are licensed to write prescriptions in three states: Illinois, Louisiana, and New Mexico. Nurse practitioners are licensed to write prescriptions in all states, but they are required to do so with oversight from physicians in twenty-nine states. Chiropractors are licensed to practice in all states even as debate continues about the efficacy of such treatment, with consumers claiming that they receive clear benefit and medical research questioning evidence of benefit and voicing concern about possible harm.

Education and licensure are entry-level credentials. After that, physicians entering into practice have decisions to make before they see patients. They aren't simply opening up an office and starting to see patients the way doctors did decades ago. Doctors had offices in the community. Everyone in the community knew the doctor and talked about the care received and how much it cost. Patients were well informed about the doctor. The doctor behaved in ways that reinforced people's trust, because everyone in the community would surely hear about it if he (invariably he) did not. The relationship between doctor and patient and trust in what the doctor recommended was essential to the treatment process. Indeed, trust stood at the core of medical professionalism, and medicine served as the model of professionalism that other occupations worked hard to emulate.

Writing in 1991, Arnold Relman, former editor of the *New England Journal of Medicine*, explained the contrast between medical practice then and the time he was writing the editorial.

> Today's market-oriented, profit-driven health care industry therefore sends signals to physicians that are frustrating and profoundly disturbing to the majority of us who believe that our primary commitment is to patients. Most of us believe we are parties to a social contract, not a business contract. We are not vendors and we are not merely free economic agents in a free market. Society has given us a licensed monopoly to practice our profession protected in large part against competition from other would-be dispensers of health services. We enjoy independence and the authority to regulate ourselves and set our own standards. Much of our professional training is subsidized, and almost all the information and technology we need to practice our profession have been produced at public expense.[3]

In the past, the majority of doctors were in solo practice or in a partnership. The office was staffed by a receptionist who managed appointments, billing, and patient files. There was relatively little medical equipment. A number of basic medical tests could be carried out in the office—an X-ray and some basic lab tests if the doctor chose to hire a trained assistant. Doctors are not entering solo practice these days for a number of reasons. For one, they can no longer afford to set up an office because of the expense associated with electronic record keeping, which is required by law to collect health statistics. Not only does it require purchase of expensive electronic record keeping software but it also means paying a trained staff person to do the entry work. The fact that health insurance differs so much from one carrier to another means that doctors cannot maintain an office without staff to manage third-party reimbursement. The fact that doctors must repay educational debt is now a much bigger factor in making a choice about the setting the doctor chooses to practice in than was true in the past. In short, setting up an office requires considerable investment before the doctor can generate any income. Indeed, where are the patients going to come from? There are third-party payer contracts to consider. The result is that newly certified doctors are now more likely to begin practicing medicine by joining an established group practice on a contractual or salary basis.

Not only are doctors banding together in group practices but group practices are also getting larger. More importantly, the groups are linking up with hospitals or being purchased by hospitals, which turn doctors into hospital employees. This trend has accelerated at an unprecedented rate in recent years. The result is that 42 percent of all physicians in this country are now hospital employees.[4] The advantage to doctors is that the employer takes on responsibility for all the administrative tasks that doctors have no interest in carrying out—hiring, firing, training staff to maintain patient files, arranging appointments, handling complicated billing calculations, and so forth. Not to be forgotten, malpractice insurance premiums are generally covered by the hospital or the group. And, of course, there is the need to deal with the expenses associated with electronic record keeping: buying the software and paying trained staff to do data entry. Doctors join large practices on the assumption that doing so will result in more time to spend on patient care. Contrary to expectation, doctors are increasingly discovering that turning over administrative responsibilities to others does not produce more time to see patients and may introduce a range of unexpected and unwelcome problems.

Physicians are expressing growing levels of frustration regarding their efforts to carry out the social contract between doctor and patient that Relman talked about nearly three decades ago. The results of a 2016 survey of physicians found physicians saying that they are struggling to "maintain morale levels, [to] adapt to changing delivery and payment models, and to provide patients with reasonable access to care."[5] A majority, 72 percent, said that "external factors such as third party authorizations significantly detract from the quality of care they are able to provide." It is widely believed in physician circles that "professional satisfaction has sunk to an all-time low."[6]

The "cognitive specialists," that is, family practitioners, internists, and pediatricians, have apparently experienced greater frustration than their colleagues who carry out more highly technical procedures. They find that they must work longer hours, see more patients, and devote less time to each patient. The main source of professional satisfaction according to most doctors, namely, the doctor's relationship with the patient, is deteriorating.

A graphic account provided by one disillusioned doctor expresses it well.

> I work one week a month in the ICU. I spend the other three weeks of the month in an outpatient clinic. This is a nightmare. The Electronic Health Record they have in place makes me so slow and inefficient I want to scream when I come to work every day. They want me to see new complex pulmo-

nary consult patients on the hour every hour. Frequently, just to review their imaging, labs and special studies takes 15 minutes before I even walk in the door to meet the patient. Today I saw 8 new patients in eight hours. I need at least 60 minutes per new patient and a buffer of at least 15 minutes between patients to complete my EHR charting. I am so frustrated and just want to walk away but where does one go. It is the same everywhere now in the USA. HER [health electronic records] and conveyer belt, output-driven medicine. I feel trapped and betrayed. I did not go to medical school to sit on my butt for four to six hours a day doing data entry in a computer.[7]

One well-known physician-author, Atul Gawande, writing in the *New Yorker*, asserts that doctors hate their computers and explains why.[8] He says that doctors are frustrated by the fact that they must spend two hours a day doing computer work for every hour of face-to-face time with patients. He writes that this is his experience as a surgeon and that his colleagues who are not surgeons have even more difficulty managing the time needed to care for their patients. He says that doctor's workdays have expanded to eleven and a half hours. Is it any wonder that they hate their computers?

Fee-for-Service: How Doctors Get Paid

As will quickly become clear, current arrangements for paying doctors are convoluted, even byzantine. A very big share of what is troubling doctors these days revolves around the paperwork connected to reimbursement arrangements. As I have already mentioned, fee-for-service is the way that doctors were traditionally paid. That doctors were likely to do more because they were rewarded for each medical service they provided may be true, but it is also a major oversimplification. What explains why doctors choose to do what they do is far more complicated. Back to that shortly.

What is especially interesting about the fee-for-service arrangement is its two-sided nature. In the past, the fee-for-service practice model was considered to be emblematic of professionalism. The doctor provided the kinds of care the patient needed and wanted without interference from third parties. Doctors charged patients according to the patients' ability to pay. Patients who did not have the cash sometimes paid by providing goods—such as freshly butchered game—or services—like fixing the doctor's roof—in exchange for medical care. Of course, it is also true that people who had little to share could not participate in such arrangements. In such cases, the patient had to rely on charity and the doctor had to extend it. The result is that a doctor could not collect enough money to support himself in a poor community, meaning that not everyone in the country had access to medical care.

At the same time, fee-for-service in those days meant the doctor was an independent business proprietor. The doctor sold services, and the patient bought those services directly from the doctor. That certainly sounds like the essence of a market-based arrangement. It is exactly what the most doctrinaire market-based advocates would like to see happening. However, medical care is now much too complex to be carried out in a doctor's office and permit this arrangement. And it is much too expensive to be compensated by trading simple goods and services for medical care rendered.

Other reimbursement arrangements have always existed but were the exception, not the rule. Accepting a salary was one. Most medical school faculty fell into this category. Another alternative is capitation or prepaid care. In this case, the doctor is paid a set amount for every patient who signs up with the doctor, regardless of whether the patient seeks health care services or not. This arrangement evolved in isolated but notable cases, for example, the Mayo Clinic or, as mentioned in the previous chapter, Kaiser Permanente in California. It is also true that the medical establishment, as represented by the American Medical Association, regarded fee-for-service as the primary indicator of professionalism during the first half of the twentieth century and beyond. It made every effort to discourage alternative arrangements.

The way things work these days is that doctors who sign on to work in a hospital generally accept a salary paid by the hospital. Signing on with a medical group may involve salary or a more complicated contractual reimbursement arrangement. In all cases when doctors accept a salary, they become employees. They work under conditions set by the employer, including hours of work, tasks to be performed, pace of work, and set amount of pay. Pace is reflected in the number of patients the doctor is expected to see in a day or in an hour. Because the doctor-employee receives the same salary no matter how many patients the doctor sees, the logic is clear. Processing more patients benefits the employer, who collects the fees from third-party payers.

Critics say that this amounts to the industrialization of medicine. They say that doctors have become assembly-line factory workers, where patients are looked upon as products requiring assembly. The imagery may be extreme.

Doctors are, however, complaining bitterly, as illustrated by the disillusioned doctor quoted earlier and the assessment by Atul Gawande, that they are being confronted with a common assembly-line tactic—"speed up"—in the time allotted for seeing patients. Speed-up is causing physician burnout, a topic to which we will return in chapter 9.

The solo practitioner who was engaged in a fee-for-service practice has been relegated to a disappearing era when doctors set the fee. Only 17 percent of doctors are currently in solo practice, which is basically fee-for-service practice.[9] Even in the case of doctors who are still engaged in fee-for-service practice, doctors are no longer in charge of fees. Fees are set through negotiation by medical practice groups and/or hospital-owners of medical practice groups with various third-party payers. Fee-for-service practitioners have little alternative but to accept the going reimbursement rate.

More on How Doctors Get Paid

Medicare, more precisely the Centers for Medicare and Medicaid Services (CMS), does not negotiate over fees. It does however play a significant role in determining medical care reimbursement schedules. It has been relying on the resource-based relative value scale (RBRVS) for the last few decades to determine the value of the services provided by doctors. The American Medical Association explains it this way: "Payments are calculated by multiplying the combined costs of a service times a conversion factor (a monetary amount determined by CMS) and adjusting for geographical differences in resource costs." This results in the Medicare fee for the work the doctor performs.

A committee of doctors organized by the AMA, called the Relative Value Update Committee (RUC), took on the task of assessing how to evaluate the work component in 1989. It assigns monetary value to all medical services reported in the Current Procedural Terminology (CPT) code. Medicare generally accepts the committee's recommendations without change. The composition of the committee is revealing. There are thirty-one members: twenty-one are representatives of medical specialty societies, four seats rotate (two for internal medicine, one for primary care, and one for any other specialty). The remaining six seats include an American Osteopathic Association representative, and five AMA appointees or representatives of committees associated with the AMA.

Primary care practitioners, the so-called cognitive specialists, say that this goes a long way in explaining why they earn less, a lot less, than surgical and procedural specialists. They generally do their work in an office rather than performing hospital-based procedures—read those as costly procedures for which the hospital and specialist are both reimbursed. Primary care practitioners say that what they do is not valued sufficiently in the process the RUC uses to assess the value of medical services doctors provide. They say that the value of the time they spend taking patient histories and listening to patients report initial symptoms and response to treatment is not being recognized. They say that dominance by procedural specialists means that doing procedures is more highly rewarded than listening to what patients say. The result is that Medicare pays primary care practitioners far less than surgical and other technically oriented procedural specialists. The sparring between specialists and primary care practitioners makes clear that not all doctors are the same.

While health policy experts repeatedly say that what this country needs is fewer specialists and more family practitioners, there is good evidence to indicate that the trend is going in the opposite direction. The turning point came in 2013, when the number of patient visits to specialists first outnumbered visits to primary care practitioners.[10]

The New and Improved Payment Arrangement: MACRA

In the interest of clarification of the formula used to determine the value of medical services, the American Academy of Family Practice (AAFP) presents a detailed outline of legislation covering how doctors get paid, the Medicare Access and CHIP Reauthorization Act of 2015 (MACRA), that is scheduled to go into full effect in 2019. The legislation has been undergoing continuous revision since it came into existence and is likely to continue to do so. AAFP states that MACRA was presented with the intent of giving doctors "the opportunity to select and use clearer, more manageable, more meaningful measures that will improve reporting accuracy and effectiveness—and reduce waste." However, it goes on to state that the time required to respond to quality measures is 785 hours per year according to a 2016 assessment.[11] More on that shortly.

It is worth noting that the 2016 Survey of American Physicians found that only 20 percent are familiar with MACRA.[12] CMS as well as other organizations offer videos, podcasts, and webinars to help doctors understand what is expected. Some observers predict that the complicated nature of the formula and the need to rely on electronic record keeping will force more doctors to join larger practices that have the funds and staff to deal with the enormous amount of detail involved. Some physicians who are already dissatisfied and threatening to quit may do that. One does not have to be much of a cynic to predict that for-profit electronic record keeping services will be appearing shortly to help physicians handle the reporting burden—for a price. And it will be a price that someone, presumably consumers, will have to pay, based on the explanation that the for-profit electronic records experts will be more efficient, therefore less costly to practices and ultimately to consumers.

- Sound familiar? (Recall that the entry of management companies to help doctors deal with reporting requirements is exactly what happened in the case of Accountable Care Organizations discussed in chapter 4.)

Critics say that the new legislation was necessary to overcome the flaws in the prevailing CMS reimbursement schedule, which rewarded volume. Accordingly, Medicare responded to pressure to come up with payment mechanisms to pay for the "quality" and not "quantity" of medical care. Passage of MACRA was designed to achieve this. It replaced the sustainable growth rate (SGR) reimbursement formula created in 1997 that was specifically designed to control for increasing costs by tying reimbursement to inflation. However, SGR was ineffective because Congress passed legislation increasing the reimbursement rate nearly every year after that. This happened because the rate of inflation has been close to flat over the last decade or so. Doctors argued that a reimbursement increase was necessary to cover medical practice costs, which were rising faster than inflation. "Cumulatively from 2001–2014, while general inflation increased 33.4 percent and physician practice expense increased 60.6 percent, Medicare payment rates only went up by 2.9 percent!"[13]

MACRA was legislated promising to achieve several objectives: overcome the problem of uncertainty about reimbursement increases from year to year, reward quality, and contain costs. To understand how well it is working requires knowing a lot more about what is in the law. This is where the idea that reimbursement arrangements are byzantine comes in. So why make an effort to understand MACRA? Part of the reason is all third-party payers, private sector payers, and Medicaid rely on the reimbursement formula used by Medicare in negotiations over reimbursement rates. It is reasonable to have a plan in place to assess how much doctors are to be reimbursed for the services they provide. Neither Medicare nor any other third-party payer is prepared to pay doctors whatever they might wish to charge. The continuing concern about the need to rein in health care costs means that there needs to be some way to assess the value of the services doctors provide. The pressure to build assessment of the quality of care is now in the forefront of the focus on reimbursement arrangements. In short, designing the methodology to be used to set medical care fees constitutes a very big challenge. That explains why MACRA is continuing to be revised after it went into effect. At this point, we can look at the thinking behind how it is supposed to work, not how it does/will work. Get ready to encounter a tremendous amount of complexity.

MACRA requires that doctors who treat one hundred or more Medicare patients join the Quality Payment Program. That requires participation in the Merit-Based Incentive Payment System (MIPS). Doctors may choose to report as members of a group or as individuals if the group does not choose to submit a single report. Doctors who are affiliated with health care delivery organizations that operate under prepaid care arrangements, that is, work in Accountable Care Organizations or patient-centered medical homes (PCMHs) and are paid in bundled model reimbursement arrangements are to be covered by Alternative Payment Models (APMs). (Bundled payments are being reconsidered in light of new criticism—more on this below.) PCMHs may choose to participate in a different version of the APM, the Advanced Alternative Payment Model, by accepting a higher level of (financial) risk. Doctors covered by the APM models may choose to participate in MIPS but are not required to do so, because their reimbursement is more closely related to the number of patients they see and not the number of services they provide. They will receive an annual bonus connected to evidence of delivering quality care.

Under the MIPS reimbursement formula, doctors are scored on the basis of four factors: cost, quality, advanced care information (ACI), and improvement activities (IA). Cost is calculated by CMS. Doctors may choose up to 6 measures of quality from a list of 284 measures plus one outcome measure. They may select from 15 ACI measures. IA consists of 92 activities, which are weighted as medium for ten points or high for twenty points. Doctors are required to perform activities that add up to forty points for a minimum of ninety consecutive days. This involves participation in activities being carried out by community organizations whose work is overseen by certain accrediting agencies.

Total scores on each of the four factors are weighed. The weights will shift over the course of the payment program on an annual basis. In the most recent (as of 2019) version to be effectuated in 2020, quality makes up 50 percent of the score, ACI is 25 percent, IA is 15 percent, and cost is 10 percent.[14] By 2022, quality drops to 30 percent and cost rises to 30 percent of the total score. Payment adjustments will occur based on the MIPS score, ranging from plus or minus 5 percent during the first year and 9 percent plus or minus by 2022. Lump sum and performance bonuses will end by 2024, and all physicians will then be covered by APMs which will be updated by 0.75 percent per year.[15]

Doctors will undoubtedly find the shift—from allocating fifty points to quality and ten to cost in the first year to allocating thirty points to cost and thirty points to quality within a three-year period—striking. This is clearly intended to signal a major change in how the value of health care services is viewed. But whether the measures being introduced do what they are purported to do depends on two things: (1) whether they are good measures to begin with and (2) how accurately they are calculated. Computing how much services cost is something that Medicare does as a matter of course in paying out reimbursements. Gauging quality is a whole different matter. Determining an estimation of quality—based on the 284 quality measures, 15 ACI measures, and 92 IA activities—is obviously a monumental task.

There is more to the MIPS formula that doctors have had a good deal to say about over past years. MIPS is adjusted for three components: (1) the physician work component, which encompasses such factors as technical skills, physical effort, and stress due to the potential risk to patients; (2) the practice expense component; and (3) the professional liability component. The practice expense component involves the cost of living and practicing in different parts of the country: land values, wage rates, heating costs, and so forth. Professional liability refers to malpractice premiums. The data on the second and third components are readily available. It is the work component part of the formula that requires definition.

Organizations dedicated to the task of measuring quality of care are operating at every level of the health care system. And they have been engaged in creating a stream of new measures to complete the task. Healthcare Effectiveness

Data and Information Set measures are used by most private sector third-party payers and differ from the measures used by Medicare. I suspect you will not be surprised to find that the number of measures out there is quite problematic in the view of most doctors.

The number of quality measures is astounding—1,700 used by federal agencies plus another 546 commonly used by private sector insurers.[16] Responding to quality measure requirements is time-consuming, as already mentioned; it adds up to 785 hours per year, which amounts to 15.1 per week per physician practice. Critics point out that physicians spend 2.6 hours per day on this task, time that could be used to care for approximately nine patients. Staff spend about 12.5 hours per week. Translating the time into money means that it is costing $15.4 billion per year. Responding to quality measure requirements is clearly burdensome and a major cause of dissatisfaction voiced by physicians. Their references to "conveyer belt" medicine makes that strikingly clear.

Okay, so quality measure reporting is time-consuming, costly, and frustrating to doctors. The question for which there is no answer at present is,

- Are the cost and the hassle involved in measuring quality of care having a noticeable effect on the quality of care?

An early answer to the question was published in February 2018:

> While the first performance year of the MIPS program just ended, some observers, including the Medicare Payment Advisory Commission, have already raised concerns that MIPS will fail to improve patient care, even as it generates substantial administrative burdens.[17]

As a number of observers have noted, it is easy to measure what doctors do, which is not the same as measuring quality of care. Counting tests generates data but, in some cases, deciding not to do more for the patient would be better. However, the decision not to do more testing or provide more treatment is hard to track. Watching and waiting may save money, reducing risk and improving quality, but there are no dollar amounts involved. And there is no way to measure the psychological costs and financial waste of testing that produces uncertain results, leading to more testing.

It is worth considering how doctors respond to being presented with measures that reward carrying out tests and procedures. As one astute observer points out, doctors are good at responding to evaluation criteria. They are good test takers. That is how they got through medical school. If they are rated on how many tests they perform, they will perform loads of tests.[18] In other words, it is likely that they are not responding to financial incentives but to the kinds of performance measures that got them where they are—through medical school, residency training, licensure exams, and so on.

An article in the *British Journal of Medicine* supports this assessment. It presents a sophisticated analysis of how doctors respond to evaluation of their performance:

> It is difficult to improve care without the risk of falling into the kinds of decontextualized measures and incentives that promote better care. Personal, social, and comorbid complexities force increasing levels of sophisticated tailoring of clinical action, a simultaneous attention to biology and to biography. Today, that attention often places clinicians in a soul-killing bind to either be patient-centered or to gain quality points and rewards.[19]

If that sounds too vague or convoluted, the authors make the meaning perfectly clear by saying, "Measurement misleads when it fails to award the best score to the best care, but instead rewards the best player."[20]

The question of why doctors deliver unnecessary care is hard to answer. Shannon Brownlee offers a list of possible explanations:

> Doctors lack the evidence they need to know which treatments are most effective and which drugs and devices really work. They also lack the training to interpret the quality of the evidence that's available. They overtreat patients out of a desire to help even when they don't know the right thing to do. Malpractice fears drive defensive medicine, and then there is medical custom, which varies from region to region of the United States.[21]

Perhaps doctors, who do know a lot more about high-quality as opposed to low-quality health care, have not been given a platform for indicating what they think about the kind of care that has little value and should not be reimbursed. Letting third-party payers make such judgments has put weight on cost and broad measures of quality. Little attention has been directed at identifying low-value health care, which, as it turns out, is actually more costly than has been previously recognized.

All of this is related to the new criticism of what seemed like such a reasonable idea: bundled payment. A set fee for "episode-specific" care—that is, for a particular medical diagnosis and the care it requires—was expected to give physicians more control over testing and treatment, improving quality and reducing cost. It did not take long to discover that the model works better in the case of surgery than medical care. Surgery can be defined as an episode. Medical care cannot. It is continuous. Of course, if bundled payment is a good idea but not comprehensive enough to cover all services, then maybe a "global budget" would be an even better idea. But that moves us beyond what individuals do to what institutions do. We return to that topic in the final pages of the book.

An initiative on the part of the American Board of Internal Medicine Foundation in partnership with *Consumer Reports* led to the Choosing Wisely campaign in Washington state.[22] The campaign brought together 75 medical societies that together had 490 recommendations regarding issues that doctors and patients need to discuss. The Choosing Wisely Task Force ended up identifying the top five services that should not be reimbursed or purchased at any price:

- Diagnostic testing and imagining for low-risk patients prior to low-risk surgery
- Population-based vitamin D screening
- Prostate-specific antigen (PSA) screening in men age 75 and older
- Imaging for acute low-back pain for the first six weeks after onset, unless clinical warning signs are present (red flags)
- Use of more expensive branded drugs when generics with identical active ingredients are available

The Choosing Wisely Task Force found that "more than $500 million was spent in 2014 on 44 low-value health services in one U.S. state."[23] The authors of the report, published in a *Health Affairs* blog, go on to say:

> At first glance, many of the items on this list seem inexpensive; however, these
> services are so ubiquitous that based on their sheer high volume, they rank

among the most costly items in health care. In fact, US health care purchasers spend more than $25 billion annually on these top five services—and that's before taking into account the costs of downstream services and complications.[24]

The authors say that an alliance of "leading purchasers, patient advocates, employer coalitions, and other health care stakeholders . . . has a clear message: 'start here.'"[25] It is worth noting that it is not competition but cooperation that is identifying steps leading to both better quality and lower cost. This is an observation that deserves a great deal more attention. It is explored more fully in the final sections of the book.

Getting back to relying on financial incentives aimed at altering doctors' behavior, this is how the APM reward system is designed to operate. It promises to present the doctor with a bonus payment at the end of the year. Critics say that the bonus is not likely to alter doctors' behavior if only because it is not large enough to notice and will not make an impact. In economic theory terms, the bonus is not enough to drive an increase or decrease in supplier-induced demand. There are other, more convincing explanations for doctors' treatment patterns. Explaining why some doctors choose to engage in a more aggressive form of care while others choose a less aggressive and less costly form of care is worth considering. The variation in rates of tests and treatments across the country, tracked by the Dartmouth Atlas, shows that the patterns reflect systemic differences among doctors in a particular region. The variables that explain the differences between one region and another indicate that how doctors were trained matters. If they were trained by highly regarded doctors who do a lot of testing, they will do that as well. If they move into a practice setting in which senior doctors value certain tests but not others, they will adopt those practices.

Sociologists would interpret this to mean that socialization and norms play a big role in how doctors practice. The Dartmouth Atlas, developed by doctors, graphs patterns of practice across the country that illustrate this observation. Its origins make for an interesting story: Shannon Brownlee offers a captivating account of what led Dr. John Wennberg to notice and then begin tracking variation in practice patterns.[26] The highly persuasive interpretation of the account indicates that the opinion of colleagues, especially those who are highly regarded, is a critical element in judging one's own performance as a doctor. Being assured that one is taking the right steps in providing care translates into confidence. Confidence on the doctor's part has a reassuring effect on the patient by reducing anxiety, which in turn has a positive effect on the patient's health. From a sociological perspective, the trick is not to try to influence the behavior of the recently minted doctor directly through financial incentives but to make sure the performance of the senior doctors the young doctor interacts with is superior. That requires making sure that the senior doctors use fewer resources and attain higher quality of care. Needless to say, placing young doctors is such settings is a lot harder to arrange than turning to a financial-incentive/reimbursement arrangement. And the fact that financial incentives fit market-based health care theory if not reality explains the continuous fiddling with incentive arrangements, in the expectation that different results will suddenly be achieved than were achieved in the past.

If this discourse seems to have gone far afield, I want to make very clear that the point of the discussion on evaluating quality has to do with the expectation that consumers will go into the market and choose medical care services based on their evaluation of the quality and price. Given how difficult evaluating quality is even when experts, those closest to the matter, try to do it, the idea that consumers can determine the quality of health care makes little sense.

CONSUMER CHOICE

Consumers of medical care services aren't going to the doctor whom everyone in the neighborhood goes to anymore. Many have no alternative but to seek medical care services from the list of providers in the network that their insurance company signed up or pay a penalty for going outside of the network to seek care. The fact that it is not always possible to determine whether one is being treated by a doctor who is part of the network just makes it all the more frustrating. To illustrate, consumers are generally not told the names of doctors who read the results of certain kinds of tests. They are typically not the doctors whom patients see face-to-face. Surprise medical bills from doctors not in the network have become so objectionable that politicians have begun to focus on it. For now, there is no way to know what that will lead to.

Doctors, who have traditionally operated as solo practitioners or members of small group practices, have been moving to join together at a much greater pace over the last decade or so. As of 2017, the majority, 65 percent, of specialists are members of groups. Primary care practitioners have been slower to join groups; 39 percent are concentrated into groups.[27] Recent evidence suggests that more than a third of physicians belong to groups of fifty or more, which means that about a fifth of physicians' markets are highly concentrated and another fifth moderately concentrated, based on federal merger guidelines.[28]

In short, sellers have been responding to market pressures to compete by combining into increasingly larger entities, which are becoming smaller in number. Buyers, that is, consumers of medical care services, were herded into an increasingly smaller number of groups much earlier by the shrinking number of major third-party payers.

Private sector third-party payers are in a position to hold out access to the consumers on their list of enrollees. This gives third-party payers clout in negotiations with groups of physicians over the reimbursements they will accept. Doctors who have less bargaining power are forced to agree to be part of a "narrow network" and enter into contracts in which they accept a lower level of reimbursement. The networks also specify the hospitals that are included in the network (see the discussion of hospitals in chapter 6).

Even concerted efforts to shop for a doctor do not always work, because network directories may not be accurate. The frustration registered by one shopper about an inaccurate network list makes this clear.

> Penny Gentieu did not intend to phone 308 physicians in six different insurance plans when she started shopping for 2017 health insurance. . . . "It's just not fair to be baited and switched. . . . It's just so crazy that you're presented with this big list of doctors then you call them you realize there's nobody there."[29]

Contract negotiations between doctors and private sector third-party payers over network membership take place on an annual basis. The contract can be broken by either side if some aspect of the contract is not fulfilled. If the costs to the third-party payer turn out to be higher than projected, individual doctors might be pressured to withdraw from the arrangement or the whole group might be cut off. Or doctors may drop out because disagreements develop over restrictions on reimbursement for particular services.

The fact that large medical practice groups are increasingly being bought out by hospitals casts a very different light on the circumstances under which supplier-induced demand occurs. Doctors are certainly performing the tasks that generate fees that are paid by third parties. But the pressure to generate those fees is increasingly coming from the organization, not the individual doctor, because it is now the organization that is benefiting from supplier-induced demand. Indeed, there is evidence to confirm the logical expectation, that health care services delivered in the hospital outpatient department will cost more than the same services delivered in a physician's office.[30]

Physicians are clear about who they believe is promoting supplier-induced demand. They report that the pressure to see more patients per hour results in the need to do more tests to identify the patients' problems, and to enter a report on all the tests and services the doctor performs, because this is what brings in the money. Doctors may be discouraged about what they see as assembly-line medicine, but they are not in a position to do much about it. But somebody must be interested in promoting this form of practice, generating more charges that bring more fees, because the cost of medical care keeps rising.

The ability to pay for the goods and services a consumer wishes to buy is characteristic of all markets, but consumers in other markets do not face the impediments that consumers of medical care face, for several reasons. First, consumers in most sectors of the economy are under no obligation to enter the marketplace by signing up with a vendor—not the doctor but the insurance company that restricts their choice of sellers of medical care services to a selected list, that is, doctors and hospitals in a particular network. Second, consumers in other sectors can obtain information on price far more readily than is true of medical care services. Third, information on quality is especially hard to find because, as the discussion above indicates, assessing quality of medical care is so confounding. If the Medicare formula for measuring quality of care is any indicator of the challenges involved in evaluating quality, how likely is it that consumers can identify it? It is difficult to see how market-based health care advocates who promote the idea that health care is consumer-driven can ignore each of these obstacles.

Getting Information on Quality and Cost of Care

It matters where consumers go to get information on cost and quality especially because quality means different things to different people—patients, doctors, health policy experts, and third-party payers, among others.

The result of the 2014 Gallup Poll survey on health care, a poll that has been conducted every year since 2001, indicates that TV continues to be the

main source of health care news that consumers are turning to. Of those sur-
veyed, 55 percent said they rely on TV, 21 percent rely on the internet, and
9 percent rely on print. More of those over the age of fifty rely on TV than
younger respondents.

The answers to questions regarding what kind of information consumers
of health care are looking for are highly revealing. A 2011 Pew survey found
that "symptoms and treatments continue to dominate internet users' health
searches."[31] More specifically, people said they were searching for information
on the following topics:

- A specific disease or medical problem (66 percent)
- A certain medical treatment or procedure (56 percent)
- Doctors or other health professionals (44 percent)
- Hospitals or other medical facilities (36 percent)
- Health insurance, including private insurance, Medicare, or Medicaid (33
  percent)

The Pew survey found that that when respondents were asked to identify the
main source of information that they relied on, 70 percent said they relied on
doctors or health care professionals, 60 percent relied on family and friends;
and 24 percent turned to someone who has the same condition.

Health policy experts are very good at assessing quality when looking at
large population groups as opposed to individuals. Such a group, assembled
by the Institute of Medicine, issued a spectacular report in 2000, *To Err is
Human*, which issued the finding that ninety-eight thousand deaths in this
country could be attributed to error. That stimulated continuing debate about
what is meant by quality of care and about the measures that capture quality,
with the result that specific indicators have been identified. And changes have
been implemented. This is not to say, however, that the problems associated
with measuring quality have been resolved. Government efforts to address
quality of care are obviously ongoing. That is certainly the objective of the
MACRA legislation discussed earlier.

The Agency for Healthcare Research and Quality (AHRQ), a branch of
HHS, created for the purpose of improving "quality, safety, efficiency, and effectiveness of health care," has been trying to develop measures focusing on
evidence-based medicine for many years. Progress on what this means has

been moving ahead albeit at what the AHRQ admits is a slow pace. Clearly, the fact that there is a great deal of variation in both quality and price of medical care services has been known for a very long time without good understanding how to change things for the better. Quality as indicated by measures of evidence-based medicine is very different from quality considered by factors that the public looks at.

Consumers' Sources of Information on Quality of Care

In 2014, *Consumer Reports* announced that it would be rating primary care doctors in the future. In the meantime, it came up with a list of ten websites that consumers could turn to. The list included AMA DoctorFinder, Angie's List, Castle Connolly, Healthgrades, National Committee for Quality Assurance, Physician Compare, RateMDs, Vitals, U.S. News & World Report, and Yelp. The measures from one site to another vary, but the primary indicator involves consumer satisfaction.

According to a 2017 Pew poll, 87 percent of respondents who saw a provider in the past year said that their "symptoms or concerns were carefully listened to" and 84 percent said they "felt their doctor really cared about their health/well-being."[32]

A 2014 National Opinion Research Center (NORC) study found that "when it comes to defining provider quality, most Americans tend to focus on certain aspects of quality relating to doctor-patient interactions and doctors' personality traits, rather than the effectiveness of care provided or the patient's own health outcomes."[33] Whatever indicators health care consumers are looking for, they seem to be finding them, because they are reporting very high levels of satisfaction with the quality of care they receive from the physicians they see.

Consumers' Sources of Information on Cost of Care

Given the challenges involved in obtaining meaningful information on quality of medical care, NORC's finding on consumers' views of information on cost of care is interesting. Respondents reported that "getting information on the cost of provider care is even more challenging for Americans than finding information about provider quality. A third of Americans say it is easy to find information they trust related to the costs of provider care. Fewer say it's easy to find data that compares a provider's costs and quality."

Costs increase when test results indicate that something falls out of the normal distribution of test results, which happens because the recipients of medical care services do not come in a standardized form. Inconclusive tests require follow-up testing. How many tests and what kinds of tests are required to assure diagnostic certainty is unclear. Thus the costs involved in diagnosis are unpredictable. The costs involved in the next step, treatment, are therefore unpredictable because there is no guarantee that the prescribed treatment will work the way it does in most cases. Whether the drugs prescribed work or whether new drugs must be tried before finding a drug that works is unpredictable. That may require additional tests and so on.

Given how murky this process can be, the announcement that CMS created a database in 2014 with information on payment information for physician services was greeted with great enthusiasm. The CMS website introduced the Physician Fee Schedule Look-Up by saying that it provided information on ten thousand physician and nonphysician practitioner services. The announcement stated the following when it was introduced.

This easy to use look-up tool allows you to:

- Search payment amounts, relative value units (RVUs), various payment policy indicators, and geographic practice cost indexes (GPCIs) for a single procedure code, a range of procedure codes, or a list of procedure codes.
- Find the national payment amount, the payment amount for a specific Carrier/Medicare Administrative Contractor (MAC), or the payment amount in a specific locality.

The news media were quick to check out what some referred to as a "data dump." The names of a few doctors who received the highest reimbursements got special attention. Three were already known to the Justice Department and had already been charged with fraud. A few others issued responses indicating that the payments they received were distributed to a larger number of physicians engaged in a large research project—claims supported by the institutions involved. Others complained that the reimbursements were as high as they were because the physicians were relying on high-cost drugs used in treating patients in their offices. Ophthalmologists made this claim, noting that there are no generic versions of the drugs they use.

Enthusiasm ebbed after a very short time because people could not open the file. Inquiries asking CMS why the file would not open produced the following reason: "The file includes over 9 million lines of data. As a result, this file is too large to be opened in Excel."[34]

The wording quoted above has since disappeared from the CMS site. Once the tool was established, CMS went on to create an online booklet to explain all the terms employed by the tool. The booklet and the site continue to be revised, becoming far more user-friendly.[35]

A big factor in understanding pricing has to do with third-party policies that define which tests, treatments, and drugs will be covered, all of which may not be specified in sufficient detail. That has a major effect on the cost of the care for which the patient is ultimately responsible. Thus not only are the prices of medical services hard to get but information on the part of the bill that the consumer is expected to pay may be equally hard to get.

We keep returning to a basic question:

- Why is getting information on the quality and cost of medical services so difficult?

My answer goes back to the fact that medical care is a service and not a product. Products can be standardized and compared. The results of medical care are difficult to standardize and compare because the recipients of the services do not come in standardized form. Patients come with different histories; different genetic makeup; different reactions to symptoms, which are not always easy to predict; and different reactions to treatment, which are not easy to interpret. In short, medical services that are highly effective in the case of some patients may not be nearly as effective in the case of other patients, and there is no absolutely sure way to predict which will be which. Yes, there are a lot of routine forms of care, but there is no guarantee that something will not go wrong even in such instances.

BEFORE SUMMING UP

Before attempting to close with a summation of the material discussed in this chapter, I would like to digress to comment on medical professionalism and the pursuit of collective interests by health care practitioners—that is, unionism.

As noted earlier in this chapter, the values associated with professionalism, namely, the understanding that physicians are dedicated to working first and foremost in the interest of their patients, served medicine well for much of the twentieth century. Other occupational groups used the professionalism model provided by physicians to shape their identities. However, professionalism no longer carries as much authority as it did in the past when doctors were primarily engaged in independent, fee-for-service practice. This is not to suggest going back to that era. It is to point out that individual doctors continue to be in a strong position to affect patient care of individual patients but have far less influence over the rules, regulations, and policies set in place by organizations. In recognition of this, doctors have been banding together to increase their influence. They did that initially by joining groups that grew in size but, as they discovered, not so much in influence. The groups themselves began coming under the umbrella of hospitals, which have at the same time been expanding into hospital networks. It has not taken long for physicians' groups to discover that becoming a single actor in a corporate network is not the best way to exert influence.

Enter the physicians' union. The American Union of Physicians and Dentists (UAPD), the largest union for doctors in the country, illustrates what an organization that represents doctors' interests can accomplish.[36] Established in 1972 in California, its spokespersons are now being invited to talk to physicians across the country about the benefits of joining. The UAPD recruits both employed doctors and private practice doctors. It bargains collectively on behalf of the employed physicians. A July 2018 case provides an illustration, which is also documented on its website:

> For instance, the Alameda Health System (AHS) decided to contract out psychiatric emergency services to a private contractor in violation of the UAPD contract and California statute. The case went to arbitration. The arbitrator ruled against the AHS, returning all the jobs to UAPD member psychiatrists.

The only option nonunionized psychiatrists would have at their disposal would be to sue over contract violation on an individual basis. Having the union sue on behalf of all the psychiatrists involved clearly caused the AHS to rethink its decision.

What the UAPD offers private practice doctors, who are prohibited by law from bargaining collectively, is expertise in addressing issues with which the union has considerable experience and is ready to share with members. It provides high-level legal and political advocacy to individuals, which may translate into institutional policy that benefits many more physicians, including nonmembers. It provides benefits that doctors would have to pay for on an individual basis, for example, Continuing Medical Education classes. It offers review of contracts individual members enter into with a range of organizations, including hospitals and insurance companies. It offers legal assistance to individual members in dealing with malpractice suits.

Nurses

We have not focused on the part that nurses play in the health care system. There is considerable evidence to indicate that nurses play a central role in how patients fare in hospitals. Nursing has a long history, but I will not attempt to review it here. I propose to limit the discussion regarding nurses to consideration of how they have been reacting over the last few decades to the way they are treated by the hospitals that employ them.

Historically, hospitals, the primary employers of all levels of nursing personnel, dealt with the ever-present shortage of nurses without incurring a significant increase in labor costs by importing nurses trained in other countries. They dealt with the continuing shortage of more highly trained American nurses by increasing workloads and hours of work. Nurses in some parts of the country responded by forming unions. The California Nurses Association (CNA) is a case in point. Taking the position that increased workload was a threat to patient safety, the CNA pushed for nursing staffing ratios. This resulted in the state of California mandating nursing staffing ratios for all hospitals in 1999. When then governor Schwarzenegger attempted to overturn the ratios in 2004, the CNA campaigned to have the ratios reinstated—in fact, expanded in some cases—and won. The CNA demanded that hospitals use a one (patient) to one (nurse) ratio in departments such as intensive care units, operating rooms, and ER trauma units, and a one-to-five ratio on medical/surgical floors. They argued for limits on the number of continuous hours they would be required to work in order to prevent mistakes due to fatigue. In other words, the nurses' union succeeded in having an influential voice in hospital organizational arrangements related to quality of care. The AHRQ provides citations to dozens of articles on research indicating that nurse staffing is a critical variable associated with hospital mortality.

A decade ago, the California Nurses Association joined together with the United American Nurses and the Massachusetts Nurses Association to establish the National Nurses United (NNU), which now represents approximately 150,000 nurses across the country. The NNU website describes its mission as follows:

> At its founding convention in December, 2009, NNU adopted a call for action premised on the principles intended to counter the national assault by the healthcare industry on patient care conditions and standards for nurses, and to promote a unified vision of collective action for nurses with campaigns to:
>
> - Advance the interest of direct care nurses and patients across the U.S.
> - Organize all direct care RNs "into a single organization capable of exercising influence over the health care industry, governments, and employers."
> - Promote effective collective bargaining representation to all NNU affiliates to promote the economic and professional interests of all direct care RNs.
> - Expand the voice of direct care RNs and patients in public policy, including enactment of safe nurse to patient ratios and patient advocacy rights in Congress and every state.
> - Win "healthcare justice, accessible, quality healthcare for all, as a human right."

I introduce the topic of health care practitioner unions to raise some thought-provoking questions. The basic question is,

- What are the chances that health care practitioner unions, particularly doctors' and nurses' unions, will continue to expand enough to be instrumental in achieving goals such as those outlined by the UAPD and the NNU?

Then there is this question:

- What is the relationship between health practitioner unionism and professionalism?

Michael Ash and Jean Ann Seago find that union membership enhances nurses' ability to achieve reduced mortality because it allows them to speak up to improve patient care—something that could be "career-jeopardizing without union protection."[37] They determined that unionized nurses achieve lower rates of heart-attack mortality. In other words, unionism embodies professionalism by furthering the ability of nurses to achieve the health care delivery standards concomitant with their occupational identity, which their employee status does not further.

As to doctors' unions, there is reason to think that physicians' unions may expand with the number of doctors accepting salaried positions. This raises a number of questions. For a start, what does this portend for patient outcomes? Beyond that, what are the implications for professionalism of physicians in particular and for other occupations more generally? The following may be a question of greater interest to academics than policy makers, but the answer does have important implications for both cost and quality of care. Does the success of physicians' and nurses' unions provide a model for other occupational groups to emulate, just as physician professionalism did during the first half of the twentieth century?

FINAL THOUGHTS ON DOCTORS AND THE MARKET-BASED APPROACH

Where does the discussion presented in this chapter leave us in trying to answer the basic question posed at the chapter's beginning, which was, How is the market-based health care approach working out in advancing health care quality while containing costs? The approach is clearly not succeeding in containing health care costs. The explanation offered by market-based health care advocates involves laying the blame on both providers and consumers of health care services. They maintain that the model is right—that financial incentives built into existing reimbursement arrangements offered to individual physicians is the best way to improve quality of care and lower costs. They hold fast to this perspective even as they criticize providers for violating model expectations by generating supplier-induced demand. They fault consumers for failing to shop for health care services based on price and quality. In short, they continue to argue that there is nothing wrong with the model. They hold that the reason this approach is not producing promised results, primarily cost control, is that neither the sellers of health care services nor the buyers of those services are behaving in line with model expectations.

NOTES

1. Aaron Young et al., "A Census of Actively Licensed Physicians in the United States, 2016," *Journal of Medical Regulation* 103, no. 2 (2017): 7–21.

2. Robert Lowes, "Malpractice Insurance Premiums Nudge Down Again," Medscape, October 13, 2014, https://www.medscape.com/viewarticle/833151.

3. Arnold Relman, "Shattuck Lecture—The Health Care Industry: Where Is It Taking Us?" *New England Journal of Medicine* 325, no. 10 (September 1991): 854–59.

4. "Updated Physician Practice Acquisition Study: National and Regional Changes in Physician Employment 2012–2016," Physician Advocacy Institute, March 2018, http://www.physiciansadvocacyinstitute.org/Portals/0/assets/docs/2016-PAI -Physician-Employment-Study-Final.pdf.

5. Physicians Foundation, *2016 Survey of America's Physicians: Practice Patterns and Perspectives*, September 21, 2016, https://physiciansfoundation.org/wp-content/ uploads/2018/01/Biennial_Physician_Survey_2016.pdf.

6. Robert Pearl, "Why This Is the Hardest of Times to Be a Physician in America," *Forbes*, August 6, 2015.

7. Pamela Wible, "Depressed Doctor: 'I'm Angry and Frustrated and Lost,'" *Patient Care*, September 16, 2015, https://www.patientcareonline.com/blog/depressed-doctor-im-angry-and-frustrated-and-lost.

8. Atul Gawande, "Why Doctors Hate Their Computers," *New Yorker*, November 12, 2018.

9. David Squires and David Blumenthal, "Do Small Physicians Practices Have a Future?" Commonwealth Fund, May 26, 2016, https://www.commonwealthfund.org/ blog/2016/do-small-physician-practices-have-future.

10. Andis Robeznieks, "More Patients Chose Specialists over Primary-Care Docs in 2013," *Modern Healthcare*, April 21, 2014, https://www.modernhealthcare.com/ article/20140421/blog/304219936.

11. Lawrence Casalino et al., "US Physician Practices Spend More than $15.4 Billion Annually to Report Quality Measures," *Health Affairs* 35, no. 3 (2016.): 401–6.

12. Physicians Foundation, *2016 Survey of America's Physicians*.

13. Robert Smoldt et al., Medicare Physician Payment: Why It's Still A Problem, And What to Do Now," *Health Affairs Blog*, January 27, 2017, https://www.health affairs.org/do/10.1377/hblog20170127.058490/full/.

14. Billy Wynne, "Breaking Down the MACRA Final Rule," *Health Affairs Blog*, November 9, 2017, https://www.healthaffairs.org/do/10.1377/hblog20171109 .968225/full/.

15. Smoldt et al., "Medicare Physician Payment."

16. Casalino et al., "US Physician Practices Spend."

17. Matthew Fiedler et al., "Congress Should Replace Medicare's Merit-Based Incentive Payment System," *Health Affairs Blog*, February 26, 2018, https://www .healthaffairs.org/do/10.1377/hblog20180222.35120/full/.

18. Gilbert Welch, *Less Medicine, More Health* (Boston: Beacon Press, 2015).

19. Marleen Kunneman, Victor Montori, and Nilay Shah, "Measurement with a Wink," *BMJ Quality and Safety* 26, no. 10 (October 2017): 849–51. https://quality safety.bmj.com/content/26/10/849?utm_source=trendmd&utm_medium=cpc&utm _campaign=bmjqs&utm_content=consumer&int_source=trendmd&int_medium= trendmd&int_campaign=trendmd.

20. Kunneman, Montori, and Shah, "Measurement with a Wink."

21. Shannon Brownlee, *Overtreated: Why Too Much Medicine Is Making Us Sicker and Poorer* (New York: Bloomsbury, 2008).

22. Jason Buxbaum, John Mafi, and A. Mark Fendrick, "Tackling Low-Value Care: A New 'Top Five' For Purchaser Action," *Health Affairs Blog*, November 21, 2017, https://www.healthaffairs.org/do/10.1377/hblog20171117.664355/full/.

23. Buxbaum, Mafi, and Fendrick, "Tackling Low-Value Care."

24. Buxbaum, Mafi, and Fendrick, "Tackling Low-Value Care."

25. Buxbaum, Mafi, and Fendrick, "Tackling Low-Value Care."

26. Brownlee, *Overtreated*.

27. Young et al., "Census of Actively Licensed Physicians."

28. Cory Capps, David Dranove, and Christopher Ody, "Physician Practice Consolidation Driven by Small Acquisitions, so Antitrust Agencies Have Few Tools to Intervene," *Health Affairs* 36, no. 9 (2017): 1556–63, https://www.healthaffairs.org/ doi/10.1377/hlthaff.2017.0054.

29. Jay Hancock, "Insurers' Flawed Lists Send Patients Scrambling," *New York Times*, December 4, 2016.

30. "Updated Physician Practice Acquisition Study: National and Regional Changes in Physician Employment 2012–2016," Physician Advocacy Institute, March 2018, http://www.physiciansadvocacyinstitute.org/Portals/0/assets/docs/2016-PAI -Physician-Employment-Study-Final.pdf.

31. Susannah Fox, Health Topics: 80% of Internet Users Look for Health Information Online (Washington, DC: Pew Research Center's Internet & American Life Project, February 1. 2011).

32. Mark Strauss, "Most Patients in U.S. Have High Praise for Their Health Care Providers," Pew Research Center, August 2, 2017, http://www.pewresearch.org/fact -tank/2017/08/02/most-patients-in-u-s-have-high-praise-for-their-health-care -providers/.

33. "National Survey Examines Perceptions of Health Care Provider Quality," National Opinion Research Center, July 20, 2014, http://www.norc.org/NewsEvents Publications/PressReleases/Pages/national-survey-examines-perceptions-of-health -care-provider-quality.aspx.

34. "Medicare Provider Utilization and Payment Data: Physician and Other Supplier PUF—Frequently Asked Questions," Centers for Medicare and Medicaid Services, updated May 4, 2018, https://www.cms.gov/Research-Statistics-Data-and-Systems/ Statistics-Trends-and-Reports/Medicare-Provider-Charge-Data/Downloads/ Physician_FAQ.pdf.

35. Physician Fee Schedule Look-Up Tool. Centers for Medicare and Medicaid Services, updated March 8, 2019, https://www.cms.gov/Medicare/Medicare-Fee -for-Service-Payment/PFSlookup; How to Use the Searchable Medicare Physician Fee Schedule (MPFS) https://www.cms.gov/Outreach-and-Education/Medicare -Learning-Network-MLN/MLNProducts/Downloads/How_to_MPFS_Booklet _ICN901344.pdf.

36. Grace Budrys, When Doctors Join Unions (Ithaca, NY: Cornell University Press, 1997).

37. Michael Ash and Jean Ann Seago, "The Effects of Registered Nurses' Unions on Heart-Attack Mortality," IRL Review 57, no. 3 (2004): 422–42.

6

Hospitals

This chapter focuses on the role of hospitals in the delivery of health care goods and services. It starts by outlining hospital growth trends, which are closely related to the three market-based health care principles identified in previous chapters: (1) many buyers and many sellers, (2) easy entry and exit, and (3) consumer choice. The core of the chapter is devoted to discussion of how hospitals set prices and how they are reimbursed for the care they provide. It gives special attention to the ability of consumers to determine the price and quality of hospital care.

The fact that 32.3 percent, the largest share of the country's total $3.2 trillion health care bill, is for hospital care means that it stands as the biggest target for cost-reduction efforts. This is in contrast to 19.8 percent for physician services and 10.1 percent for drugs.

The pressure on hospitals to reduce costs began decades ago. Proponents of market-based health care said the nonprofit, mission-driven hospitals, which were in the majority especially in urban areas, were inefficient. Hospital boards of directors and administrators responded. They adopted a businesslike approach. Critics saw it as a shift "from mission to margin." The emphasis on business practices that was set in motion decades ago continues to evolve.

The result of the emphasis on the businesslike approach to hospital management is this: it is not easy to differentiate nonprofit from for-profit hospitals, which are now identified as "investor-owned." According to the American

Hospital Association, as of 2017 there were 4,840 community—that is, short-term—hospitals; 2,849 were nonprofit and 1,035 were investor-owned. I will return to discussion of the differences between the two later in this chapter.

Most of the remaining 956 community hospitals were owned and operated by state and local governments; a portion, 209, were owned and operated by the federal government. Hospitals created by state and local governments to care for the poor did not respond to pressure to become more businesslike, because the majority of the consumers of their services are not paying customers. Public hospitals depend on government funding, that is, tax monies. Because government intervention in the delivery of health care services is always under debate, the amount of funding public hospitals can expect to receive is not assured. They struggle to keep their doors open. Many have closed.

Teaching hospitals associated with medical schools operated by universities, both public and private sector universities, have not ignored the pressure to operate in a more businesslike manner, but doing so is more complicated for them because teaching and research stand at the core of their mission. The two activities are governed less by market forces than by the availability of government and private funding.

MANY BUYERS AND MANY SELLERS

Hospital Growth Trends

An observation made by Milton Roemer in 1986 regarding hospital growth was so convincing that it became known as Roemer's Law. The law held that a "built bed was a filled bed." The supplier-induced demand phenomenon was the driving force in this scenario. The observation produced a lot of talk about preventing what seemed like the spontaneous "filling of beds." The number of beds, the basic measure used in hospital counts, declined, but this happened for reasons that were not necessarily due to what we think of as market-forces. It became clear that people got better sooner when they went home to familiar and comfortable surroundings. Another thing that became clear was that hospitals were dangerous places where people picked up hospital-based infections. Short hospital stays became the norm whenever possible. Turnover meant that there were always beds available and no need to build more beds. That had another effect: the building of more clinics to provide outpatient care. More on this later.

The number of hospital beds per one thousand persons in 1975 was 4.6. By 2014, that number dropped to 2.5 beds per one thousand patients. The average length of stay in a hospital bed dropped from 7.7 days in 1975 to 5.5 in 2014. The occupancy rate, that is, the percentage of beds that were in fact "filled beds," dropped from 75 percent in 1975 to 62.8 percent in 2014.[1] This was happening even as the population was aging and presenting an increasing need for health care services, and as a steady stream of new tests requiring expensive new equipment was introduced.

The history of hospital development in this country provides the background for understanding where and why they were established. It makes for interesting reading. Because there was no sure way to control infection prior to the discovery of penicillin, which happened around 1950, people were reluctant to go to a hospital. Surgeons who were increasingly relying on hospital facilities wanted to assure the public that they should turn to hospitals for the services that surgeons could provide. Surgeons were largely responsible for a nationwide study earlier in the century that identified low-quality hospitals and forced them to close. The effort led to creation of an organization charged with reviewing hospital quality on a voluntary basis, the Joint Commission on Accreditation of Hospitals in 1951, now known simply as the Joint Commission. The review became not-so-voluntary, since Medicare began requiring Joint Commission approval to qualify for Medicare reimbursement. Other hospital review organizations have come into existence over the years, but the Joint Commission remains the primary reviewer.

Hospital development was greatly advanced in the post–World War II era by a law, the Hill-Burton Act, passed in 1946 to provide government funding to support the building of new hospitals and the expansion of existing hospitals. Communities that could raise the funds to develop a hospital could expect to have half of the cost covered by the government. Many of those hospitals were mission-driven, created by religious organizations, ethnic communities, and civic-minded residents of newly developing suburban communities. The distribution of hospitals reflected the ability to raise funds rather than the need for hospital care. This became clear as founders moved away and interest in and/or ability to maintain the hospital declined. Many closed.

Hospitals owned by one or several doctors, were common during the first half of the twentieth century. That is, they operated as for-profit, privately owned establishments. Some privately owned hospitals grew into large corporate

organizations. Others struggled to survive because they did not have the financial resources needed for expansion, unlike larger entities such as religious
orders, flourishing communities, or shareholders willing to invest.

In rural areas, particularly in the southern part of the country, privately
owned hospitals continued to operate. However, the socioeconomic changes
that occurred in the country over the second half of the twentieth century
eventually began to turn the tide against rural hospitals. As manufacturing
jobs declined in rural communities across the country, people lost health
insurance, younger people left for the city to seek better opportunities, and
the population that remained was older and poorer. The economics simply
couldn't work. A 2012–2013 study of rural hospitals found that rural hospitals
had an average of fifty beds, with a median of twenty-five beds. The average
census was 7 patients and 321 employees.[2] Small urban hospitals in poor communities faced similar demographic challenges.

There is evidence to show that the small for-profit hospital sector is experiencing an upsurge—just not in rural areas. A large part of the explanation
is that new for-profit hospitals have been opening in suburban communities.
More on this shortly.

It seems that midsize hospitals, those with between 100 and 499 beds,
which were the most numerous until the 1980s, declined at a greater rate than
either the small or the large hospitals.

> The United States relies on competition to balance costs and quality in the
> health care system. But concentration is increasing throughout the hospital,
> physician, and insurer markets. Midsize community hospitals face declining
> demand and growing competition from both larger hospitals and smaller free-
> standing diagnostic and surgical centers, leaving midsize hospitals vulnerable to
> closure or merger with other facilities.[3]

EASE OF EXIT AND ENTRY

The decade of the 1970s brought a shift in social attitudes in the country. The
focus changed from the social values that prevailed during the 1960s, which
held that the government is obligated to address the needs of all members of
society, especially the poor, to social support of values associated with individual responsibility and the benefits of a market-based approach. (Medicare and
Medicaid were legislated in the 1960s with the aim of extending access. Health

Maintenance Organizations [HMOs] were introduced during the 1970s in the effort to contain health care costs.) This is when hospitals, especially mission-driven hospitals, were charged with being inefficient. They did become more businesslike regardless of whether this occurred by choice or recognition that they would not survive if they did not do so. What changed is pretty easy to observe. Just look at hospital lobbies. They have come to look a lot like lobbies in high-end hotels and Fortune 500 companies.

Hospitals entered into an early horizontal consolidation phase during the 1970s and 1980s, forming hospital chains. This allowed them to negotiate better deals with sellers of everything from paper products to medical equipment. It also gave them greater power in negotiations with health insurance companies over reimbursements. Armed with success in horizontal consolidation, hospitals extended the consolidation efforts to vertical integration. They began by building outpatient clinics, moving on to buying out physician practices. "Health care markets became increasingly concentrated between 2010 and 2016, as hospitals and physician organizations merged horizontally and vertically. In 2016, 90 percent of all metropolitan areas had highly concentrated hospital markets."[4]

A study of the effects of hospital consolidation in California over the last decade is provocative because, as the researchers point out, what happens in California is often predictive of what will happen in the rest of the country. Consider the effects of consolidation between 2004 and 2013. Hospital prices increased by 76 percent per hospital admission across all hospitals during this period. The prices at hospitals

> that are members of the largest, multi-hospital systems grew substantially more (113%) than the prices paid to all other California hospitals (70%). Prices were similar in both groups at the start of the period (approximately $9,200 per admission). By the end of the period, prices at hospitals in the largest systems exceeded prices at other California hospitals by almost $4,000 per patient admission.[5]

One might wonder whether hospital networks have been getting so big that insurers are now unable to exert enough pressure to keep them from raising their prices. That is certainly what major insurers say. There is evidence to indicate that it may be true. A study of emergency department spending over the last two decades indicates that private insurance expenditures exhibited the highest expenditure-to-charge ratio over that period when compared to Medicare, Medicaid, and no insurance.[6] Private insurance companies paid higher rates to hospitals for emergency room care than other payers even though hospital charges were the same for all payers. The difference between expenditures and charges is determined by how much of a reduction the payer negotiates. Previous research indicates that private insurers also pay higher rates for inpatient care.

Isn't this in direct contradiction to what advocates of market-based health care tell us—that the government is inept and wastes money and that private insurers are sure to do a better job controlling prices? That is clearly not what is happening. The authors of the emergency department study offer an explanation for the higher prices paid by private insurance companies, stating that private insurance companies are unable to negotiate lower prices because they are in a weaker bargaining position. They represent fewer consumers of emergency department services than the number of consumers that Medicare and Medicaid represent.

At the same time, there is reason to believe that insurers may be benefiting more than they are losing. Research confirms the idea that greater concentration of hospitals results in less competition. That in turn allows hospitals in areas with highly concentrated markets to keep prices high. And it allows insurers to share in those profits, what economists call "rents," that is, what consumers end up paying for hospital services. In other words, insurers seem to be adjusting to the situation by adopting an "if you can't beat them, join them" philosophy.

The consolidation trend has resulted in a steady drop in the number of organizations selling hospital services. What about the buyers? Have the buyers been consolidating as well? Yes, that is exactly what happened as more people gained health insurance coverage. Clearly, people would not choose to act as buyers of hospital services on an individual basis if they could avoid it. Individuals have zero bargaining power in dealing with hospitals.

Indeed, uninsured consumers are often charged the highest prices. Hospitals may reduce the charges in response to pleading and the likelihood that the individual doesn't have the funds to pay the entire bill in any case. For their part, hospitals were willing to accept such losses because they could report unreimbursed costs as a charitable, community benefit. That has changed.

Nonprofit hospitals enjoy tax-exempt status, freeing them from some local, state, and federal taxes. In order to qualify, hospitals are required to provide "community benefit." How this was interpreted did not receive much attention until the beginning of the twenty-first century. The Affordable Care Act (ACA) made it clear. Nonprofit hospitals are now required to conduct community health need assessments in cooperation with public health officials and community representatives and develop plans to provide those community services. Writing off unreimbursed costs is no longer considered to be the same as provision of community benefit. Whether the activities that hospitals engage in actually bring noticeable community benefit is not all that clear.

Private Sector Hospital Reimbursement

The two sides—the buyers and sellers of hospital services—have evolved in response to each other's efforts to deal with pricing of hospital services.

The private sector third-party payer response is based on pressing hospitals to negotiate over rates. Insurers came up with the "network" mechanism. This involves pressuring smaller stand-alone hospitals that are unaffiliated with larger incorporated entities to participate in what are known as "narrow networks." The narrow network hospitals have little bargaining power so have little alternative but to accept lower reimbursement from the private insurance companies if they want to continue to serve patients, that is, to stay open. The result is that consumers who sign on for the narrow networks pay a lower premium in return for being restricted to the hospitals and doctors in such networks. Health care services obtained outside of the network are generally not reimbursed.

Hospital chains that have become horizontally and vertically integrated have continued to grow, developing various kinds of clinics and specialized testing operations. Third-party payers have little alternative but to treat the integrated systems as a single hospital care network. Thus the largest and most successful networks are in a very powerful bargaining position in negotiations over reimbursement. Insurers have been heard to complain that large hospital systems have gotten so big and so powerful that they are simply not willing to engage in bargaining. In some cases, insurers have threatened to drop hospitals from the list of organizations that the policy covers. The largest, most successful hospital enterprises have not been intimidated. However, in other cases, less well-established hospitals have been dropped, and enrollees have had to scramble to find alternative plans if they wanted to use a hospital that has suddenly been dropped from the insurer's list.

Medicare Hospital Reimbursement

The response of the public sector, as represented by Medicare, to the onset of businesslike practices of hospitals has been to develop comprehensive payment schedules to achieve greater control over pricing. Medicare does not negotiate reimbursement. It employs a set schedule—one for inpatient services and another for outpatient services. Medicare has a tremendous impact on pricing arrangements. Because it is the single largest third-party payer and does employ a detailed reimbursement schedule, other payers follow its lead. It is understood that private payers will pay more than Medicare and that Medicaid will pay less than Medicare. Accordingly, it is important to understand how Medicare arrives at the prices it sets. (Medicaid has more enrollees, but it bargains with providers of health care services on a state-by-state basis.)

Hospitals receive about 31 percent of their net revenues from Medicare. Medicaid accounts for about 17 percent. Private health insurance and payment by individuals cover the rest.

Medicare has been using a diagnosis-related group (DRG) system since 1983 to set reimbursement rates for *inpatient* care. This is a prospective payment arrangement originally based on about six hundred possible diagnoses.

Analogous to DRGs, the Ambulatory Payment Classification (APC) schedule is the Outpatient Prospective Payment System schedule (OPPS) Medicare uses to reimburse hospitals for services provided on an *outpatient* basis.

> For outpatient services, Medicare originally reimbursed hospitals retrospectively for allowable, incurred costs, for which beneficiaries were required to make copayments. By 1997 these copayments had come to equal about 50 percent of total Medicare payments to hospitals for outpatient care. . . . Congress mandated Medicare to replace that inherently inflationary, retrospective, full-cost reimbursement system with a prospective fee schedule. . . . This schedule went into effect in 2000.
>
> In developing the new fee schedule, Medicare bundled—as much as is sensible—entire sets of supplies and services associated with each major procedure into one lump-sum fee for that procedure. . . . The grouping was made accord-

ing to an ambulatory payment classification (APC) scheme developed through health services research.[7]

The DRG inpatient reimbursement system is based on the procedure, patient's age, sex, discharge status, presence of comorbidities, plus regional variations in cost of labor and other hospital inputs. The DRG begins with an International Classification of Diseases (ICD) diagnosis. According to the Centers for Disease Control the ICD codes are the "cornerstone of classifying diseases, injuries, health encounters and inpatient procedures in morbidity settings."[8] The codes are used to document morbidity statistics and for billing purposes. (The statistics establish morbidity and mortality rates used for comparative purposes nationally and internationally.) The tenth revision of the coding system, ICD-10, replacing the ICD-9 version, was instituted in 2015. The ICD-10 code has 71,924 procedure codes (the ICD-9 version had 3,824) and 69,823 diagnostic codes (ICD-9 had 14,025). Doctors and hospitals have had to make adjustments by purchasing new software, training coders to use the new system, and possibly having to upgrade computer systems. It has been challenging and expensive.

Reimbursement for outpatient care, the APC system, is complicated by the fact that physicians, the providers of health care services, are reimbursed using a different system from the one used to reimburse hospitals. The OPPS requires CPT codes for all services and supplies to determine the APC. (As you may recall from the previous chapter, the CPT code was created and is managed by the AMA CPT Editorial Panel. It provides a code for all services and supplies used by physicians in delivering health care. I don't actually expect you to recall that in any detail; why would anyone who is not directly involved make any effort to remember the names of these things? But I do think taking notice of the complexity involved cannot be ignored.)

What makes determining charges complicated is that the APC is based on two sources—the ICD-10 code and the hospital's price list, called a *chargemaster*. More on the chargemaster shortly. Armies of coders do this work in hospital health information management departments. They are assisted by software, called a "grouper," created to merge the CPT code and the ICD-10 code, to arrive at an APC code.

If the hospital bill that the consumer of hospital services receives is confusing, it is no wonder. Coders face a monumental challenge figuring out how to produce a hospital bill. "An individual hospital might be paid by a dozen or more distinct third-party payers, each with its own distinct set of rules for and levels of payment, which are negotiated separately with each private insurer once a year."[9]

The point is not to throw up one's hands and say that it so complicated, there is nothing we can do about it. It is to ask whether it has to be as complicated as it is.

A growing number of observers, both those who favor a market-based approach and those who do not, believe that hospitals are now in the phase of competition that occurs when competition has eliminated too many competitors and has left too few to be truly competitive.[10] These observers are calling for government to intervene.

> To combat the negative effects of increased market concentration, the author recommends policy responses, as follows: government regulators should scrutinize proposed mergers and acquisitions for their impact on competition; policies that restrict market entry should be evaluated to determine the impact on consumers; anticompetitive behaviors should be restricted—particularly in markets that are already concentrated; and reimbursement policies that reduce competition should be revised.[11]

CONSUMER CHOICE

Consumer choice is a matter of making purchases based on need and preference, right? This brings us back to shopping—in this case, shopping for the goods and services provided by hospitals. Paul Krugman captures the absurdity of shopping for hospital care perfectly: "I hear they've got a real deal on stents at St. Mary's!"[12]

While hospitals don't advertise sales, they do advertise. They announce being highly rated for quality by one or another rating entity, *U.S. News & World Report*, for example. They publish photographs of top doctors outlining their achievements. They tell stories about especially notable cases. How far does this go in informing you about the quality and price of the health care the hospital delivers?

To shop for the best buy in hospital goods and services, you need to be able to compare price and quality. As I have already said in earlier chapters, it is good to be able to do so before—not after—you have received the services. But that is not so likely to happen in the case of hospital services.

Price Transparency

Health policy types who identify themselves as consumer advocates have been pressing for price transparency, which they say will have a positive effect on quality. Here is the argument:

> If consumers realized that they could receive high-quality services from lower-cost providers, they would seek them out. This, in turn, could encourage competition among providers based on the value of the care—not just on reputation and market share.[13]

But, as the same authors also point out,

> There are many challenges to making comparative pricing information available. A September 2011 report from the U.S. Government Accountability Office outlined some of the most significant, including the difficulty of determining in advance the health services any given patient will need. The wide variety of insurance benefit structures, a lack of standard formatting for reporting prices, and the difficulty of determining prices when charges originate from multiple providers further complicate these efforts.[14]

I see this as policy built on the *if* factor. There is a lot of that going on: *if* we had transparency, prices would go down and quality would go up. Just like that? In fact, when California introduced a price transparency tool to help public employees and retirees to shop for hospital services, it found that few people used the tool. Researchers concluded that offering the tool did not decrease health prices or spending.[15]

Other observers try to explain why transparency is not enough.

> All of which makes this kind of transparency similar to rubbernecking a freeway accident. There's a brief moment of anxiety and tension and then everyone speeds on their way. Assuming data accuracy, releasing healthcare pricing is a hollow objective because there is almost nothing anyone can do with it. We simply have no way to influence it—either individually or collectively—and absent

quality (or clinical outcomes), there's no way to equate any value. We might as well use random number generators.[16]

Transparency was the motivating force behind the relatively recent comprehensive analysis of hospital pricing carried out by the Centers for Medicare and Medicaid Services (CMS). The CMS report, released in 2013, was based on one hundred of the most common inpatient procedures carried out in more than 3,300 US hospitals. The results revealed wide variation in charges for the same procedures. Comments in the media indicated astonishment at the differences. People were talking about the variation in pricing before the release of the CMS report, but the public now had factual evidence. Hospital pricing was suddenly more transparent. What accounted for the differences in price did not get nearly as much attention.

A study in the *American Journal of Surgery* released in 2017 indicates that, yes, there is significant variation: the median cost of surgery between 2009 and 2013 was $23,845.[17] Extreme differences occurred in some cases. The researchers do not focus on transparency. However, the analysis of factors responsible for variation in costs makes clear that transparency is unlikely to reduce prices. The researchers determined that more than 86 percent was due to differences in patient characteristics, around 8 percent to variation in surgeon practices, and around 6 percent to differences between surgical specialties. In short, unless you can do something about the patient population—that is, the buyers rather than the sellers—you are not likely to achieve much of a reduction in costs.

This is not to ignore the significance of the role played by sellers of health care and, more specifically, hospital services. Consumers do not walk up to the door of a hospital to buy stents and have them installed, as Paul Krugman's tongue-in-cheek observation suggests. In order to receive hospital care, a consumer must transform himself or herself into a patient who has received a diagnosis to be confirmed through further testing and addressed through a treatment regimen outlined by the doctor. A consumer cannot simply walk up to the door of a hospital and announce that he or she is shopping for an MRI or a colonoscopy or an endoscopy. One can't even drop in and try to sign up for a simple X-ray or blood test without a doctor's order. Calling up and asking how much one of these tests will cost is unlikely to produce a price. (That is not necessarily true in some instances; it can happen in the case of care outside of a hospital, in a clinic. Back to that shortly.) Nor would it do the consumer that much good, because the test is just the beginning of the treatment process. It is hard to see how getting a price for hospital care can happen without being absolutely sure about what other tests and procedures will be involved.

Talking about buyers and sellers of hospital services requires attending to what is at the heart of the hospital price transparency problem: the chargemaster—again, the hospital's price list for all goods and services. This is a privately held list not open to anyone but the hospital coders who use it in determining charges for hospital services. In other words, no one—not the government, not large insurance companies, certainly not an individual consumer—can see it. California is the only state that has passed legislation requiring hospitals to make their chargemasters public. That means that, outside of California, one hospital's list of prices cannot be compared to another hospital's list.

- Returning to Paul Krugman's observation, how do you know you can get a good deal on stents at St. Mary's if what the hospital next door and the one down the street are charging are not stated on a publicly available price list?

What about asking your doctor for the price you will be paying for hospital care? Part of the answer is that your doctor doesn't have access to the chargemaster either. Why not go to someone who has access to the list and see if you can entice one of the coders to tell you? Coders have no idea ahead of time what tests and treatments you will have. They can only tell you what your charges are after the fact. They do tell you in the form of the hospital's final bill.

In an online story entitled: "How Many Doctors Does It Take to Read a Hospital Bill?" a doctor explains his efforts to help a young woman, Anna, figure out her bill. The young woman who was covered by student health insurance went in for treatment for a sexually transmitted infection. She was treated and given a clean bill of health. She was told that her care was covered by her insurance. Then the bills from the hospital started to come. It turned out that her student insurance plan did not cover sexually transmitted disease.

All in all, the episode cost Anna somewhere from $350 to approximately $1200. Despite our best efforts, the health system still cannot tell us the final amount that she owes and seems content to continue sending bills. I knew that under the new health care price transparency law that went into effect at the beginning of the year, physicians were theoretically responsible for informing patients of medical prices upfront. I also knew that most physicians have no idea whatsoever how much the services they provide or request cost.

Several weeks ago I played a dinner game with a few of my physician friends; each of us would try to read the bills and figure out exactly how much Anna would owe if she paid the full amount.[18]

In the end the doctors at the dinner party concluded that they could not be sure whether they had figured out the bill correctly.

The hospital bill is not the only bill a person may have to figure out. Bills can come from doctors who are members of the staff but not members of the (third-party payer) network the consumer signed up with. The doctors bill for their services independently. You say you did not agree to getting their services? Too late. It already happened. The issue of "surprise bills" has become a hot topic that politicians have been pressed into talking about. So far there don't seem to be any good solutions in the offing.

Then there is the "facility fee." If the doctor's practice is owned by a hospital, the hospital can add an additional charge to whatever the doctor charges. The justification is that the hospital is responsible for maintaining "the facility" in which doctor sees the patient. It is just another instance of charging separately for every aspect of the event.

If you were unlucky enough to need an ambulance to get to the hospital, you will probably be billed for that separately too. Most ambulance companies are privately owned and are generally not part of networks. This may be true of ambulance service operated by the local fire department. The advice from policy experts is to take a cab or an Uber if you are able to manage that.

If one does make the effort to examine the hospital bill in detail, one might find some interesting charges such as the ones reported in a *Reader's Digest* article: fifteen dollars per Tylenol pill, fifty-three dollars for each pair of plastic gloves, and eight dollars for a "mucus recovery system," otherwise known as a box of tissues.[19] Outrageous, right? Hospitals argue that the requirement that they treat everyone who comes through the emergency room door means that they are treating people who have no insurance and no resources to pay for their care. (This is required by the Emergency Room Medical Treatment and Labor Act passed in 1986.) In some cases, this involves hospitalization to stabilize the patient. In the most extreme cases, it means having the patient spend days in the intensive care unit, which is the most expensive form of hospitalization. Hospital administrators ask, How are hospitals supposed to cover those costs? Their answer is that they are forced to overcharge patients who have insurance coverage. Those who are uninsured are charged the full price rather than the discounted price negotiated with insurance companies.

The federal government instituted the requirement that all hospitals publish chargemaster prices on their web sites as of January 1, 2019. Full transparency is not likely because chargemaster prices involve codes and because they not fixed. They are discounted in negotiations with health insurance companies. I will leave the question of whether this means that the market is working to achieve supply and demand equilibrium when giants negotiate for others to answer. The question of how consumers of hospital services fit into this scenario is easier to answer: they don't.

I must admit that I have never been sure at what point the consumer is supposed to be in a position to influence hospital pricing. Is it once the person is released from the hospital and receives the bill? The consumer's bargaining power is obviously diminished once the services have been consumed. Yes, people do try to bargain at that point. And there is a chance the bill will be reduced, especially if it looks as if the person has no way of paying the full amount. But there is no assurance of that happening. It is completely at the discretion of the hospital. The consumer's bargaining position can be helped a lot by a media spotlight. Kaiser Health News and NPR have established a "Bill of the Month" series. In August 2018, a Texas hospital that charged a teacher $108,951 to treat him for a heart attack reduced the bill to $332.29 after the charge became a national news story.[20]

How about bargaining before receiving the services? Consumers are told to shop before going to the hospital. But that assumes that the admission to the hospital is a matter of choice and is comparable to choosing a hotel based on amenities and price. By the time a person knows he or she needs to be admitted to the hospital, the person is very likely beginning to look more like a patient than a consumer. That is, he or she is likely to be far more concerned about the procedures to be undergone than about amenities and price comparisons. After all, most people are not eager to be admitted to a hospital. They are not eager to consume hospital care without good reason. In other words, price transparency is probably a secondary concern. If that is the case, then price transparency matters less than market-based health care would have us believe.

Quality Transparency

What about transparency with regard to quality? That raises a number of questions, such as, Who do you trust to give you information about hospital quality? Are you interested in a particular indicator of quality or a comprehensive evaluation?

People generally start by asking their friends and relatives about the quality of products they are thinking of buying or of services they are seeking. The complaint that health policy experts have about that is the public tends to focus on hotel amenities provided by the hospital—how attractive the room is, how beautiful the lobby is—and how nice the nurses are. How competent and attentive the nurses are matters a lot. Unfortunately, one cannot be sure that there is a high correlation between niceness and competence. And hospital amenities may be desirable features, but they don't have a lot to do with the outcome of hospital care.

As I have already said, it is far easier to get information on products than services. Products that come in a standardized form are comparable. Even if one does not understand how a highly sophisticated product works, one can generally find some rating service that reviews the strengths and weaknesses of the product, which generally has a specific numerical identifier.

Services are harder to standardize. The more complicated the service, the harder to compare. But hospital quality ratings are being developed by various entities. In fact, the Advisory Board Company, a consulting firm that advises hospitals on best practices to improve performance, found twelve hospital ratings groups in 2017. It carried out an evaluation of the ratings provided by each of the reviewers. The list includes among others: Leapfrog Group, which provides data to large employers and other purchasers; Healthgrades, which is a commercial entity; *Consumer Reports*, which is a nonprofit entity; *U.S. News & World Report*, a national magazine; and the Joint Commission, a private sector nonprofit organization that carries out accreditation of twenty-one thousand health care organizations as required by Medicare to qualify for reimbursement. Two government agencies are on the list: AHRQ, which is primarily engaged in research and issues advisory information; and CMS, which issued a report in 2016. More about the CMS report shortly.

The fact that there are so many different raters, each with its own rating system, is bound to be confusing to consumers especially if the ratings are inconsistent. That is exactly the problem according to one observer who says that a survey of readers conducted by the journal *Modern Healthcare*

> indicated that healthcare executives are ambivalent about hospital ratings efforts. Of more than 230 respondents, 53% said that their facility had received a poor rating from at least one ratings organization while receiving a high rating on similar measures during the same time period from another group.[21]

A spokesperson for *Consumer Reports*, another one of the rating organizations on the Advisory Board list, points out that the inconsistency is not stopping health care executives from taking advantage of the positive ratings:

> It's hypocritical for hospitals to complain about ratings groups when they often use favorable rankings in their marketing and advertising or make claims about having the 'best doctors' or 'the most innovative technology' without good evidence.
>
> I chuckle when I get reports that hospital CEOs are worried or confused about ratings. . . . They're not so confused that they are not using comparisons in their own advertising.[22]

Incidentally, I think it is interesting that the Advisory Board Company announced that it was splitting its educational consulting business from its health care consulting business. It put the two halves on the market for $2.6 billion in the autumn of 2017. I mention this to make the point that there is a great deal of money to be made in the health care sector. Providing ratings can be profitable. This is an observation to which I will return in the final two chapters.

Before leaving the topic of hospital quality, let's consider the first-ever hospital quality ratings released by CMS in 2016. CMS published hospital quality star ratings on the Medicare Hospital Compare website (https://www.medicare.gov/hospitalcompare/search.html) with the following announcement:

> Today, we are updating the star ratings on the Hospital Compare website to help millions of patients and their families learn about the quality of hospitals, compare facilities in their area side-by-side, and ask important questions about care quality when visiting a hospital or other health care providers. . . . The new

Overall Hospital Quality Star Rating summarizes data from existing measures publicly reported on *Hospital Compare* into a single star rating for each hospital, making it easier for consumers to compare hospitals and interpret complex quality information.

The ratings are based on sixty-four quality measures from seven quality domains. The three domains allotted the greatest weight are mortality, readmission, and patient safety. The other four include patient experience, effectiveness of care, timeliness of care, and efficient use of medical imaging. The results for the 3,662 eligible hospitals (937 were not rated because they did not meet reporting thresholds) are as follows:

5-star rating—102 hospitals

4-star rating—934 hospitals

3-star rating—1,770 hospitals

2-star rating—723 hospitals

1-star rating—133 hospitals[23]

Given that the CMS star ratings report is a comprehensive review based on highly reliable data collected on all hospitals in the country and is free to anyone who wishes to access it, it should have had a bigger impact. Maybe the report came out at a time when there were already too many ratings out there, and it is just adding more numbers rather than better, easy-to-use information.

Another reason the release of the ratings did not receive as much attention as might be expected is the reaction of health policy experts who analyzed the methodology CMS used. The authors of one of the few thorough assessments start by saying that the ratings are "confusing at best and misleading at worst." They go on to say that the names of some of the hospitals receiving the highest ratings are unfamiliar and that some receiving the lowest ratings are highly regarded university teaching hospitals. The explanation has to do with the methodology used to compile the data.

The disconnect is the result of the fact that when a hospital has insufficient data to report on one or more quality domains, the "weights" of those miss-

ing domains are reallocated to the domains for which there is sufficient data.
. . . This is simply inconsistent with the rating system's original intention of
making performance on clinical outcomes the predominant influence on the
overall rating.[24]

Because teaching hospitals provide comprehensive services and collect statistics on those services, they are in a position to report on them. The CMS rating scale penalizes them for having more data on serving patients with more
serious illnesses. The authors conclude their assessment with the following
observation: "While all improvement efforts can be challenging, we believe
that it takes more to improve clinical outcomes—for example, saving a patient's
life—than to improve delivery process, such as reducing the use of imaging."[25]

In sum, coming up with hospital quality ratings is fraught with glitches.
Picking a hospital based on the idea that high prices serve to indicate consen-
sus that the medical care it offers is superior because so many consumers are
flocking to its doors, as a market-based view of transactions would suggest,
is also not a reliable indicator. It seems that list prices have little relationship
to quality.[26] Highly advanced shopping efforts may not, in the end, be much
better than asking one's friends and relatives. What one has to keep in mind is
that the big hurdle, one that is very difficult to overcome, is that your experience may turn out to be very different from that of your friends and relatives
because your problem is not exactly the same as theirs.

I always like to turn to evidence that can be confirmed, so I offer the following as worth considering. There is a lot of evidence to indicate that people's
attitudes are shaped by physiological—more specifically, neurological—factors.
For example, holding a glass of warm as opposed to cold liquid affects a person's attitude, making the person either more or less generous.[27] If one were to
look for one measure of patient satisfaction with a hospital stay, it is likely that
how much sleep the person was able to get would be the single best determining variable. It seems that the more sleep patients get, the better they feel and
more satisfied they are with their hospital experience.[28] Maybe that is not such
a bad indicator or quality, but still, it's not quite enough, is it?

So, we are back to the *if* factor. If we could only measure quality, then all
kinds of good things would happen: the best hospitals could be rewarded and
lower-quality hospitals could be penalized. An article in the *New England
Journal of Medicine* authored by twenty-three persons involved in health

policy making presents exactly that argument.[29] The idea is that the market would be highly responsive, consumers would flock to the better hospitals *if*, . . . followed by a quite a few *ifs*.

Investor-Owned Hospitals

In order for the market-based approach to health care to be convincing, shouldn't the performance of investor-owned hospitals be superior to that of non-investor-owned hospitals? Shouldn't there be clear evidence that they are more efficient and successful than other hospitals, most notably, nonprofit hospitals? That proposition has clearly come into question.

What is clear is that for-profit hospitals charge more. In a study calculating how much hospitals charge beyond the Medicare-allowable cost compared to what hospitals charge based on their respective chargemasters, researchers found the following: government hospitals charge 3.47 percent more, non-profit hospitals charge 3.47 more, and for-profit hospitals charge 6.31 more.[30]

A closer look reveals that over the last couple of decades, investor-owned hospitals went through a period of expansion, which some are now saying was a "merger and acquisition binge." The binge apparently caused more debt than the hospital organizations could tolerate. The result is that the for-profit sector hospital chains are selling off individual hospitals to nonprofit hospital groups.[31] Whether this is the beginning of a "great unraveling" remains to be seen. Watching the unraveling does, however, mean that the efficiency attributed to the market-based approach is not producing the results promised by advocates. In the meantime, nonprofit chains are becoming increasingly bigger. Catholic Health Initiatives and Dignity Health announced a merger that would give them a presence in twenty-eight states. Ascension, the largest nonprofit system, is currently in the process of adding more hospitals.[32]

- Does that mean that the nonprofit hospitals are becoming increasingly more efficient—more efficient than the for-profits, which are having financial difficulties?

If we were to go back to see how the for-profit sector hospitals were performing over past decades, the picture would reveal other kinds of problems, including some really unpleasant ones. One of the earliest in a list of spectacular revelations about for-profit hospital practices was the 1998 FBI raid of the

Health Corporation of America (HCA) offices. The FBI confirmed that the company was keeping two sets of books—the real set and one used for reporting to Medicare. HCA was the biggest for-profit chain at the time. The FBI also found that CEO salaries were tied to meeting financial targets based on increasing patient admissions. This was the biggest case of Medicare fraud to date. The company paid $1.7 billion in fines. Rick Scott, the CEO at the time, resigned. He went on to become governor of Florida and, as of 2019, a senator.

The Tenet Healthcare organization provides another troubling example. In 2002, when it was the second-largest for-profit chain, it paid a $54 million fine when doctors at one of its hospitals in California were found to be admitting healthy people and subjecting them to unnecessary heart surgery. In 2016, the chain paid a $513 million fine for defrauding Medicare, making illegal payments in exchange for referrals. Do you think this may help to explain why Tenet is selling off some of its hospitals?

In 2013 a CBS *60 Minutes* report revealed that administrators at the Health Management Associates hospital chain were telling emergency room doctors that they would be fired if they did not admit more patients to the hospital. The hospital chain, the fourth-biggest at the time, reportedly made $5.8 billion in profit over the previous year, about half of which came from Medicare and Medicaid.

I am not suggesting that all big, for-profit hospital chains are engaged in fraud. But efficiency, as touted by proponents of market-based health care, has been quite closely linked to colossal cases of fraud, and that should give one pause for thought.

Investor-Owned Facilities Other than Hospitals

Evidence of price gouging, fraud, and poor quality in the for-profit nursing home industry has been around for decades. The newest kinds of health organizations enjoy a very different reputation. These are the stand-alone health care facilities, which may or may not be connected to hospitals. MRI facilities in shopping centers are one example. Many are privately owned, for-profit operations. They charge about half of what a hospital charges for an MRI.

Another kind is the freestanding emergency department (FSED). As of 2016, 387 were hospital owned and 172 were independently owned, 17 percent by for-profit entities.[33] Freestanding outpatient ERs first surfaced in the 1970s.

Until recently, the idea of an FSED in suburbia was almost inconceivable. But FSEDs are now proliferating, thanks to cheaper, faster innovations in advanced imaging and testing; an almost insatiable demand for immediate, 24/7 access to care; and, of course, the potential for profit. . . . Unlike hospital-based FSEDs, which receive 10% to 40% of their patients by ambulance, more than 95% of FSED patients are walk-ins, and very few require hospital admission.[34]

There is considerable debate about FSEDs. On the upside, many provide high-quality care, score high on patient satisfaction, and are open 24/7. On the downside, they charge the same fees as hospitals with a fraction of overhead costs; and they may steer patients away from low-cost, continuing care by primary care physicians, escalating health care costs and fragmenting the care continuum. They are being established in areas with higher household incomes not because there is greater need but because they are more profitable, since the patients are healthier, are well-insured, and are less costly to treat.

The Medicare Payment Advisory Commission (MedPac), which has been tracking the growth of these entities, found that from 2010 to 2015 outpatient visits to the ER (freestanding and hospital-based) increased by 13.6 percent; this is in contrast to the 3.5 percent increase in physician visits.[35] A MedPac analysis of five markets (cities) found that 75 percent of the freestanding ERs were within six miles of a hospital. In response to this finding and the fact that the ERs are paid the same as hospital ERs, which must be open 24/7 to deal with serious trauma, MedPac has proposed a 30 percent reduction in Medicare reimbursement rates.[36]

The growing number of freestanding surgical centers is also raising concerns. As of 2017, there were 5,616 Medicare-certified surgical centers which took in $4.1 billion in Medicare reimbursements.[37] The procedures may go well, but when something unexpected occurs, there isn't much that can be done for the patient other than calling 911. Part of the problem is that the centers are engaging in increasingly more complicated procedures. According to one study, there have been 260 deaths over the last four years. But there is no official record. No one is tracking complications at surgical centers. Is there reason to institute tracking? . . . to impose restrictions on the types of procedures that can be performed in off-site centers? Is there reason for the government to become involved?

Stand-alone facilities are not a new phenomenon. Specialty hospitals that perform a specific procedure—back surgery, for example—evolved a couple of decades ago. By 2010, there were about two hundred across the country. This is when ACA was passed. It prohibited new specialty hospitals from developing. The explanation is as follows: the specialty hospitals were private sector operations, often owned by physician entrepreneurs on staff at traditional hospitals who were touting high quality at a lower price than traditional hospitals could offer. No one disputed the claims. What traditional hospitals said was that the doctors involved screened patients, admitting low-risk patients who were likely to present few complications. That meant that the patients with comorbidities were going to the traditional hospital. Such patients were at greater risk of complications, likely to stay in the hospital for a longer time and run up higher costs. The established hospitals objected, saying that this was unfair competition. They disputed claims of efficiency on the part of the specialty hospitals. Yes, the specialty hospitals could claim to be more efficient, but the playing field was not the same. They weren't responding to needs presented by the same kinds of consumers. The authors of ACA agreed.

It is not clear what the future holds for stand-alone MRI centers, freestanding emergency departments, and surgical centers. Will they be viewed from the same perspective as specialty hospitals or will they be encouraged to compete with traditional hospitals with the aim of reducing traditional hospital prices? The effect of continuing competition from the freestanding entities on traditional hospitals is also unclear. One administrator quoted in the podcast mentioned above made the point that hospitals are required to treat each person who comes to the emergency room and admit the patient for expensive treatment if necessary, even if the person cannot pay for the care. As long as that is the case, hospitals will have to find a way to cover those costs. If they reduce the price of MRIs, they will charge more for something else. He compared it to squeezing a balloon: you can contract it on one side, but it will balloon up on the other side.

Competition on a procedure-by-procedure basis may affect the price of the procedures but is unlikely to reduce costs attributable to the hospital sector as a whole. Indeed, freestanding centers may be responsible for increasing total health care costs by seeking out healthier consumers who cost less to treat while charging the same fees that full-service hospitals charge—fees that have not, at least not so far, been reduced to match reduced costs of operation. In short, efficiency and competition must be examined in context; otherwise they are slogans, and misleading slogans at that.

NOTES

1. National Center for Health Statistics, "Table 89. Hospitals, Beds, and Occupancy Rates, by Type of Ownership and Size of Hospital: United States, Selected Years, 1975–2014," CDC/National Center for Health Statistics, 2017, https://www.cdc.gov/nchs/data/hus/2016/089.pdf.

2. Jane Wishner et al., "A Look at Rural Hospital Closures and Implications for Access to Care: Three Case Studies," Kaiser Family Foundation, July 7, 2016, https://www.kff.org/medicaid/issue-brief/a-look-at-rural-hospital-closures-and-implications-for-access-to-care/.

3. Sherry Glied and Stuart Altman, "Beyond Antitrust: Health Care and Health Insurance Market Trends and the Future of Competition," *Health Affairs* 36, no. 9 (2017): 1572–77.

4. Brent Fulton, "Health Care Market Concentration Trends in the United States: Evidence and Policy Responses," *Health Affairs* 36, no. 9 (2017): 1530–38.

5. G. A. Melnick and K. Fonkych, "Hospital Prices Increase in California, Especially among Hospitals in the Largest Multi-Hospital Systems," *Inquiry* 53 (June 9, 2016): 1–7.

6. Jonathan Yun, Kathryn Oehlman, and Michael Johansen, "Per Visit Emergency Department Expenditures by Insurance Type, 1996–2015," *Health Affairs* 7 (July 2018): 1109–14.

7. Uwe Reinhardt, "The Pricing of U.S. Hospital Services: Chaos Behind a Veil of Secrecy," *Health Affairs* 25, no. 1 (2006): 57–69, p. 60.

8. National Center for Health Statistics, "International Classification of Diseases, (ICD-10-CM-PCS) Transition—Background," CDC/National Center for Health Statistics, https://www.cdc.gov/nchs/icd/icd10cm_pcs_background.htm.

9. Reinhardt, "Pricing of U.S. Hospital Services," 59.

10. Annabelle Fowler et al., "Corporate Investors Increased Common Ownership in Hospitals and Postacute Care and Hospice Sectors," *Health Affairs* 36, no. 9 (2017): 1547–55.

11. Fulton, "Health Care Market Concentration Trends."

12. Paul Krugman, "Why Markets Can't Cure Healthcare," *New York Times*, July 25, 2009.

13. Martha Hostetter and Sarah Klein, "Health Care Price Transparency: Can It Promote High-Value Care?" Commonwealth Fund, 2012, https://www.common wealthfund.org/publications/newsletter-article/health-care-price-transparency-can -it-promote-high-value-care.

14. Hostetter and Klein, "Health Care Price Transparency."

15. Sunita Desai et al., "Offering a Price Transparency Tool Did Not Reduce Overall Spending among California Public Employees and Retirees," *Health Affairs* 36, no. 8 (2017): 1401–7.

16. Dan Munro, "Avoiding Healthcare Cost with Pricing Transparency Hype," *Forbes*, April 22, 2014, https://www.forbes.com/sites/danmunro/2014/04/22/ avoiding-healthcare-cost-with-pricing-transparency-hype/#5ae0d7f933bd.

17. Faiz Gani et al., "Variations in Hospitals Costs for Surgical Procedures: Inefficient Care or Sick Patients," *American Journal of Surgery* 213, no. 1 (2017): 1–9.

18. Sylvia Romm, "How Many Doctors Does It Take to Read a Hospital Bill?" Costs of Care, June 30, 2018, https://costsofcare.org/how-many-doctors-does-it-take-to -read-a-hospital-bill/.

19. Lauren Gelman, "10 Wildly Overinflated Hospital Costs You Didn't Know About," *Reader's Digest*, https://www.rd.com/health/wellness/wildly-overinflated -hospital-costs/.

20. Chad Terhune, "The $109K Heart Attack Bill is Down to $332. What About Other Surprise Bills?" Kaiser Health News, August 31, 2018, https://khn.org/news/ the-109k-heart-attack-bill-is-down-to-332-what-about-other-surprise-bills/.

21. Sabriya Rice, "Experts Raise Questions about Hospital Raters' Methods and Lack of Transparency," *Modern Healthcare*, May 31, 2014, https://www.modernhealthcare .com/article/20140531/MAGAZINE/305319980/experts-question-hospital-raters -methods.

22. Rice, "Experts Raise Questions."

23. "First Release of the Overall Hospital Quality Rating on Hospital Compare," CMS, July 27, 2016, https://www.cms.gov/newsroom/fact-sheets/first-release-overall

-hospital-quality-star-rating-hospital-compare; "The First-Ever CMS Overall Hospital Quality Star Ratings Are Out. See How Hospitals Fared on Our Map," Advisory Board, July 28, 2016, https://www.advisory.com/daily-briefing/2016/07/28/cms-star-rating.

24. Susan Xu and Atul Grover, "CMS' Hospital Quality Star Ratings Fail to Pass the Common Sense Test," *Health Affairs Blog*, November 14, 2016, https://www.health affairs.org/do/10.1377/hblog20161114.057512/full/.

25. Xu and Grover, "CMS' Hospital Quality."

26. Michael Batty and Benedic Ippolito, "Mystery of the Chargemaster: Examining the Role of Hospital List Prices in What Patients Actually Pay," *Health Affairs* 36, no. 4 (2017): 689–96.

27. Lawrence Williams and John Bargh, "Experiencing Physical Warmth Promotes Interpersonal Warmth," *Science* 322 (October 24, 2008): 606–7.

28. Shefali Luthra, "For Hospitals, Sleep and Patient Satisfaction May Go Hand in Hand," Kaiser Health News, August 17, 2017, https://khn.org/news/for-hospitals-sleep-and-patient-satisfaction-may-go-hand-in-hand/.

29. Ezekiel Emanuel et al., "A Systemic Approach to Containing Health Care Spending," *New England Journal of Medicine* 367 (September 5, 2012): 949–54.

30. Ge Bai and Gerard Anderson, "US Hospitals Are Still Using Chargemaster Markups to Maximize Revenues," *Health Affairs* 35, no. 9 (September 2016): 1658–64.

31. Dave Barkholz, "Nation's Largest Investor-Owned Hospital Systems Are in Full Retreat," *Modern Healthcare*, January 28, 2017, https://www.modernhealthcare.com/article/20170128/MAGAZINE/301289983/nation-s-largest-investor-owned-hospital-systems-are-in-full-retreat.

32. Reed Abelson, "To Fend Off Competition, Hospitals Consolidate," *New York Times*, December 19, 2017.

33. Caitlin Kenney, "Shopping for an MRI," in *Planet Money*, podcast, November 6, 2009, https://www.npr.org/sections/money/2009/11/podcast_shopping_for_an_mri.html.

34. Nir Harish and Jennifer Wiler, "How the Freestanding Emergency Department Boom Can Help Patients," NEJM Catalyst, October 24, 2016, https://catalyst.nejm.org/how-the-freestanding-emergency-department-boom-can-help-patients/.

35. Harish and Wiler, "Freestanding Emergency Department Boom."

36. Michelle Andrews, "Congress Urged to Cut Medicare Payments to Many Stand-Alone ERs," Kaiser Health News, April 17, 2018, https://khn.org/news/congressional-advisers-urge-medicare-payments-to-many-stand-alone-ers-be-cut/.

37. Christina Jewett and Mark Alesia, "As Surgical Centers Boom, Patients Are Paying with Their Lives," Kaiser Health News, March 2, 2018, https://khn.org/news/medicare-certified-surgery-centers-are-expanding-but-deaths-question-safety/.

7

Pharmaceuticals

This chapter starts by examining public attitudes toward pharmaceutical prices and the role of government in doing something about those prices. The discussion that follows focuses on laws, regulations, and other forms of government intervention in this arena, including decisions in court cases that govern pharmaceutical market operations. The laws have a clear impact on the three, now familiar, market-based health care theory principles: ease of market entry and exit, many buyers and many sellers, and consumer choice.

The pharmaceutical sector of the health care market has moved to the center of public debate in recent years as increasing numbers of people have come to believe that drugs are unaffordable and that drug prices are outrageous. A Kaiser Family Foundation survey conducted in 2016 reported that 74 percent of the population said that making drugs affordable was a "top priority." More surprising is finding that 63 percent said that "government action to lower prescription drug prices" was a "top priority."[1] The government responded to the growing sense that drugs are too expensive by holding hearings and introducing two dozen bills between 2016 and 2017 aimed at curbing drug prices over the following year.[2]

The announcement coming from the executive office in October 2018 indicated that pharmaceutical companies would be required to charge Medicare Part B the same prices as it charges other economically advanced countries.[3] No one seems to have a good answer to the puzzling question this raises: Why depend on other countries to do the negotiating? Wouldn't it make sense to allow Medicare to conduct its own negotiations? On the other hand, it is not clear at the time of this writing how the announcement will be followed up.

It is of course important to stop here for a moment and remember that legislation created in the past is what allows pharmaceutical companies to charge as much as they are charging. That observation is central to the discussion to follow.

I probably don't need to point out the contrast between the popularity of government action aimed at imposing controls over pharmaceutical prices and the opposition to government control of health insurance. Why members of the public and politicians alike are willing to have government intervene in the pharmaceutical market but not in other health care markets raises an interesting question, one that has not been fully explored.

A number of answers come to mind. Headline stories in the media have probably played a big part in influencing public opinion. Reports on the amount of money involved are eye-popping. According to a Government Accountability Office (GAO) report, pharmaceutical and biotechnology companies' sales revenues increased from $534 billion in 2006 to $775 billion in 2015. Profit margins are about 20 percent.[4]

That kind of information tends to produce nodding and shaking of heads—maybe a call to arrange for a stock purchase by some—but it generally does not elicit more of a reaction, because most people view it as important only in the abstract since they don't feel they can do anything about it.

Doctors say that patients ask them why health insurance covers all but a small fraction of a $100,000 hospitalization but they are required to pay 20 percent or more of the cost of a life-saving $100,000 drug. Doctors don't have an answer.

Media attention to exorbitant increases in the price of certain drugs and the individuals responsible for those increases has helped fuel public anger and frustration. Martin Shkreli is the main actor in an especially riveting story. After making a fortune with a business he founded in 2009, he established a pharmaceutical company in 2011. In 2015, he launched Turing Pharmaceuticals and bought out the rights to Daraprim, an AIDS and cancer drug. Shortly thereafter he raised the price of a single pill from $13 to $750. A few months later, he bought a major share in another company, KaloBios, "a hot bio tech company," with the understanding that he would raise prices.[5] The stock of that company increased by 400 percent in response to this announcement. At this point, the Senate Committee on Aging opened an investigation of the Turing company. The following month Shkreli was arrested for securities fraud, not for price gouging. While most people would agree that a 5,000 percent increase in price was outrageous, what cannot be ignored is that the stockholders had no reservations about investing in Shkreli's new venture knowing that it would have a devastating effect on the price of yet another drug. What this sequence of events says about market-based health care in general and the pharmaceutical market in particular is obviously thought-provoking.

The EpiPen story is another attention-grabbing tale. EpiPens are used to deliver an injectable drug in reaction to a life-threatening allergic reaction to bee stings and food allergies. Peanut allergies in children receive more attention than other cases because it is not always possible to know that peanuts are used in food preparation and children cannot be expected to monitor the food they get outside of their homes. The fact that children are often the victims helps to explain the level of public outrage in response to the sudden increase in the price of EpiPens.

The EpiPen story begins with the purchase of the EpiPen brand by Mylan Pharmaceuticals from Merck in 2007. The pen injects about a dollar's worth of epinephrine, which produces an instantaneous resolution of the allergic threat. In 2009, Mylan raised the price of a twin pack of injectors from $57 to $100. It raised the price to $600 in 2017. This is when the public reacted with demands that the government do something. The company said it would reduce the price in special cases but would not budge on the basic price. At the same time, it used political influence to try to force schools to buy EpiPens.

While these two cases grabbed public attention, the increase in price of other, more commonly used drugs has not attracted much media attention. But it is certainly something that consumers of those drugs have noticed. For example, the price of Humira, "the best-selling prescription drug in the world," rose from $19,000 per year in 2012 to $38,000 in 2017.[6] That is a 100 percent increase over a five-year period. The drug is used to treat arthritis, psoriasis, and colitis—that is, chronic diseases, meaning that the numbers of consumers who depend on the drug can be expected to increase.

The opioid epidemic that is receiving a great deal of attention these days is directly related to the role played by drug companies, which market the drugs to patients as pain relief "without addiction." News stories have pointed to the link between the unprecedented drop in life expectancy in this country over the last two years and the rise in opioid deaths. The CDC estimates that this amounts to about ninety-one deaths per day. About sixty-four thousand persons died of overdoses in 2016, which is more than those who died in the Vietnam war and more than those who died of HIV in 1995 at the height of that epidemic, when forty-three thousand persons died.[7]

Doctors are being blamed for overprescribing. But it is worth noting that the government played a part in pressing physicians to treat pain more aggressively some years ago. Orrin Hatch took on this campaign in 1999 during the 106th Congress by proposing the Pain Relief Promotion Act, arguing that undertreating pain should be treated as a criminal offense. The proposal did not pass but apparently increased consumer demand for prescription pain medications, which are now recognized as a gateway to addiction.

Other branches of government have begun investigations focusing on the five companies that manufacture opioid drugs and the three drug distributor companies. Forty-one states attorneys general have joined together to serve the companies with subpoenas requesting information on how they market and sell opioids. This is in addition to separate lawsuits filed by about one hundred cities and states demanding compensation for financial loss, for example, the cost of doing autopsies to confirm cause of death.

Having witnessed recent events involving the pharmaceutical industry, the public is apparently ready to see someone punished for what certainly appears to be excessive greed on the part of the industry. Members of government are being pressed into doing something about two issues: high drug prices and availability of addictive prescription drugs.

MARKET-BASED HEALTH CARE THEORY AND THE REALITY IN THE PHARMACEUTICAL MARKET

The traditional solution to consumer complaints about high prices, one that is embraced by fans of the market-based approach—namely, greater reliance on market forces—does not present an obvious answer in this case. Drug companies are private enterprises. They are market-driven. They do not need to be encouraged to compete. They are aggressively competitive, which in this instance means doing a lot of advertising to increase sales, making the industry extremely profitable.

Is this enough to conclude that pharmaceutical sector operations conform to the principles inherent in the market-based model? Not really, mainly because government has been playing such a large role in the operations of the pharmaceutical market. The relationship is complicated. It doesn't work the way the market-based health care model says it should work—that the government should stay out of the way. The fact is that the government has been heavily involved in the pharmaceutical sector for decades with the intent of promoting research and development by providing a profit incentive. It has done this through patent law. Patents translate into a "time is money" formula. While the patent is in effect, the pharmaceutical company that brought the drug to market enjoys monopoly rights over the drug formula and the right to sell that drug.

The 1980 Bayh-Dole Act constitutes an important turning point in the government's interest in providing incentives to drug researchers and manufacturers. The law allowed universities and businesses to patent discoveries even when the research was sponsored by government funding through the National Institutes of Health (NIH). The law serves as an incentive to universities and individual researchers to enter into partnerships with drug companies in order to share in the benefits that monopoly rights produce.

The 1984 Hatch-Waxman Act increased patent life from eight years to fourteen years. Patent life was extended to twenty years in 1994. In 1997, a six-month extension was added for the purpose of testing on children. The average length of patents currently may be well over twenty years because the companies can employ a variety of tactics to gain further extensions.

The 21st Century Cures Act of 2016 did more than provide $4.8 billion to the NIH to fight cancer and mental health problems through lab research leading to new pharmaceuticals. It provided vouchers for six-month drug approval in cases of pediatric disease and gave each pharmaceutical company the right to sell to other companies. The vouchers can sell for hundreds of millions of dollars.

In other words, Congress has intervened in the pharmaceutical market by passing legislation that sanctions exclusive control over the production and distribution of highly lucrative products for what now amounts to a period of at least twenty years, making the pharmaceutical industry enormously profitable.

At this point let's turn to the question of how this affects the answer to the basic question raised in this book, namely, How closely does the pharmaceutical sector conform to the basic principles of the market-based theoretical model? Accordingly, we now turn to our three principles: ease of market entry and exit, many buyers and many sellers, and consumers' ability to choose.

EASE OF ENTRY AND EXIT

Ease of entry and exit in this market has a different meaning than it does in other markets. The Federal Drug Administration is the gatekeeper. Anyone can start a company, as is confirmed by the Shkreli story. Permission to enter the pharmaceutical market, that is, sell a new drug, requires evidence of drug safety and efficacy. Because this takes years of evidence gathering, drug companies take out patents on new entities before they proceed to test their efficacy. This is also when the US Patent and Trademark Office (USPTO) gets involved.

The development of a new drug occurs in stages. The preclinical stage involves identification and testing molecules in the lab; next is testing on animals. If a molecule looks promising, the company takes out a patent. The clinical stage involves testing on humans. This requires application to the FDA. After clinical trials are complete, which may take a few years, the company must turn to the FDA again for permission to go to market.

Discoveries that ultimately lead to drug formulations occur in a variety of research settings including universities and biotech startups. Original research conducted in these settings is typically sponsored through grants offered by the NIH.[8] In other words, research at this stage is largely paid for by the public sector, through tax dollars, not by private sector pharmaceutical companies.

Innovators, often university-based researchers, who create biotech start-ups can participate at the edge of the pharmaceutical market without investing in setting up full-fledged clinical testing, manufacturing, and sales operations. They do not have to establish new pharmaceutical companies. There are no barriers to creating a biotech start-up, an enterprise designed to conduct original lab research aimed at producing a molecule to be transformed into a drug. Selling the product that results from research at this stage to a large company is not the same as exit. The innovators can continue to stand at the edge of this market and simply repeat the process of innovation and sale of newly developed molecular products, which may or may not include the expectation of a share in profits resulting from development of the product. The relationship between innovators and giant pharmaceutical companies is symbiotic. The innovators are interested in arranging the sale of the product they identify to the giants and are not competing with them. They profit from success at the lab research stage, not from producing and marketing the product. The giants are happy to buy the end product of lab research rather than doing start-from-scratch research.

Patents and User Fees

Patents are issued by the USPTO and by the FDA. The USPTO patent can apply to the chemical composition of the drug, the method of use or medical condition for which it is used, or the formulation—that is, capsule, liquid, injectable—and/or process of making the drug. Its role is interesting to consider. Pharmaceutical companies pay a "user fee" for patent review. Reviewers at the USPTO are paid bonuses that depend in part on the number of patents they process.[9] User fees play a role in the operations of both the USPTO and the FDA.

The role of the FDA as gatekeeper deserves more public attention than it receives. Pharmaceutical companies pay substantial user fees in applying to have a drug approved for distribution. The fee schedule is updated periodically. The 2017 fee is $2,038,100 for approval, required prior to the initiation of clinical trials. The fee is half of that amount for approval that does not involve clinical trials or for approval of supplemental application (when a change in a drug that has received previous approval is being made). Two other fees, establishment and product, are paid at later stages in the approval process.

User fees constitute half of the FDA's annual budget. That means that taxpayers pick up less of the bill for the FDA's activities. It also means that the agency is heavily dependent on the money coming from the "users," whose applications the agency must approve. No one, to the best of my knowledge, is prepared to argue that taxpayers should cover more of the cost in order to avoid undue influence on the part of users. But that would presumably free the FDA from even the hint of suspicion that it is approving more drugs than it should in order to keep the agency funded.

Patents and the Value of Exclusivity

Pharmaceutical companies have good reason to take advantage of every patenting opportunity to maintain exclusivity over their drugs.

Going to court to sue over patent infringement offers a way to obtain thirty extra months of exclusivity. Suing even when there is little evidence of infringement is risk-free because the thirty extra months kick in when the suit is filed. By the time the suit is settled, the company has gained thirty months of exclusivity. The label applied to the process of repeatedly applying for patents whether they are warranted or not—"evergreening"—is clearly apropos.

Another avenue is to "pay for delay." Brand-name corporations have been able to negotiate payment to a generic company ready to produce the drug in exchange for agreement on a set, future date for generic entry. More on this shortly.

Another way government intervention benefits brand-name pharmaceutical companies is by providing incentives to encourage the companies to pursue certain kinds of new drugs. It does so by permitting shorter clinical research trials to suffice for drug approval by the FDA. The law requires companies to compensate for the shortened clinical trial period through post–drug release clinical trials. There is no mechanism to ensure that this happens. Shorter approval time is presented by drug companies as something that consumers want. In cases where patients have been diagnosed with a fatal disease and have run out of options, those patients have a good case to make. However, shorter approval time for drugs that do not serve that purpose is beneficial to drug companies, not patients. There are good reasons to avoid rushing into release of drugs since there is no sure mechanism for identifying drugs that present safety issues without time to observe effects.

The FDA does not have the authority to recall unsafe drugs. Since it does no long-term monitoring, it is not clear how it would know to do so. "In fact, the FDA has mandatory recall authority for only five categories of products: infant formula, food, medical devices, biologic products (for example, blood products) and tobacco products."[10] Pharmaceutical companies can decide whether or not to take drugs off the market if and when they determine that they have received enough reports of damaging side effects.

Exactly when drug manufacturers discover that a drug might be unsafe is difficult to know. That may have occurred during the regular course of clinical trials or at any time afterward. Drug companies release the results of trials that they want to release, the ones that make their products look good.

> For years, researchers have talked about the problem of publication bias, or selectivity in publishing results of trials. Concern about such bias gathered force

in the 1990s and early 2000s, when researchers documented how time and time again, positive results were published while negative ones were not. . . .

Problems with data about high-profile drugs have led to scandals over the past decade, like one involving contentions that the number of heart attacks was underreported in research about the painkiller Vioxx. Another involved accusations of misleading data about links between the antidepressant Paxil and risk of suicide among teenagers.[11]

What allows misrepresentation of the efficacy of drugs is the FDA's long-standing policy of not making public its reasons for rejecting applications. According to some observers,

[the lack of transparency] prevents patients, researchers, and healthcare providers from gaining insight into why a drug's application was not approved. The FDA's policy is particularly troubling in cases where the agency has found a currently marketed drug to be ineffective or unsafe for a newly proposed indication.[12]

Making the results of trial data public may be moving ahead on several fronts. The European Union is tackling the issue. The Cochrane Collaborative, an international network of experts based in Oxford, England, has pressed drug companies to release data on particular drugs. Some researchers say that they are ready to seek the information through litigation and Freedom of Information Act requests.[13]

MANY BUYERS, MANY SELLERS

Counting the number of consumers who are buyers of pharmaceuticals is an impossible task. Counting sellers is complicated as well because many companies are global. Some are large enterprises that sell a wide variety of products to vast numbers of buyers. Others are small enterprises that sell only one or two products to a very limited number of buyers. And the number of companies is unstable because the companies are themselves being traded—bought and sold at a rapid rate.

List prices of drugs get most attention in discussions that revolve around the high cost of drugs. But that is just the tip of the iceberg, given the number of organizations that stand between producers of drugs and consumers of drugs. This is captured in a unique 2017 study of the flow of money in the pharmaceutical sector based on financial information disclosed to the US Securities and Exchange Commission. The distributional chain looks like this: Health plans or employers contract with a pharmacy benefit manager (PBM), which negotiates with drug manufacturers and processes pharmacy claims in exchange for rebates and other fees. The PBM also negotiates with pharmacies to set prices. Pharmacies negotiate with drug wholesalers. "When a beneficiary fills a prescription at a retail pharmacy, the pharmacy collects the beneficiary's copayment or coinsurance and dispenses the drug from inventory. The pharmacy passes the copayment to the PBM, and the PBM pays the pharmacy the negotiated reimbursement."[14]

Using a hypothetical $100 expenditure on a prescription drug, the split of profits looks like this:

> Roughly $58 goes to the manufacturer and $41 is captured by intermediaries. (Numbers do not sum to 100 due to rounding.) Of the $58 received by the manufacturer, $17 is spent on drug production and the remaining $41 is spent on other expenditures (such as marketing and R&D) or kept as net profit. Total net profit on a $100 expenditure is $23, of which $15 goes to manufacturers and the remaining $8 goes to intermediaries including $3 to insurers, $3 to pharmacies, and $2 to PBMs.[15]

The role PBMs play is important because health insurance companies rely on them to negotiate the price of drugs with manufacturers. In cases where there are two or more competing drugs, the PBM makes the selection that the insurance company uses in its "formulary," which is the list of drugs available to the insurance enrollee. How that selection is made is now coming into question. PBMs say that they negotiate the lowest price and pass on the savings to the consumer. Investigators claim that this may be true in some cases but that in other cases the PBM selects the drug for which it receives the biggest rebate, which is not necessarily the one that carries the lowest price. The negotiations are not made public, so whether the decision is made on the basis of getting a kickback or not is unclear.

It is also interesting to note that competition among an earlier array of PBMs has resulted in three survivors in the race—CVS Caremark, OptumRx, and Express Scripts. Their role was not receiving much attention until the *Washington Post* and the *60 Minutes* television show presented data showing that the PBMs were delivering "hundreds of millions of pills," of opioid drugs, to certain towns that could not have possibly used the drugs. The reports cast the PBMs, "some of which were fined for repeatedly ignoring warnings from the agency to shut down suspicious sales," as distributors of drugs responsible for the rise in opioid-related deaths. The nominee to head the Drug Enforcement Administration (DEA), who had proposed legislation weakening the DEA's authority, withdrew his name from consideration the morning after the *60 Minutes* program was aired.[16]

There is no question that there are many more levels of sellers in the pharmaceutical sector of the health care system than a superficial look at drug pricing would suggest. Doing something about high drug prices would mean examining the practices of each level of sellers—obviously a monumental challenge.

Consider the difference in distribution of brand-name versus generic drugs. Manufacturers of generic drugs make $18 rather than $58. But other stakeholders make much more. "PBMs make four times as much on generic drugs compared to brands, while wholesalers make 11 times as much, and pharmacies make almost 12 times as much, $32 compared to $3."[17]

No sooner than there were three survivors in the PBM business, the picture changed. They were either bought out or merged with one of the big health insurance companies. OptumRx was bought out by UnitedHealth Group; Cigna took over Express Scripts. The last to go was CVS Health, which merged with Aetna in the autumn of 2018. The stated objective of the mergers was making health care products and services easier for consumers to access. Standing on the sidelines of the Justice Department decision, antitrust lawyers warn that the mergers could leave consumers with fewer choices and higher drug costs. We will have to wait to see how the changes introduced at this stage turn out.

Generic Drugs

The generic drug market is huge. It is still evolving in interesting ways. Given that the price of a brand-name drug falls about 85 to 90 percent when it loses its patent and a generic version comes on the market, big-name pharmaceutical companies have good reason to try to keep the generic from becoming available.

As of 2019 nine out of every ten prescriptions are generics. Between 2007 and 2014, the generic share of the drug market grew from 28.5 percent to

64 percent. According to the Generic Pharmaceutical Association, "generic products saved the U.S. health system nearly $1.68 trillion" over the ten-year period from 2005 to 2014.[18]

The generic drug company sector of the pharmaceutical market has been highly competitive. In fact, the race has been going on long enough to whittle down the number of competitors in this sector as well. The remaining competitors are engaging in behavior that characterizes competitive races in other sectors—they are combining to reduce competition. Teva, the largest generic company, announced that it was acquiring the third largest company, Allergan's generic unit, for $40.5 billion. Allergan is probably best known as the maker of Botox. The deal was closed in August 2016 when Teva paid $33 billion in cash and one hundred million shares.

The company's rationale for the acquisition reminds one of how the top health insurance mergers were described by potential merger partners. Teva stated that it expected to achieve $1.4 billion in savings annually. It projected "cost synergies and tax savings by eliminating duplication and inefficiencies on a global scale." That expectation was not fulfilled, possibly because Teva's ambitions were extreme. Teva went on to pursue a $500 million acquisition the day after the Allergan deal. It sought to acquire Anda, a drug distributor representing three hundred manufacturers. In other words, it did not move to reduce prices but to expand its enterprise.

The effect of this "changing market has shifted the balance of power in favor of a smaller group of massive generic-drug manufacturers" causing generic drug prices to rise. "Half of all generic drugs saw an increase in cost from July 2013 to July 2014. Nearly one in 10 generic drugs more than doubled their previous price over that period, and some saw increases of more than 1,000 percent."[19]

As stated previously, lawsuits instituted to stall the introduction of generic drugs constitute a common practice used to extend a brand-name drug's patent period. The pay-for-delay tactic is newer. To reiterate, in this case, the brand-name drug company negotiates settlement of the patent lawsuit by a generic company in exchange for setting a future date for introduction of the generic drug.[20]

That, in turn, delays the start of the erosion of the brand-name price—even in cases where the underlying patents are eventually deemed invalid. These pay-for-delay agreements have been challenged by antitrust regulators with some success. However, federal courts have not agreed with antitrust authorities that there should be a bright-line rule defining those agreements as anticompetitive, prompting proposals for legislation to address this issue directly.[21]

What this means is that government is taking an active role in this matter, but the role is basically undefined. For example, when the FTC took a pay-to-delay case to the Supreme Court in June 2013, the Court held that the practice could be considered a violation of antitrust regulations. The impact of that decision was a drop from forty such deals in 2012 to twenty-one in 2014. In other words, government action has not stopped the practice but has slowed the rate at which it was growing before 2013. It is worth noting that no one has been punished for engaging in this practice.

If it seems that there is a lot of action in this corner of the industry, there really is. Brand-name drug manufacturers have engaged in at least four different strategies designed to delay generic drug entry:

- Secondary patents—obtaining new patents on secondary aspects of the drug, such as its coating or method of administration
- Reverse patent settlements—settling litigation by offering compensation in exchange for having generic manufacturers drop legal challenges and market their products later. This is the pay-for-delay tactic. "The Federal Trade Commission (FTC) estimates that these settlements cost consumers $3.5 billion annually."
- Restrictions on distribution—some brand-name manufacturers have tried to restrict access to drug samples hoping to prevent generic companies from completing FDA-required bioequivalent testing.
- Frivolous petitions to the FDA—typical petitions challenge bioequivalence and ask that approval of the generic be withheld pending further testing. "Between 2013 and 2015, the FDA received 67 such petitions but approved only three."[22]

An example of the extreme tactics that pharmaceutical companies can think up to extend patent rights is captured by the Restasis saga.[23] The patent for Restasis, a dry-eye medication, granted to Allergan in 1995 and which was due to expire in 2014, is a $1.5 billion-dollar seller. As mentioned above, Allergan's leading moneymaker is Botox, but Restasis is the company's second-biggest moneymaker. Allergan has gone to court to seek extensions of the Restasis patent using a variety of ploys. A few examples make clear that the company will do whatever it takes. It claimed that the product's efficacy was eight times more effective than previous studies had shown. Actual results indicated no significant difference in efficacy. It sued generic companies pre-emptively to block them from producing the product, claiming violation of intellectual property rights even though the rights were set to expire. While the suits were not successful, the fact that they were filed was enough to ex-tend the patent. This worked until 2014, when the company went to court to obtain yet another extension. In an unconventional but creative maneuver, the company transferred patent rights to New York State's Saint Regis Mo-hawk Tribe, gaining a ten-year extension. The rationale was that the tribe had sovereign immunity, so competitors would be prevented from violating the tribe's patent rights. Competitors sued. The patent extension was found to be invalid in 2017.[24]

Just when it looks like the generic drug story has stabilized and is going in a well-established and predictable direction, a new development makes clear that continuing innovation is at the heart of health sector developments. In this case, it is the entry of a unique new generic company, Civica Rx.[25] It is the creation of seven large health systems together with three philanthropic groups and is led by an industry insider who is taking no salary. The com-pany is a nonprofit, meaning that it does not have stockholders interested in pursuing dividends or higher stock prices. The company will offer fourteen generic drugs commonly used by hospitals at a base price without the expecta-tion of profit. According to a representative of one of the member hospitals, the drugs on the list were included because they underwent a 50 percent or more price increase between 2014 and 2016, were essential medicines, and were on national shortage lists. Spokespersons say that they anticipate that companies currently producing the generics will cut their prices to maintain market share. Their aim, they say, is not to win market share, but to make the marketplace work better by guaranteeing a steady supply of drugs at a fair and transparent price. They also say that they that may add new drugs if their ef-forts to achieve this objective succeed. The fact that Civica Rx is coming into existence as a seller with a committed body of buyers and does not expect to make a profit makes it a formidable player in this market.

Orphan Drugs

A distinctive characteristic of the pharmaceutical market is its volatility. As the entry and exit discussion above makes clear, organizations engaged in research and development of new products that announce that they are ready to bring a highly innovative product to the market are quickly bought out by one of the giant companies. The small innovative company then has the resources to turn to developing new discoveries. Both parties are satisfied.

Specialty or orphan drugs are used by a small number of patients—under two hundred thousand—whose numbers are not expected to increase. What is special about this designation is that it revolves around therapeutic interventions defined not by biology or medical specialty but by the prevalence of the treated condition in a small segment of the population. Given that the market for such drugs is not expected to grow, legislation was thought to be necessary to encourage drugmakers to develop the drugs required by these patients. Accordingly, the Orphan Drug Act of 1983 was established to provide "economic incentives—including tax credits, research grants, and special market exclusivity protections—to encourage drug developers to invest in drugs for rare diseases."[26]

The effect of the legislation has helped to make the drugs into attractive venture capital investment opportunities. Drug companies do not need to invest as many resources in bringing the product to the market. For a start, the FDA does not require a $2 million plus application fee investment. Orphan drugs do not require as many drug salespersons, since there are no other drugs physicians can turn to. The small market for orphan drugs is not a source of discouragement. The drugs present an excellent investment opportunity, providing a corner of the market that is not likely to be affected by competition.

The upshot is that nearly half of the drugs approved by the FDA between 2011 and 2015 were orphan drugs. Additionally, the top ten world's most expensive drugs are orphan drugs.[27]

Biologics

Biologic medicines constitute the newest entrants into the pharmaceutical market. They include such products as vaccines, blood and blood components, gene therapies, and recombinant therapeutic proteins. These medicines are harder to produce than those based on small molecules. The production process involves multiple steps and use of living cells. Laws governing generics that allow pharmacists to substitute existing drugs or generics for biosimilar drugs do not apply, which helps to keep the prices high.

However, patents provide a nearly impenetrable shield. With $16 billion in sales, Humira, made by AbbVie, is the planet's best-selling drug.[28] It is used to treat rheumatoid arthritis and psoriasis. Approved in 2002, it has applied for and been granted more than one hundred patents. Its exclusivity was not challenged until 2016, when Amgen Inc. "decided the prize is too rich not to try breaching AbbVie's patent defenses."[29] AbbVie reacted by filing a lawsuit insisting that Amgen Inc. violated sixty patents. When a German company started to explore developing a generic version, AbbVie filed another suit, claiming that it violated seventy-four patents. The court fights are not about to end. In 2019, Amgen was sued by Coherus, which had entered into a deal with AbbVie, for patent infringement on Coherus' biosimilar version of Humira.[30]

Johnson & Johnson holds a similar number of patents on its blockbuster drug Remicade. It is receiving less attention because it is not as aggressive as AbbVie in touting the patent shield approach.

CONSUMER CHOICE

Consumer choice in the pharmaceutical market is unlike choice in other consumer markets. Although consumers may hold strong views about the drugs they wish to buy, they are restricted from going into the market to purchase drugs on their own. They must go through an agent, a health care provider who is licensed to prescribe drugs, but whose decision may be rejected by the insurance plan and/or PBM. Accordingly, sellers of drugs engage in a two-pronged approach to influence choice: direct-to-consumer marketing and provider education.

Direct-to-Consumer Marketing

The sentence that you hear in all pharmaceutical ads is, "Ask your doctor." The reason you hear the same sentence is that this is the admonition that FDA requires in allowing companies to engage in direct-to-consumer advertising. It is worth noting that, as critics repeatedly point out, only two economically advanced countries permit this kind of advertising, the United States and New Zealand. Other countries consider it to be objectionable. In my view, this does have to make you wonder, given so many economically advanced countries have decided to prohibit direct-to-consumer advertising, whether the reasons for the prohibition deserve to be revisited.

One answer to this question that is offered by some critics is that advertising actually creates sickness where there is none, that direct-to-consumer advertising amounts to selling sickness, not selling a cure. The charge is that drug companies use drugs to go in search of disease rather than the other way around is certainly a damning charge. The practice has been labeled "medicalization." Medicalization of what is normal is promoted when ads give it a catchy label. ED (erectile dysfunction) or low T (low testosterone) are especially prominent. Feeling less than ready to take on the world is suddenly reason to believe one requires drugs for depression, which ads sometimes suggest is likely to result in progressive disease, a claim for which there is no evidence. Hyperactivity disorder diagnoses are on a steadily increasing growth curve.[31] Promotion of highly addictive pain-relief medications is, of course, what many observers point to as the cause of the opioid epidemic in this country.

No one who watches TV or uses the internet is unaware of how pervasive direct-to-consumer advertising has become, but the statistics are still staggering. "The average American television viewer watches as many as nine drug ads a day, totaling 16 hours per year, which far exceeds the amount of time the average individual spends with a primary care physician."[32]

Prior to 2005, the Government Accountability Office (GAO) had estimated that DTCPA [direct-to-consumer pharmaceutical advertising] was growing at approximately 20% per year, or twice as fast as spending on pharmaceutical direct-to-physician (DTP) advertising or on drug research and development. The growth in DTC advertising expenditures was not without reason, being that it was estimated that every dollar spent on DTCPA would increase sales of the advertised drug by an estimated $2.20 to $4.20. Still, in 2005, DTCPA accounted for only 14% of industry expenditures, whereas DTP advertising totaled 24%.[33]

How much money is involved is also pretty remarkable. A 2011 estimate puts industry spending at $1 billion for a five-to-one return on its investment in advertising.[34] A *Consumer Reports* study found that "over the 12-month period ending in July 2014, in fact, manufacturers spent $1.9 billion in ads for just the top 10 drugs."[35] A review of the "safety and efficacy" of seven of the ten drugs is revealing. The following list focuses on advertising expenditures and drug prices. Many of the names of the drugs will surely be familiar even if you have no reason to pay attention to ads focusing on the health problems the drugs are supposed to address.

- Cialis and Viagra for erectile dysfunction. Cialis, which may not be covered by insurance, costs $70 for ten 5 mg pills and $332 for ten 50 mg pills of Viagra. Pfizer spent $218 million on Viagra ads, and Eli Lily spent $263 million on Cialis ads.
- Humira for Crohn's disease. AbbVie spent $293 million, more than what was spent for any other drug. It costs more than $5,000 per month.
- Eliquis and Xarelto for atrial fibrillation. The cost is $300 per month.
- Lyrica for fibromyalgia, $260 per month.
- Celebrex for arthritis, $181 to $282 per month.
- Xeljanz for rheumatoid arthritis, $2,380 per month.
- Abilify for depression, $900 per month.

The report ends with the following statement:

> *Consumer Reports* has long held that drug ads should be banned. . . . For one, they encourage patients and doctors to turn to medication when nondrug options might work. And when drugs are needed, ads often promote more expensive options, not the best or safest. In addition, a 2014 review in the *Journal of Internal Medicine* of 168 drug ads found that 57 percent of claims were potentially misleading and 10 were outright false.[36]

The pharmaceutical industry perspective is interesting to consider in light of the information on accuracy of the claims made in marketing campaigns. Comments made by industry representatives indicate that drug companies are more interested in appealing to consumers' emotions than in presenting them with facts. In discussing pharmaceutical marketing, Sidney Wolfe refers to an observation made by the Canadian economist Stephen Leacock, that advertising is "the science of arresting the human intelligence long enough to get money from it."[37]

The industry says that the amount of money spent to influence consumer buying decisions is done to advance the consumer's right to choose. There is no reference to the fact that it is hard to establish the price of products and engage in comparison shopping. There is apparently good reason to think that accuracy of information on quality is questionable. Information on price is no better. A 2013 "secret shopper" survey of two hundred pharmacies by *Consumer Reports* aimed at obtaining the price of five blockbuster drugs is revealing; it found "a whopping difference of $749, or 447 percent, between the highest- and lowest-priced stores."[38]

The market-based, consumer health care–driven approach depends on consumers to be dedicated shoppers. Stories in the media abound on how shopping results in a vastly cheaper price for one drug but not others. But these stories make the news because the practice is so unusual that it is newsworthy. What may or may not be included in such stories is that shopping and getting a good price on one drug says nothing about the prices the supplier charges for other drugs. According to Elisabeth Rosenthal, the physician author of the *New York Times* series, "Paying Till It Hurts":

> Drugs that sell for $150 a month at one pharmacy are given away to members of a loyalty program at another. I discovered that a generic prescription anti-inflammatory medicine for which I now pay a $20 monthly copay through my insurer is on Target's limited list of $4 prescriptions, although other drugs are far more expensive there.[39]

If you stop to think about it, for someone who takes several drugs, shopping not only involves checking the prices at different stores but driving around to all those stores—and becomes worse if it means taking a bus and changing buses—to pick up each of the drugs. One does have to ask, How much of a difference in price would make this effort worthwhile on a regular basis? Of course, some people simply can't afford to ask themselves that question.

Shopping may be even more onerous for some people than others because of where they live. In one study of pharmaceutical prices in Florida, the highest prices were found in the poorest zip codes, 9 percent above the statewide average.[40]

Provider Education

Pharmaceutical companies engage in provider education through conferences that include lectures on drug applications. Pharmaceutical reps go to doctors' office to provide more detailed information on new drugs and provide samples. The GAO assessment mentioned above puts the amount spent on direct-to-consumer advertising at $3 billion but the amount spent on promotions directed at health care professionals at $24 billion.

Concern about undue influence of monies spent to influence doctors' prescribing decisions is reflected in numerous studies indicating that it makes a difference. The findings indicate that receiving something as small as a ballpoint pen made the doctor more favorably inclined to prescribe the medication being promoted. This should not be surprising; social psychologists have made similar observations for years about the impact that a token gift can have on people's attitudes.

The concern about the relationship between gifting on the part of pharmaceutical and medical device companies led to the Physician Payment Sunshine Act. Part of the Affordable Care Act of 2010, it mandates disclosure of payments of amounts over ten dollars in value. The Open Payments database established in conjunction with the act required reporting beginning in 2013. An analysis of reports dating from August 2013 through December 2015 was conducted by researchers associated with ProPublica and published as "Dollars for Docs." It revealed that doctors received $6.25 billion from pharmaceutical companies during that time period.[41] The report lists names of doctors and hospitals and analyzes rates by specialty and by state.

The same ProPublica researchers published an earlier report analyzing the impact of industry payments on doctors' prescribing practices:

> Doctors who got money from drug and device makers—even just a meal—prescribed a higher percentage of brand-name drugs overall than doctors who didn't, our analysis showed. Indeed, doctors who received industry payments were two to three times as likely to prescribe name-brand drugs at exceptionally high rates as other in their specialty.[42]

INDUSTRY EXPENSES

The cost of doing business in this sector is interesting to look at. To start, there is the cost of carrying out research, which the pharmaceutical companies claim is the reason drug prices are high. Then there are the costs of all those lawsuits to extend patent life, which the industry does not talk about. But it is the cost of settling cases in which a given company is charged with malfeasance that really runs up costs.

Marketing versus R&D

Pharmaceutical companies repeatedly claim that they must spend a vast amount on research and development (R&D) of new drugs. They do spend a considerable amount of money conducting clinical trials. This is not the same as original research that leads to patents, which, as we have already mentioned, goes on in universities and in start-up research organizations. The clinical trial stage is expensive because of the time involved. It takes time to organize a study involving enough doctors and patients, to collect and analyze the data, and to do so for enough time to show the effects of the drug. It is when the amount spent on R&D is compared to the amount spent on marketing that critics make their point.

The 2015 expenditures by Johnson & Johnson, which led the field in spending on marketing, attracted a good deal of business media attention when the company's financial report was made public. A story in the *Washington Post*, based on an analysis of those financial reports, among others, indicated that the company spent 17.5 percent of its budget on marketing while spending 8.2 percent on R&D.[43] The ratio may not be quite as high in other companies, but the investigators found that the amount spent on marketing by most companies is consistently higher than the amount spent on research.

A breakdown of pharmaceutical industry spending reported by the Pew Charitable Trusts in 2013 speaks to the industry claim that it spends a major proportion of its resources on clinical trials.

Promotion activities to physicians

Face-to-face sales	$15 billion
Samples to physicians	$5.7 billion
Education/promotion meetings	$2.1 billion
Promotional mailings	$1.2 billion
Advertising (print)	$90 million
Direct-to-consumer advertising	$3.1 billion
Clinical trials	$130 million[44]

Fraud and the Courts

The industry spends far more in settlements of cases brought to court based on charges of fraud than it does on research and development of drugs. A review of legal settlements over the 1991–2015 period conducted by researchers at the advocacy organization Public Citizen reveal a breathtaking degree of swindling and scamming.[45] The record shows 140 federal lawsuits settled for $31.9 billion and 233 state lawsuits settled for $3.8 billion. The settlements constitute $28 billion in civil settlements and $7.8 in criminal penalties. The most common violations involved overcharging government programs (48 percent) and unlawful promotion (25 percent).

GlaxoSmithKline achieved singular recognition for paying out the largest legal settlement in history, at $3 billion for violations involving multiple drugs. It made $28 billion in sales on just three of the drugs: Paxil, Wellbutrin SR, and Avandia.[46]

Johnson & Johnson distinguished itself by having the third-largest health fraud settlement in history. It pleaded guilty to off-label promotion of the blockbuster antipsychotic drug Risperdal and agreed to pay a $2 billion fine—this on top of the $181 million fine for the unlawful marketing of another antipsychotic, Inuega. While a fine of $2 billion for violations related to marketing Risperdal may seem staggering, taken in context it can be seen as good business practice. The drug brought in $11.7 billion in sales in the first twelve years after approval.[47]

Looking at the industry as a whole, "the $35.7 billion paid in penalties from 1991 through 2015 is a miniscule fraction of drug company profits—just 5% of the $711 billion in net profits made by the 11 largest global drug companies during only 10 of those 25 years (2003–2012)."[48]

A March 2018 update of an earlier report is interesting for what it says about the government as much as about pharmaceutical companies:

> The report's most striking finding is a precipitous drop in federal criminal penalties against drug companies. In 2016–2017, federal criminal penalties totaled just $317 million from four settlements. This represents a nearly 90-percent plunge in financial penalties compared with 2012–2013, when criminal penalties totaled $2.7 billion from 10 settlements.[49]

What accounts for the 90 percent plunge? Is it a change in pharmaceutical company practices or a change in the political party responsible for oversight of fraudulent pharmaceutical practices? Might it have something to do with the contributions political action committees, or PACs, have given to members of Congress over recent years? (We'll return to this shortly.)

Then there are the fines the companies paid for violations of the Foreign Corrupt Practices Act enacted in 1977. A few examples include the following: In 2013, GlaxoSmithKline was implicated in a scheme involving $400 million in bribes in China. The attraction is that China is rapidly becoming the world's largest pharmaceutical market. In 2012, Eli Lilly paid $29 million for engaging in bribery in Russia, Brazil, China, and Poland. Johnson & Johnson paid $70 million in 2011 for bribery in several European countries and in Iraq. Pfizer paid $45 million for bribing other foreign officials.[50]

If some courts have been holding pharmaceutical companies responsible for misrepresenting their products, other courts have taken the opposite stance. The outcome of the 2012 *United States v. Caronia* case has added to the complicated picture of what pharmaceutical companies can and cannot say about their products:

> The government brought the case against Alfred Caronia, a former sales representative for Orphan Medical who was charged with marketing the company's drug, Xyrem, for unapproved use. Although Xyrem was approved only for narcolepsy, Caronia was accused of promoting the drug to physicians for a number of other conditions, including insomnia and fibromyalgia. After his conviction in 2008, Caronia appealed, arguing that the federal government's prosecution violated his right to free speech. The United States Court of Appeals for the Second Circuit agreed with Caronia and overturned the conviction, ruling "that the government cannot prosecute pharmaceutical manufacturers and their representatives under the FDCA [Food Drug and Cosmetic Act] for speech promoting lawful, off-label use of an FDA-approved drug."[51]

Evidence of a range of other anticompetitive practices continues to receive attention. An observation in the *Journal of the American Medical Association* that insulin prices nearly tripled between 2002 and 2013 led to a lawsuit accusing three drug makers of conspiracy: Sanofi, Novo Nordisk, and Eli Lilly.[52] The same month, Mallinckrodt Pharmaceuticals agreed to pay a $100 million dollar fine for engaging in "anti-competitive behavior by acquiring the rival drug to their costly H.P. Acthar Gel—which goes for $38,000 a vial—and keeping it off the market to protect their profits."[53] The rival drug, Synacthen, is sold for a tiny fraction of the price of Acthar.

In February 2017, Marathon Pharmaceuticals received approval to market Deflazacort, a drug used to treat a fatal wasting disease, Duchenne muscular dystrophy. The company announced that it would be priced at $89,000 but that it should cost consumers with health insurance only $20 per prescription. Critics were outraged, pointing out that the drug has been available for years outside of the United States for $1,200 a year. The company responded by saying that it would pause its "commercialization efforts" and hold the product off the market until management could discuss the issue.[54]

Senator Bernie Sanders and Representative Elijah Cummings wrote a scathing letter calling Marathon's pricing outrageous. Having followed the developments in the pharmaceutical markets for a while, they came up with an imaginative piece of legislation in 2015. It called for removing patent exclusivity in cases when companies have been found guilty or have admitted to misrepresentation of drugs. While it did not receive enough congressional support to pass, Sanders and Cummings are not about to stop focusing on pharmaceutical fraud.

Politicians, Former Politicians, and Lobbying

Unfortunately, in too many cases, a period of service in Congress opens the revolving door that leads to a lobbyist position. Members of Congress who leave are in position to trade on their friendships and connections in Congress to produce legislation favorable to their new employers. It is not clear how many pharmaceutical lobbyists are former legislators, but the ones who are can be assumed to have special access and potentially exceptional influence. As of June 2017, there were 12,553 reported pharmaceutical lobbyists addressing members of Congress. Drugmakers spent $2.3 billion over the last decade on lobbying.[55]

After they exit public service jobs, some politicians find even better places to land, in corporate positions with stupendous CEO salaries. A few have been called out for exactly that by Public Citizen. Deborah Autor, who was deputy commissioner for global regulatory operations and policy at the FDA, left after eleven years to accept a position at Mylan Teva. The company is the highest individual spender in the generics lobby. Billy Tauzin, former chair of the House Energy and Commerce Committee, coauthored and was instrumental in pushing through the Medicare Part D program that bans negotiation between Medicare and pharmaceutical companies. He left Congress to head up PhRMA, the industry's professional association and lobbying group.

The revolving door can also sweep health care executives into government offices. For example, Alex Azar became secretary of the Department of Health and Human Services, stepping into that office directly out of the office of the presidency of the Eli Lilly pharmaceutical company.

Not all politicians become lobbyists after they leave office. Henry Waxman is one who has taken a different route. He was one of the two authors of the 1984 law that was intended to help the generic drug industry but actually ended up benefiting the brand-name drug industry by extending the life of pharmaceutical patents by eight years. Waxman now heads up a nonprofit organization that works to develop policy solutions to health care issues including the high cost of drugs. He is the senior author of a statement on the steps that Congress and regulators can take "to begin to rebalance incentives for innovation and price competition." The guiding principle driving the discussion is that "discovery and development of innovative therapies . . . should not come at a price that leaves patients without access." In identifying drivers of high drug prices, the policy statement emphasizes the need to maximize availability of information to "facilitate patient-centered decision-making." It concludes with a powerful directive: "Drug manufacturers should be able to clearly articulate and justify their drug pricing decisions in a clear, straightforward manner to the public."[56]

MARKET-BASED HEALTH CARE, THE GOVERNMENT, AND THE PHARMACEUTICAL SECTOR

To sum up, the government has played a significant role in balancing stockholder value and the social value of curative medicines by extending monopoly rights to manufacturers. This has implications for arguments that begin from the premise that the pharmaceutical industry is market-based and only needs to follow free-market model guidelines more closely with greatest reliance on increased competition. These observations may raise a whole host of questions. I offer the following questions as the place to begin the discussion.

- Is anyone ready to argue for getting government out of the way in response to the problems linked to government intervention in the pharmaceutical industry? How feasible would that be?
- Has the government gone too far in favoring the pharmaceutical industry in its efforts to balance the need of companies to make a profit and society's need to develop and distribute lifesaving drugs?

NOTES

1. Ashley Kirzinger, Elise Sugarman, and Mollyann Brodie, "Kaiser Health Tracking Poll: October 2016." Kaiser Family Foundation, October 27, 2016, https://www.kff.org/health-costs/poll-finding/kaiser-health-tracking-poll-october-2016/.

2. Jay Hancock, "Everyone Wants to Reduce Drug Prices. So Why Can't We Do It?" *New York Times*, September 23, 2017.

3. "Trump Announces Plan to Lower 'Unfair' Prescription Drug Prices," CBS News, updated October 25, 2018, https://www.cbsnews.com/news/trump-prescription-drug-pricing-costs-speech-today-10-25-18-live-stream-updates/.

4. US Government Accountability Office, "Profits, Research and Development Spending, and Merger and Acquisition Deals," GAO-18-40, GAO, November 17, 2017, https://www.gao.gov/products/GAO-18-40.

5. Arlene Weintraub, "Shrekli Is Out as Shareholder and Influencer of KaloBios—Well Almost," *Forbes*, July 7, 2016, https://www.forbes.com/sites/arleneweintraub/2016/07/07/shkreli-is-out-as-a-shareholder-and-influencer-of-kalobios-well-almost/#17c6f9ca5754.

6. Danny Hakin, "Humira's Best-Selling Drug Formula: Start High. Go Higher," *New York Times*, January 6, 2018.

7. Josh Katz, "Drug Deaths in America Are Rising Faster than Ever," *New York Times*, June 5, 2017.

8. Marcia Angell, *The Truth about the Drug Companies* (New York: Random House, 2005).

9. "U.S. Patent and Trademark Office, Hiring Efforts Are Not Sufficient to Reduce Patent Application Backlog," U.S. Government Accountability Office, September 2007.

10. Michael Carome, "A Dangerous Gap in FDA Recall Authority," *Worst Pills, Best Pills News* 20, no. 9 (2014): 2.

11. Katie Thomas, "Health Law Drug Plans Are Given a Check-Up," *New York Times*, October 8, 2014, B1.

12. Sammy Almashat and Michael Carome, "Withholding Information on Unapproved Drug Marketing Applications," *Journal of Law, Medicine & Ethics*, January 10, 2018.

13. Thomas, "Health Law Drug Plans."

14. Neeraj Sood et al. "Follow the Money: The Flow of Funds in the Pharmaceutical Distribution System," *Health Affairs Blog*, June 13, 2017, https://www.healthaffairs.org/do/10.1377/hblog20170613.060557/full/.

15. Sood et al., "Follow the Money."

16. John Wagner, Lenny Bernstein, and Scott Higham, "Trump Drug Czar Nominee is Withdrawing; Administration 'Very Concerned' about Law He Championed," *Washington Post*, October 17, 2017.

17. Sood et al., "Follow the Money."

18. "The Rising Cost of Generic Drugs," *Worst Pills, Best Pills News* 22, no. 12 (2016): 1, 7.

19. "Rising Cost of Generic Drugs."

20. Mike McCaughan, "Patent Settlements," Health Policy Briefs, *Health Affairs*, July 21, 2017, https://www.healthaffairs.org/do/10.1377/hpb20170721.583967/full/.

21. McCaughan, "Patent Settlements."

22. Kerstin Vokinger, Aaron Kesselheim, and Jerry Avorn, "Strategies That Delay Market Entry of Generic Drugs," *Journal of the American Medical Association, Internal Medicine* 177, no. 11 (2017): 1665–69.

23. Katie Thomas, "Patents for Restasis Are Invalidating Opening Door to Generics," *New York Times*, October 16, 2017.

24. Joe Mullins, "Judge Throws Out Allergen Patent, Slams Company's Native American Deal," ARS, https://arstechnica.com/tech-policy/2017/10/judge-throws-out-allergan-patent-slams-companys-native-american-deal/.

25. Carolyn Johnson, "Hospitals Are Fed Up with Drug Companies, So They're Starting Their Own," *New York Times*, September 6, 2018.

26. Dayton Misfeldt and James C. Robinson, "Orphan Diseases or Population Health? Policy Choices Drive Venture Capital Investments," *Health Affairs Blog*, July 21, 2017, https://www.healthaffairs.org/do/10.1377/hblog20170721.061150/full/.

27. Megan Brooks, "Rare Disease Treatments Make Up Top 10 Most Costly Drugs," Medscape Medical News, May 2, 2017, https://www.medscape.com/viewarticle/879422.

28. Cynthia Koons, "The Shield of Patents Protects the World's Best-Selling Drug," Bloomberg Businessweek, September 7, 2017, https://www.bloomberg.com/news/articles/2017-09-07/this-shield-of-patents-protects-the-world-s-best-selling-drug.

29. Koons, "The Shield of Patents."

30. Stanton Mehr, "More Adalimumab News, AbbVie Signs a Licensing Deal with Coherus, Coherus Sues Amgen for Patent Infringement," BR&R, January 28, 2019, https://biosimilarsrr.com/2019/01/28/more-adalimumab-news-abbvie-signs-a-licensing-deal-with-coherus-coherus-sues-amgen-for-patent-infringement/.

31. Alan Schwarz, "The Selling of Attention Deficit Disorder," New York Times, December 15, 2013, p. 1.

32. C. Lee Ventola, "Direct-to-Consumer Pharmaceutical Advertising: Therapeutic or Toxic?" Pharmacy and Therapeutics 36, no. 10 (2011): 681–84.

33. Ventola, "Direct-to-Consumer Pharmaceutical Advertising."

34. Ventola, "Direct-to-Consumer Pharmaceutical Advertising."

35. "Can You Trust Drug Ads on TV?" Consumer Reports, January 11, 2015, https://www.consumerreports.org/cro/news/2015/01/can-you-trust-drug-ads-on-tv/index.htm.

36. "Can You Trust. . . ."

37. Sidney Wolfe, "Direct-to-Consumer Advertising: Education or Emotion Promotion?" New England Journal of Medicine 346, no. 7 (2002): 524–26.

38. "Same Generic Drug, Many Prices," Consumer Reports, May 2013, https://www.consumerreports.org/cro/magazine/2013/05/same-generic-drug-many-prices/index.htm.

39. Elisabeth Rosenthal, "Good Deals on Pills? It's Anyone's Guess," New York Times, November 10, 2013, 5.

40. Walid Gellad et al., "Variation in Drug Prices at Pharmacies: Are Prices Higher in Poor Areas?" Health Services Research 44, no. 2 pt. 1 (2009): 606–17.

41. Mike Tigas et al., "Dollars for Docs," ProPublica, December 13, 2016, https://projects.propublica.org/docdollars/.

42. Charles Ornstein, Mike Tigas, and Ryann Grochowski Jones, "Now There's Proof: Docs Who Get Company Cash Tend to Prescribe More Brand-Name Meds," ProPublica, March 17, 2016, https://www.propublica.org/article/doctors-who-take-company-cash-tend-to-prescribe-more-brand-name-drugs.

43. Ana Swanson, "Big Pharmaceutical Companies Are Spending Far More on Marketing than Research," *Time*, February 11, 2015.

44. "Persuading the Prescribers: Pharmaceutical Industry Marketing and Its Influence on Physicians and Patients," Pew Charitable Trusts, November 11, 2013, https://www.pewtrusts.org/en/research-and-analysis/fact-sheets/2013/11/11/persuading-the-prescribers-pharmaceutical-industry-marketing-and-its-influence-on-physicians-and-patients.

45. Sammy Almashat, Sidney M. Wolfe, and Michael Carome. *Twenty-Five Years of Pharmaceutical Industry Criminal and Civil Penalties: 1991 through 2015*, Public Citizen, March 31, 2016, https://www.citizen.org/sites/default/files/2311_0.pdf.

46. Almashat, Wolfe, and Carome, *Twenty-Five Years of . . . Penalties.*

47. Almashat, Wolfe, and Carome, *Twenty-Five Years of . . . Penalties.*

48. Almashat, Wolfe, and Carome, *Twenty-Five Years of . . . Penalties.*

49. Michael Carome, "New Report on Big Pharma Settlements Highlights Need for Tougher Enforcement," *Covering Health*, March 14, 2018, https://healthjournalism.org/blog/2018/03/new-report-on-big-pharma-settlements-highlights-need-for-tougher-enforcement/.

50. Sidney Wolfe, "Pharma's Foreign Corrupt Practices Accompany Its Domestic Violations," *Worst Pills, Best Pills News* 19, no. 10 (2013): 2.

51. Sammy Almashat, "Pharmaceutical Lobby Reigns Supreme in Washington," Public Citizen, June 2014, https://www.citizen.org/our-work/health-and-safety/health-letter-pharmaceutical-lobby-reigns-supreme-washington.

52. Katie Thomas, "Three Drug Makers Are Accused of Conspiring to Raise Insulin Prices," *New York Times*, January 31, 2017, A22.

53. Gretchen Morgenson, "A Costly Drug, Missing a Dose of Disclosure," *New York Times*, January 27, 2017.

54. Lisa Schencker, "Muscular Dystrophy Drug Launch on Hold," *Chicago Tribune*, February 14, 2017, Business 1.

55. Gina Chan, "Rising Drug Prices Put Big Pharma's Lobbying to the Test," *New York Times*, September 1, 2016.

56. Henry Waxman et al., "Getting to the Root of High Prescription Drug Prices," Commonwealth Fund, July 10, 2017, https://www.commonwealthfund.org/publications/issue-briefs/2017/jul/getting-root-high-prescription-drug-prices.

Health Sector Occupations and Organizations

This chapter looks at the health sector as whole. It starts by outlining the rate at which health care occupations and organizations have been growing. It directs most attention to how the rate of growth relates to two of the three core market-based health care principles we have been considering: easy entry and exit, and consumer choice. The latter part of the chapter addresses the larger social and economic implications of occupational growth in the health sector.

THE HEALTH CARE SECTOR RATE OF GROWTH

New occupations cannot be separated from new organizations. Virtually all health occupations require some sort of training, education, and/or certification. In the case of newly created occupations, this involves establishing new educational programs, certification arrangements, standards-setting organizations, professional associations, and so on. All in turn generate additional jobs as well as new organizations in the health care sector. Well-established health sector occupations and the health organizations with which they are associated continue to expand as well.

According to the Bureau of Labor Statistics (BLS), "overall, there was a net increase of 2.6 million jobs in the health care sector between 2005 and 2015, accounting for 35 percent of total job growth in the United States during that period."[1] Looking toward the future, the BLS projects health care occupational employment growth at 18 percent between 2016 and 2026, much faster than the average for all occupations, adding about 2.4 million new jobs. Health care support occupations (examples cited by the BLS include home health aides, occupational therapy assistants, and medical transcriptionists) are projected to increase by 23-plus percent. Health care practitioner and technical occupations (examples include physicians and surgeons, registered nurses, and dental hygienists) are projected to increase by 15-plus percent. These two occupational categories—which according to the BLS will account for fourteen of the thirty fastest growing occupations across occupational sectors from 2016 to 2026—are projected to contribute about one-fifth of all new jobs by 2026.[2]

The BLS Occupational Outlook Handbook lists forty-six fast-growing health sector jobs indicating entry-level education requirements and average income level. There is a broad range. Because there are too many health occupations to identify and discuss them all, I will limit consideration to a sample of ones mentioned in the preceding chapters.

Clinical Care Occupations

As everyone is well aware, the clinical workforce consists of doctors, nurses, and a long list of associated health care occupational groups. Of the 2.6 million health sector jobs created between 2005 and 2015, 6 percent were for physicians. Physicians are often divided into two categories—primary care and specialists—for policy discussion purposes. The concern is that there are not enough primary care practitioners capable of treating the whole patient rather than a patient's specific problem.

> The number of primary care physician jobs grew by approximately 8 percent, while the number of jobs for specialists grew about six times faster. In an era when we might have expected (and hope for) rapid primary care physician growth, the share of the physician workforce devoted to primary care actually decreased from 44 percent to 37 percent, and the number of primary care physicians per capita has remained roughly flat.[3]

Some health care policy analysts say that the increasing number of specialists is an important part of the explanation for rising health care costs. The commonly cited explanation is, "if the only tool you have is a hammer, everything looks like a nail." In other words, specialists perform the tasks they were trained to perform even when the health issue at hand may benefit from a less specialized, that is, less expensive, approach. Additionally, the fact that greater numbers of specialists are becoming affiliated with hospital networks means that facility fees are now regularly being added to the specialists' charges.

The fact that five of the top ten fastest-growing occupations, as projected by the BLS, are health occupations and that the five do not include doctors suggests that an increasing amount of the work traditionally done by highly trained practitioners is being subdivided and carried out by others. Projected to increase between 2016 and 2026 are home health aides (by 47percent), personal care aides (by 37 percent), physician assistants (by 37 percent), nurse practitioners (by 36 percent), and physical therapist assistants (by 31 percent).[4]

There is considerable debate about what tasks can and should be shifted to health care personnel other than doctors. Some observers warn that the shift may be an indicator of the industrialization process that involves rationalization and bureaucratization of medical tasks. Observers who offer a more positive assessment say that the trend may be an indicator of the realization that patients require something more than the technical competence offered by doctors to deal with daily living challenges. It is easy to take a stand on the issue based on one or the other perspective. It is a lot harder to present an argument grounded in evidence-based data on the range of responsibilities and tasks involved, the training required, and ultimately whether there is a net benefit to patient outcomes. That is a complicated topic that necessitates introduction of technical knowledge related to the practice of medicine and is not the sort of discussion I am prepared to enter into.

More to the point of this discussion is the relationship between the continuing shortage of certain categories of highly skilled clinical health care workers and the role played by the health care organizations with which they are associated. Nurses have been effective in using the laws of supply and demand to their advantage to gain negotiating power in dealing with organizational employers. As noted in chapter 5, they have succeeded in establishing countervailing organizational power by organizing collectively into unions. Physicians, the majority of whom have had little experience to date with employee status, are expressing growing frustration in coping with demands imposed on them by the organizations that employ them. There are signs that they, too, are beginning to explore the possibility of using the laws of supply and demand for their knowledge and skills. They have begun to express interest in the traditional mechanism employees across organizations use to gain negotiating power, as members of collective entities rather than as isolated individuals.

New Types of Clinical Care Organizations

We have already addressed health care organizational growth in the hospital sector, both in inpatient and outpatient facilities, in chapter 6. Nursing home and home health care has expanded tremendously. Then there are the stand-alone health care facilities, including MRI facilities, freestanding emergency departments, and surgical centers also discussed in chapter 6. In all cases, organizational growth has been associated with occupational growth.

Nonclinical Occupations and Organizations and the Health Insurance Industry

Navigators, or assisters, whom we encountered in chapter 3, constitute a brand-new health occupation introduced once the Affordable Care Act (ACA) went into effect. In 2013, the Centers for Medicare and Medicaid Services (CMS) made fifty-four million dollars available to fund navigator training. It created a free online training program, the completion of which resulted in certification. It required an annual refresher course.

Agents and brokers who participate in the Federally Facilitated Marketplaces created by the ACA must also complete a training program and become certified. Some states require that agents and brokers accumulate Continuing Education units (CEUs) to meet licensure requirements. Private sector vendors have come into existence offering training programs. CMS-approved vendors are permitted to charge a fee.

Advocates of market-based health care argue that navigators constitute a new layer of government bureaucracy. That's true. However, it is also true that this layer would not have been necessary if the market for individual health care coverage were working effectively and efficiently. The reason the government created this new occupation was that consumers complained. They were confused and frustrated about being forced to participate in a market they could not navigate. They wanted someone to explain the products on offer. In short, the occupation came into existence because sellers of individual health insurance were not displaying the products they were selling in a way that consumers could evaluate without a lot of assistance. The navigators were there to achieve the transparency that observers on both sides of the exchange say they want and that they say is essential for competition to exist and achieve the efficiency promised by the free-market model.

The image that serves to clarify this scenario is that the government stepped in to provide a very big crutch to hold up the state-based, private-sector health insurance markets, preventing what would otherwise be a steady state of confusion. Funding in support of navigators has of course been cut drastically over the last couple of years by the president. One result is an increase in the rate of uninsurance in the country.

Then there are the coders. The insurance industry is responsible for the proliferation of jobs related to coding. It is not just the increase in the number of persons who do the coding but also the number of organizations that have come into existence alongside the coders, such as the Medical Billing and Coding Certification (MB&CC) organization or the Advancing the Business of Healthcare (AAPC) organization.

There are three categories of coders: certified coding assistant (CCA), certified coding specialist (CCS), and certified professional coder (CPC).[5] The internet provides online training, names of schools that offer courses and degrees in coding and medical billing. The AAPC offers certification.

Nonclinical Occupations and Organizations and the Pharmaceutical Industry

The pharmaceutical industry offers an excellent illustration of how the market for what is a tangible health product operates. There are multiple layers of organizations that stand between the manufacturer of pharmaceuticals and the buyer. Much of this was already discussed in chapter 7. The intermediary sellers include drug wholesalers, Pharmacy Benefit Manager organizations, and pharmacies. All are private sector organizations interested in making a profit. Not to be missed is the fact that competition has worked the way it works in any race: each of the intermediary layers may have started out with a legion of competitors but each layer moved to reduce the number of participants left in the game.

The enormous role that advertising plays in this industry means that the purchase of pharmaceutical products is less a matter of supply responding to demand than of concerted effort to drum up demand. That involves lots of people and lots of money generally not included in assessing the operations of the health care sector.

Another Nonclinical Occupation: Lobbyists

Lobbyists may not come to mind as a health occupation. However, the amount of money organized groups representing health sector operations spend on lobbying is impressive. The lobbyists are not volunteers. They are paid well for what they do. More to the point, they are in a position to transfer a colossal amount of money to persons responsible for crafting the laws and regulations governing the health care system. The source, an unwitting source, of all that money is, of course, the consumer, the consumer of the goods and services provided by the health insurance, medical care, hospital care, and pharmaceuticals industries who employ the legions of lobbyists.

So how much are we talking about? By one count, $3.4 billion changed hands in Washington, DC, between lobbyists and recipients of their largesse in 2018.[6] According to the Center for Responsive Politics, in 2018 the health sector was the top ranked spender at $556,276,018.[7]

To the best of my knowledge, there is no assessment of how much of the country's care bill can be attributed to lobbying expenses. However, it is clearly a significant amount. Who benefits from the money that lobbyists hand out is clear: the politicians who write legislation. But there is more to the story. The money handed out to regulators risks "regulatory capture." The economist George Stigler pointed out some years ago that lobbying risks having agencies designed to regulate an industry end up serving the industry's interests rather than the public's interests. A fellow economist, Luigi Zingales, extended the observation by pointing out that there are certain incentives for responding positively to the regulated that are built into the regulators' position. For a start, regulators depend on the regulated for information to do their job. The regulated constitute the audience whose evaluation of the regulators' performance receives more attention than the evaluations of others. In fact, no one else is particularly interested. Taxpayers are not ready to spend the time and effort overseeing the performance of regulators unless there is a disaster. The knowledge and experience that regulators accrue is valuable. It is most valuable to the regulated, which leaves open the option of future rewarding career opportunities. In short, regulators need not be corrupt to be pushed into catering to the regulated, because the incentive system is set up that way.

THE DRIVING ENGINE OF THE ECONOMY

Who benefits from the emergence of all those new jobs, new companies, new associations, new training programs, and so on is also clear. There are a lot of people getting paid for the work they do related to health care, work that involves services as well as products. How much of that work brings value is not nearly as clear. What is absolutely certain is that the health care sector has unquestionably become what the business media tout as the branch of the economy certain to produce high returns on investment.

Wall Street types laud the health care sector as "the driving engine of the economy." My image of health sector occupations and organizations comes closer to the Energizer Bunny that keeps on going. The energy comes from the money circulating in this sector. The Bunny does not have an overall policy or plan; it is more like a huge virtual ATM available to everyone who can link up to this sector. (I borrowed the ATM analogy from a physician complaining about rising costs of care.) The more lobbyists pay out, the more legislation comes into existence; new laws translate into new requirements that someone must track to be sure they are being met; that leads to new jobs and new training programs; the new occupational and organizational groups come together to form associations for the purpose of setting standards; the associations enter the lobbying treadmill to insist on standards, training, and certification being written into law.

Lawyers are involved at every stage of expansion in this sector. A steady source of work comes from the pharmaceutical industry, which uses lawsuits to protect patents. Patients sue doctors, hospitals, and pharmaceutical companies for a variety of reasons, keeping lawyers busy. Lawyers are involved in drawing up proposed mergers between major players. And they are involved in producing contracts governing hospital alliances and contracts between doctors' groups and hospitals.

All the occupations and organizations mentioned so far are just the tip of the iceberg. One critic who complains that 90 percent of health sector job growth does not involve doctors, offers the following job growth list: "The vast majority must be administrators, actuaries, advisors, agents, billers and coders, compliance officers, consultants, IT developers, lawyers, managers, navigators, project managers, salespersons, and writers of rules and regulations needed to tackle increased bureaucracy."[8]

The Energizer Bunny's job is to just keep going, to distributing the money all this activity generates. Of course, there is considerable disagreement about exactly how well it is being spent, which offers more job opportunities: employing people hired to analyze and interpret the data presented by persons and organizations engaged in policy debates about who should pay and how much. Understanding which parts of the system are projected to grow is valuable in anticipating investment opportunities.

Continuing with this analogy, I would say that advocating the market-based health care model is the verbal version of the Energizer Bunny. Proponents of the market-based model just keep talking about efficiency, competition, transparency, consumer choice, and, of course, the promise that prices will drop in response to the interaction of supply and demand—at some point in the future. All this in the face of reality, that is, the steady growth in costs, a large share of which is clearly attributable to new and expanding health care occupations and organizations.

Why would any of the people who are benefiting from health sector expansion want to rein in health care costs and risk having it impact their jobs and associated organizations? Is there anyone out there prepared to argue that we should look at the consequences that restraining occupational growth would have on the economic outlook? How about the effect it would have on health outcomes? It is worth trying to come up with answers to such questions. I propose to take a stab at it in the final chapters of the book.

REPEAL AND REPLACE PROPOSALS

As I said before, it is not worth taking time to analyze the ACA repeal and re-place proposals, because the repeal effort did not succeed. But the projection of the impact that passage of any of the proposed replacement plans would have had is worthy of attention.

This is a brief review of what happened in June 2017. Only one of the three proposals launched by the Republican Congress, the American Health Care Act (AHCA) was passed by the US House of Representatives but rejected by the Senate. It was presented as a market-based insurance arrangement that would allow the market to operate without the government-imposed regulations written into the ACA. The Congressional Budget Office (CBO), which is generally considered nonpartisan, was asked to assess the impact of the proposed legislation. It issued the following assessment: it reported that the legislation would likely increase the number of uninsured by twenty-three million by 2026 and that it would reduce the deficit by $337 billion over 2017–2026. This is the part of the CBO report that supporters of the repeal effort pointed to as a major benefit. They directed less attention to the CBO's assessment of the effect on the economy as a whole which was as follows: "By 2026, 924,000 jobs would be lost, gross state product would be $93 billion lower, and business output would be $148 billion less. About three-quarters of jobs lost (750,000) would be in the health sector."[9]

Let's now link the rise and fall of proposals intended to repeal and replace the ACA with the discussion at the beginning of the chapter, which focuses on job growth.

1. The AHCA and the two other proposed pieces of legislation were considered by Congress over the summer of 2017 and failed to pass.
2. The nonpartisan CBO assessment revealed that the proposed legislation that came close to passing would have reduced the national deficit but would have increased the number of uninsured.
3. The CBO projections indicated that the proposed legislation would have a serious negative impact on the economy as a whole due to significant job loss; and that the health sector would experience most job loss.
4. The CBO report did not comment on the kinds of jobs that would be lost, that is, whether they would be clinical, patient care jobs or office-based paper-processing jobs.

The CBO assessment received short-lived attention because the repeal effort failed. Millions of people did not lose their insurance coverage nor did people lose their health sector jobs. This allowed the business media to return to celebrating the health sector as the driving engine of the economy.

Like the CBO, the business media generally make little attempt to evaluate the social contribution or value of the jobs that have been proliferating in the health sector. Nor do they emphasize the fact that most job growth occurring in the health care sector involves relatively low paying jobs.

Opponents of the ACA are not about to give up. A case brought by twenty Republican states' attorneys general and the governors of Maine and Mississippi was heard in Texas and settled during the last weeks of 2018. The suit was based on the claim that because Congress eliminated the tax penalty for not purchasing health insurance in 2017—that is, it abolished the individual mandate—the whole law is no longer constitutional. The Justice Department intervened, taking the position that the entire law should not be struck down but that some provisions could be eliminated. The most controversial provision was the requirement that insurance companies cover preexisting conditions. That decision prompted a coalition of Democratic officeholders to launch a countersuit. The judge ruled in favor of the plaintiffs, that is, the Republican lawmakers, finding the ACA in its entirety to be unconstitutional, but did not set a date for the ruling to take effect. At the time of this writing, the case is expected to move up to the Supreme Court. Thus the effort to repeal if not replace the ACA is not about to stop.

EFFICIENCY AND THE HEALTH CARE SECTOR

Health care expenditures now amount to nearly 18 percent of the country's gross domestic product (GDP). CMS projections indicate that how much the country spends on health care is expected to increase steadily by 5.6 percent per year. That means that the country will be spending twenty cents of every American dollar on health care by 2025. Consider the rate of increase in expenditures over time. In 1960 we were devoting 5 percent of GDP to health care, that is, 5 cents of every dollar; in 1980 it was 8 percent; in 2000 it was 13.3 percent.[10] The steady rise did not happen without anyone noticing. Health care policy analysts have repeatedly pointed it out, adding that we spend almost twice as much as the average European country spends, yet Europeans all live longer and receive universal health insurance coverage. You would think Americans would want to know how this is possible.

The fact that some observers believe that half of health care costs are attributable to labor costs adds an important dimension to this picture.[11] It presents policy makers with a very big conundrum.

- Doesn't this mean that the country is actively choosing to spend more on health care, in fact on health care workers, in the interest of growing the economy?

The trend data are very clear. So it is hard to avoid the thought that the country, at least those in a position to do something about the trend, must want the rising rate of spending on health care in combination with job creation in the health care sector to continue.

One can bemoan the rising cost of health care or one can celebrate the health sector's ability to create jobs, but at some point, one has to recognize the relationship between the two and choose which to focus on in developing health policy in the future.

Where does that leave us? Here is the Catch-22:

- Are we prepared to have the health sector keep expanding and creating new jobs because it is functioning as the driving engine of the economy, with the understanding that the economy is heavily dependent on this sector for economic growth?
- Or do we want to control health care costs, with the direct effect of reducing the growth of health care jobs?

I am not about to argue that we should or should not be spending nearly twenty cents of every US dollar on health care. I am saying that if we are choosing to do so to advance economic growth, we should be more forthright about it. The point I want to make more explicitly is that acknowledging that the health care sector is serving this purpose would allow exploration of alternatives for achieving economic growth—possibly developing occupations and organizations in other sectors.

Without moving out of a health care discussion and into a discussion of the economic future of the society, I will just note that replacing the health sector as the driving engine of the economy requires that the alternative sectors have the potential to create jobs. We have long been told that defense spending is very effective in achieving that, because it requires a constant flow of military products that require replacement, which keeps a number of industries in business. The downside of counting on the military for jobs is that it requires an ongoing commitment to fight wars. It is good to check how well such long-standing assumptions hold up; on closer examination, we see that domestic spending outpaces military spending in fueling job growth. There is a huge range across sectors in how much more job creation can be achieved. To illustrate, for every $1 million spent on defense, 21 percent more jobs could be created in the wind energy industry. But 178 percent more jobs could be created in the elementary and secondary education sector.[12] Indeed, investment in education brings far greater economic and social reward over the long term. However, the market-based approach places greater value on short-term gains that accrue to individual investors.

I would argue that if nothing else, we could decide that spending such a large proportion of our GDP on health care would be more justifiable if we were allocating those dollars more effectively. We could direct all that money to expanding occupations and organizations that would actually improve the health of the population, to occupations prepared to engage in research aimed at advancing diagnosis and treatment, and to those dedicated to addressing social factors affecting health that medicine is not equipped to address. Instead we have been growing the economy by requiring too many people to spend their time on mind-numbing tasks that involve sitting in front of computers and entering codes.

Saying that market-based health care is a more efficient approach to health care is obviously not true and has not been true for decades, as the rise in proportion of GDP devoted to health care attests. Saying that it is government interference with the free market that is preventing the market from achieving all that it promises is disingenuous. It misrepresents the role of government in general and government funding in particular. Arguing in favor of a market-based health care approach reduces an extremely complex arrangement—in which much of what takes place in the health care market for goods and services depends on government to prop it up—to a false reality. It would not be much of a stretch to conclude that the argument is grounded in what is, in current parlance, a matter of "alternative facts."

- When it comes down to it, does the contradiction between unending job expansion in the health sector, with its negative implications for cost containment and claims of private sector efficiency, mean that the market-based approach is just a matter of overused slogans?

NOTES

1. Christopher Barbey et al., "Physician Workforce Trends and Their Growth Implications for Spending Growth," *Health Affairs Blog*, July 28, 2017, https://www.healthaffairs.org/do/10.1377/hblog20170728.061252/full/.

2. "Employment Projections," Bureau of Labor Statistics, October 24, 2017, p. 4, https://www.bls.gov/news.release/pdf/ecopro.pdf.

3. Barbey et al., "Physician Workforce Trends."

4. Ben Casselman, "Experts Foresee a U.S. Work Force Defined by Ever Widening Divides," *New York Times*, October 25, 2017, B3.

5. Julie Shay, "What is Coding & Understanding the Difference between CCA, CCS, CPC," http://dept.sfcollege.edu/business/hitprograms/content/PDFs/codingpresentation.pdf.

6. Center for Responsive Politics, "Who's Up, Who's Down?" OpenSecrets.org, https://www.opensecrets.org/lobby/incdec.php.

7. Center for Responsive Politics, "Ranked Sectors, 2018," Open Secrets.org, https://www.opensecrets.org/lobby/top.php?indexType=c&showYear=2018.

8. Deane Waldman, "Administrative Job Growth in Healthcare Isn't Good for America," The Hill, May 8, 2017, https://thehill.com/blogs/pundits-blog/health care/332372-administrative-job-growth-in-healthcare-isnt-good-for-america.

9. Leighton Ku et al., The American Health Care Act: Economic and Employment Consequences for States," Commonwealth Fund, June 14, 2017, https://www.com monwealthfund.org/publications/issue-briefs/2017/jun/american-health-care-act -economic-and-employment-consequences.

10. National Center for Health Statistics, "Table 93. Gross Domestic Product, National Health Expenditures, Per Capita Amounts, Percent Distribution, and Average Annual Percent Change: United States, Selected Years 1960–2015," CDC/National Center for Health Statistics, 2016, https://www.cdc.gov/nchs/data/hus/2016/093.pdf.

11. Michael Mandel, "Rising Labor Costs Accounted for 47 Percent of Increased Personal Health Care Spending in 2015," Blog, Progressive Policy Institute, September 30, 2016, https://www.progressivepolicy.org/blog/rising-labor-costs -accounted-47-percent-increased-personal-health-care-spending-2015/.

12. Heidi Garrett-Peltier, "Job Opportunity Cost of War," Watson Institute, Brown University, May 24, 2017, https://watson.brown.edu/costsofwar/files/cow/imce/papers/2017/Job%20Opportunity%20Cost%20of%20War%20-%20HGP%20-%20FINAL.pdf.

9

Market-Based Health Care
The Model and the Reality

In the opening chapter, I said this book stems from what I learned from my students on the first day of class. At this point, I would like to share what I learned several weeks into the course during one of those classes.

The history of hospital development in this country was the topic scheduled for the third week of class. I was just beginning to outline the literature on the differences in the operations of government-sponsored hospitals, nonprofit hospitals, and for-profit hospitals, when on the spur of the moment, I decided to ask the students if they knew which hospitals in the city were for-profit organizations. Maybe that was unfair, because it takes some effort to determine which hospitals are investor-owned. Their names do not provide any clues. And they are, from time to time, bought and sold, shifting their identity from for-profit to nonprofit and back.

My question was answered when one student volunteered a name, and others nodded. The student named a major university hospital. When I asked why she thought it was a for-profit hospital, she said she thought so because it was so expensive. Others now chimed in to say that they agreed and that they, too, knew how expensive it was. I was stunned. I explained that the hospital is not a for-profit organization but a nonprofit. I started to explain what nonprofit status means and suddenly realized that I had an excellent illustration at hand. I asked whether they believed that the university they were attending was a for-profit institution. They were unsure about that but did say that it was expensive too. Once I got into the explanation of where the money the organization receives in payment for services rendered goes—whether that involves hospital services or educational services—it was the students' turn to be amazed. They said they assumed that the top administrators of the university took home bigger checks and bonuses when it made more money. I won't speak for the university hospital they named, because the salary the administrator receives is enormous. And the lobby does look like that of a luxury hotel. But that does not make it a for-profit. However, the university they were attending was founded by a religious order. Administrators make good salaries but only a fraction of the salaries of CEOs in successful business organizations. I explained that the university does not have stockholders who benefit when the university's revenues increase. In fact, the university makes every effort to promote itself as an organization dedicated to serving first-generation students, with a large proportion of the students receiving financial support. Where did they think profit was coming from? They weren't sure. (I chose not to get distracted into discussion of for-profit colleges charged with fraud for accepting government tuition monies and students not graduating.) The issue was not something to which the students had paid much attention, nor had it translated into an understanding of what happens to the money organizations earn.

I tell this story because these are the same people who were so adamant several weeks earlier about the superiority of a business, that is, for-profit, approach to health care—who were convinced that that government screws up everything it touches. I could not help but conclude that the depth of their understanding of what it means to be a for-profit, business organization left a lot to be desired.

As I said in the first chapter, I am focusing on my students' misconceptions about the workings of the health care system because I think it is representative of understanding on the part of their parents and their parents' friends and neighbors, in other words, a substantial number of Americans. I might add that this flawed understanding of how the health care system works in this county does not speak well for the "consumer-driven" health care agenda that assumes that buyers have a good understanding of the facts regarding the choices before them.

Examples of big-time public misunderstandings about our health care arrangements abound. An October 2017 poll found that 24 percent of the public thought the ACA had been partially repealed; an additional 15 percent thought it had been totally repealed or repealed and replaced.[1] In June 2017, the same pollsters found that 17 percent of the population thought the ACA and Obamacare were different laws; another 18 percent admitted that they were not sure if the laws were the same or different.

My reaction to these findings goes further. It is to doubt whether the respondents who said that they knew the ACA had not been repealed or didn't think it had been repealed knew any more about the law than those who said that they were not sure whether it had been repealed.

Consider the fact that among those who report being uninsured because they can't afford to buy health insurance, four out of ten did not know that there were such things as state health exchanges or marketplaces.[2] So, of course, they don't know about the subsidies that might be available to them.

Another example of confusion revolves around what a single-payer or Medicare-for-all option means. A 2017 Kaiser Family Foundation poll found that 53 percent of Americans favor a national health plan, 30 percent strongly favor it, and 23 percent somewhat favor it. Only 3 percent strongly oppose it and 13 percent somewhat oppose it. My question again is, Do they know what it is that they are favoring or opposing? It seems that 47 percent of the respondents said they believed that they could keep their current insurance plan. In short, a large share of those who favor the single-payer option do not grasp the idea that everyone would be covered by the same plan.[3]

It's not that there are no highly informed members of the public out there; it is just that they are vastly outnumbered by the misinformed. At the same time, it is easy to understand why there is so much misunderstanding.

Admittedly, it may not be necessary for people to know what is in the current law or know about proposed changes to the law to engage in transactions in the health care marketplace, but people do have to know about the health care goods and services they are buying. And, as the discussion in preceding chapters indicates, they don't know nearly enough to make informed decisions. The problem is that the information is very hard to come by. Yet consumers face unrelenting pressure to shop for health care goods and services as if they were in a position to make well-informed and rational judgments. Furthermore, the idea that a person is ready to shop in the face of medical crisis is beyond reason.

A review of research on "shopping" in health care markets published in the journal *Health Affairs* reveals the following problems, with which, by now, I expect you will be familiar:

- Health care prices are notoriously opaque.
- Cost differences are not necessarily related to quality differences; there is not much difference in quality and efficiency between high-cost and low-cost providers, but information on quality is confusing.
- There is a distinction between choosing the provider of services and the services; there are many factors that impact the "shoppability" of services: how complex the service is, how urgent, if the patient knows is needed, or if the patient needs a recommendation from a doctor.
- In many cases, patients are in a vulnerable position (too sick) and unable to negotiate.
- It is estimated that only about 7 percent of health care spending is on services that are "shoppable," suggesting that other policies are needed.
- Evidence suggests that supplying consumers with more and more tools may not result in more savvy consumer behavior.[4]

The analyst who came up with this list offers the following conclusion.

> Health care is complex and shopping for a knee replacement is not the same as choosing which vendor on Amazon offers the lowest price for your preferred brand of coffee beans. Health care is complex, relationship-based and consumer preferences vary widely. The trend of increased consumer cost sharing along with increased expectations that those consumers should engage in price shopping is not going away. But it is naïve to believe that just increasing the cost burden on consumers and providing them with online tools to compare prices is going to fix the serious problem we have in the US health care system. It will take dedicated action by a number of actors, including consumers, but also insurers, employers, and providers.[5]

CONCEPTS AND THE MARKET-BASED APPROACH

While there is nothing confusing about the admonition to shop, how that is supposed to result in consumer-driven health care is where things get fuzzy. Those who volunteer to explain how it is supposed to work generally invoke economic arguments grounded in a number of commonly heard concepts.

The concepts are used so often in public discourse that no one, myself included so far, bothers to explain what they mean and exactly how they support the argument. Even less attention is directed to the underlying assumptions that serve as the foundation of free-market economic theory. Debate can be carried out without reference to the meaning of concepts and assumptions, because the public has little tolerance for debate about complex ideas, and even less tolerance for arguments that challenge the views to which the public is already committed.

Even a brief examination of some of the basic concepts involved—what they mean and how they are supposed to support the argument for consumer-driven health care—is highly revealing. Let's stop and consider more closely four of the most commonly used concepts: efficiency, competition, transparency, and moral hazard.

Efficiency

The question that I raised at the beginning of each chapter, which I have not heard satisfactorily answered by market-based health care proponents, is, If the private sector is more efficient and we have a private sector health care system, unlike the government-based systems in other countries, then why is the cost of health care continuing to rise? And, I might add, it's rising to a much higher level than in those other countries. Okay, observers say that it is increasing for lots of reasons having to do with greater demand, more expensive technology, aging population, and the old trope: government interference. Of course, the same factors affect the health care systems in other economically advanced countries, but they manage to control costs better than we do.

Peterson Center on Healthcare researchers addressed the question of what accounts for higher prices in this country compared to other countries. They considered the impact of five factors on health care costs: population size, population age, disease prevalence or incidence, service utilization, and service price and intensity. They found that population size and age did increase but not by much over the period they investigated, 1996–2013. Disease prevalence and service utilization decreased over this period in large part because the rate of heart disease dropped dramatically. The only factor that rose significantly, by about 50 percent, was the cost of health care services.[6] What is noteworthy is that the market-based approach to health care was also gaining greater traction in the health care sector over this period with proponents arguing that business sector practices and efficiency would result in lower prices.

The same researchers found that a comparison of the prices paid for inpatient hospital stays by private sector insurers and public sector insurers sheds some light on what accounts for high health care prices. Consider the trends in prices paid for inpatient hospital stays by private payers and public insurers between 1997 and 2015 (table 9.1). "Prices for inpatient hospital stays are higher and have grown faster for private insurance than for Medicare or Medicaid"[7]—in fact, 68 percent higher than for Medicare.

Table 9.1. Trends in Prices Paid for Inpatient Hospital Stays by Private Payers and Public Insurers between 1997 and 2015

	1997	2015
Private	$11,840	$19,975
Medicare	$11,186	$11,868
Medicaid	$9,379	$9,071

- Does this mean that lower prices are not a major objective that private sector third party payers aim to achieve through greater efficiency? What else is there at the center of the market-based approach if not lower prices in response to greater efficiency?

It is worth reflecting on the fact that proponents of market-based health care have never bothered to say how efficiency would be measured. I would suggest that the concept that stands at the center of discussion about the greater efficiency of the market-based approach to health care needs clarification. I would like to nominate a pretty clear and simple indicator to test the claim of greater private sector efficiency: comparison of the growth in per capita spending by the private sector versus the public sector over the last decade or so.

Per capita spending is a topic of interest to health policy experts. It is not something that is likely to be addressed by fans of market-based health care. Consider the following. According to the Federal Office of the Actuary in the Centers for Medicare and Medicaid Services (CMS), the per-person amount spent on health care between 2007 and 2013 increased by 6 percent for Medicaid enrollees, 14 percent for Medicare enrollees and 29 percent for private insurance enrollees. According to the CMS actuary, the rate of increase is expected to accelerate. By 2023, costs are projected to increase by 63 percent for both Medicaid and Medicare enrollees and 104 percent for private insurance enrollees.[8] Remember that the private sector insurance enrollee population is neither elderly nor poor, meaning you would expect this population to be healthier than the Medicare and Medicaid populations and less expensive to care for.

This raises the obvious question.

- Why isn't private sector spending dropping due to competition or, if nothing else, increasing at a slower rate than public sector spending?

A closer look at how medical spending is distributed provides more support for the argument that the private sector insurers are covering a healthier population that should be less expensive to cover. The persons who use most health care services are probably not working at a full-time job and are instead consuming vast amounts of health care goods and services. The following is the most recent assessment available at the time of this writing, based on data from the Agency for Healthcare Research and Quality and other government sources for 2010:

- Five percent of the population consumes 50 percent of total health expenditures.
- The top 50 percent consumes over 97 percent of total health expenditures.
- The bottom 50 percent consumes 2.7 percent of total health expenditures.[9]

The explanation for the 2.7 percent expenditure on the bottom 50 percent of the population has little to do with efficiency on anyone's part, especially on the part of third-party payers. It has to do with the fact that this portion of the population is made up of people who are healthy and not seeking health care. What conclusion about efficiency can one draw from these data? Market-based logic indicates that the simplest way to cut health care costs is to cut off access to the high-cost enrollees. One could argue that taking such a step would be immoral. Developing a policy based on cutting off access to health care for the high-expenditure segment of the population is also impractical because it is not that easy to predict who might fall into that top 5 percent.

What the market-based approach can do is reduce access to health insurance for anyone who exhibits any sign at all of becoming sick and running up costs. That, of course, amounts to reducing access to health care. It is the mechanism private insurers used all along prior to passage of the ACA. Moreover, they have continued to create variations of this instrument in the name of managed care in the name of efficiency and consumer preference.

This raises another familiar question:

- If the majority of Americans participate in a market-based system, why isn't consumer unhappiness about the high cost of health care and restricted access putting more pressure on the private sector sellers to actually be more efficient in the delivery of health care goods and services?

The approach used by private sector insurers, to offer a proliferation of plans that are supposed to give consumers greater choice, has done nothing to advance efficiency. The fact that there are so many alternatives simply causes customer confusion. More to the point, multiple plans require large numbers of company staff to monitor. The proliferation of plans is doing a great deal more to increase private sector insurance company administrative costs than to reduce them. That is apart from the administrative costs incurred on the other side by providers of health care services who must check to make sure the plan will cover the treatment health care providers prescribe. This is a case of administrative waste and inefficiency masquerading as competition. (I credit a health policy analyst friend, Susan Sanders, with authorship of this assessment.)

Administrative expense is not treated as an indicator of inefficiency in the private sector since it can easily be offset by increasing prices, which in turn produces increased profit. And, because profit is what is used as the primary indicator of efficiency, it comes full circle. Profitability works to advance the market-based health care argument.

The fact that somewhere between twenty-four and thirty cents out of every health care dollar spent in this country goes toward administration rather than health care is, however, significant. A precise figure is hard to come by because what are considered to be essential operating expenses are not always clear.[10] For example, a kerfuffle that hit the media occurred when pharmaceutical CEOs were called to testify before Congress. They flew to Washington, DC, using chartered planes rather than commercial airlines. Because the news media captured the event, it gave the public the opportunity to complain that the CEOs were running up charges that consumers would be paying for. The fact is that what constitutes a legitimate administrative expense is not something that is easily settled. We generally don't hear about what is included without something unusual happening on a very public stage. On the other hand, Medicare is required to report administrative costs in some detail and in a public format to justify the annual budget allocations that Congress appropriates. The allocation is about 2 percent per year. That also does not attract much media attention. There's just not much excitement in that story.

Harder to understand is how little attention the Institute of Medicine (IOM) report, *Best Care at Lower Cost*, issued in 2013 on sources of excess health care costs—that is, wasteful expenditure—has received. I highly recommend the November 2013 article by leading Canadian economist Robert Evans in *Healthcare Policy*, "Waste, Economists and American Healthcare." His take on the economic analysis of health care waste in the United States is unique. It is both technically sophisticated and entertaining.[11] Evans points out that Uwe Reinhardt, one of the leading health economists of this era, made the observation years ago, in 1988, that the reason the US health care system was so expensive was due to bureaucratic waste. Evans goes on to say that Reinhardt returned to his observations in 2013 in response to the IOM report. The IOM's assessment was that 31 percent of total health spending in 2009 was due to excess costs amounting to $765 billion. The excess costs were due to various kinds of inefficiency: unnecessary services, missed preventive care, legal costs, and fraud, among others.

Evans's characterization of Reinhardt's observations on administrative waste is worth seeing in the original. Evans says the following:

> [Reinhardt's statement on bureaucratic waste] was very rude of him because, although perfectly true, it challenged two of Americans' fundamental articles of faith: that the American healthcare system is the finest in the world (that's why it costs so much), and more fundamentally, that profit-driven private-sector organizations are necessarily and, by definition, lean and efficient. Only public-sector organizations are choked with wasteful and incompetent bureaucracies. Everybody knows that.[12]

The estimate of waste keeps increasing. It rose to 34 percent as of 2012. A 2016 update of that estimate indicates that waste now exceeds $1 trillion annually, $389 billion attributable to Medicare and Medicaid and $755 billion attributable to private payers.[13] A closer look at the six categories used to make this assessment shows that two stand out. Administrative complexity results in $47 billion in Medicare/Medicaid waste and $265 billion in private payer waste; fraud and abuse account for $83 billion in Medicare/Medicaid waste and $139 billion in private payer waste. (The other categories are pricing failures, failures of care and coordination, failures of care delivery, and overtreatment.) What that says about market-based health care seems to me to be self-explanatory.

Before we leave the topic of efficiency, let's stop for a moment to acknowledge that efficiency is the measure of success embraced by the private sector. It is powerful because it is easy to represent numerically as profit or loss. The measure of success employed by health care practitioners is *effectiveness* of care. The problem in using this indicator is that measuring effectiveness works well at the population health level where mortality and morbidity rates are represented in whole numbers or percentages, that is, in concrete numbers. That accounting reveals that people in other countries live longer and that they pay a lot less for health care than Americans do. At the individual level the measure of effectiveness is not nearly as clear. There are no measures for estimating health status; there are just vague terms such as "much better" or "somewhat better." In short, efficiency measures that reflect profit are far easier to point to than measures related to effectiveness.

Competition

Advocates of market-based health care put a lot of emphasis on the benefits of competition. I trust that the amount of attention devoted to competition in previous chapters makes clear how it is supposed to operate. It works best when the value of the product is clear, that is, when prices are known and quality is relatively easy to determine. This does not apply in any of the health care markets we considered. And as we saw in previous chapters, instead of reducing prices, competition in the health sector invariably results in a drop in the number of competitors or sellers, with an effect on prices just the opposite of what competition is supposed to achieve. This is vividly illustrated in the health insurance and pharmaceutical industries. Whether this happens because companies are pushed out or bought out through mergers or takeover bids doesn't matter. The result is the same. The number of competitors keeps dropping. Curiously, the process seems to continue until it reaches what I have come to believe is the magic number: 3. As the competition comes closer to this number, advocates of market-based health care can be heard loudly demanding that the government step in to enforce antitrust legislation. The government is suddenly viewed as not interfering with but with advancing competition. I cannot help but question the value of the magic number 3.

- Does anyone really believe that a field of three competitors produces any real competition? Isn't it likely that each can easily discover what the other two are working on, thereby eliminating the need to be innovative?

The market-based theoretical conceptualization does not deal with a number of other complications associated with competition. For example, competition in the health insurance sector has produced an enormous amount of variation in state-based health insurance markets. It's not that the insurance products are different. They are not. It is that the range of product choices available to consumers is not the same from one regional market to another, in part because the number of sellers is not the same. The result is that there is limited competition and enormous differences in the prices of policies from one region to another across the country. Counties next to one another exhibit huge differences.

The variation in the number of insurance sellers in some areas over the last couple of years has inspired talk about the threat to state markets of having only one seller in the area and what to do about it. As of 2017, the concern shifted to what to do about counties where the number of sellers continued to drop, leaving no sellers. With no sellers, there is no market.

- So is the solution that markets should operate in lucrative areas but government-sponsored insurance in nonlucrative areas? But that leads to arguments about the role of government and attempts on the part of Republicans to eliminate government provision of health insurance. So it isn't really a solution.

The explanation for failed markets is not puzzling. Without sufficient government subsidization, competition works in reverse of the way the market-based health care model says it works. The market-based health insurance market is not producing lower prices. It is producing a shrinking number of suppliers, leading to failing markets. The only alternative, which insurance companies stated they were forced to use in dealing with withdrawal of government sub-sidies, was . . . to raise the price of premiums.

At the theoretical level, this should not be surprising. If there are not enough buyers entering the market to make participation profitable, because they can't afford to buy the products on offer, sellers have no reason to enter it and good reason to exit. At the practical level, competition means that the state-based health insurance market that is supposed to make health insur-ance available to Americans simply may not have any sellers in some parts of the country for some period of time. Agents in the private sector continue to operate. They do make insurance products available for a fee. They do not deal in subsidies. The people who cannot afford health insurance without a subsidy are unlikely customers.

No one has suggested introducing measures to force the private sector companies to participate in markets in which they have no hope of mak-ing a profit. No one is ready to have the government play that role. Besides, stockholders would not put up with it. That leaves offering incentives or subsidies to the private sector, which is unpopular with some members of the political establishment.

But it does make one wonder this:

- Were consumer-driven health care champions prepared for the private sec-tor approach, grounded in competition, driving sellers out of the market, making the product unavailable? Isn't eliminating markets, thus eliminating opportunities for sellers to participate, self-defeating?

Transparency

The call for transparency has been getting louder. Everyone seems to be on board because it is never good to hide facts that are likely to be important in the health care arena. But what is it exactly that transparency is supposed to achieve? Better-armed consumers who are in a position to choose? Refusing to buy the product is usually not such a good option since there are usually few alternatives.

The core issue revolves around the extent to which transparency can overcome asymmetrical information between buyers and sellers regard-ing health care goods and services. Let's consider the barriers. For a start, consumers' choices are constrained by what economists call "agency." In other words, consumers cannot prescribe medicines, tests, or treatments for themselves. They require an agent to do that for them: a health care provider. The consumer is in an even less advantageous, asymmetrical position when it comes to supplier-induced demand coming from the health care organization the provider works for. For a start, those arrangements are far from public. And, as providers keep saying, they have little power to influence the operations of the health care organizations they are affiliated with. The call for transparency does little to overcome supplier-induced demand. And is it really possible to achieve full transparency? There is no certainty that getting a price on one service or product at a time prospectively will add up to reveal the full price of testing and treatment that will actually occur once the process is set in motion.

It is also important to keep in mind the fact that price transparency is only one dimension of transparency. Consider the reaction of policy makers in Maryland to finding that the transparency measures they had put in place aimed at increasing efficiency were "counterproductive."[14] The state introduced a system of financial rewards designed to incentivize providers to improve efficiency, that is, to reward them financially. Policy makers admit that their "relatively intuitive" assumption was that this would result in more efficient providers becoming higher-priced providers. The state was also introducing measures aimed at incentivizing consumers to engage in value-based purchasing, that is, to seek out lower-cost providers. Policy makers suddenly realized the effect of the two policies in combination. The insight may be startling but, after some reflection, not surprising. It appears that in promoting value-based purchasing, the state was steering consumers to seek out less efficient providers. Whether the providers were efficient or not is probably of less concern to consumers than the quality of the health care services they offer, which consumers are not good at judging. The observation made by Maryland policy makers does make one wonder whether the admonition to engage in "value-based" purchasing might be counterproductive more often than we have been ready to acknowledge.

It is hard to miss the fact that the pressure to shop is not having as much effect as market-based health care advocates have argued it will have, largely because price transparency is, in fact, rare. Kenneth Arrow, who is considered the "father of health economics," has this to say about this issue:

We talk about a price system, but that is not what we have. We have a system in which one buyer will pay ten times what other buyers will pay for similar medical devices, or services. So the idea of a price system as the source of efficiency fails at the most elementary level.[15]

He says, "That is what I call a-symmetric information, and I argue that was a key to understanding the health economic issue." This is the way he describes it:

> From the individual's point of view, you know you're going to get sick, but you don't know if medicine will save you, if medications will work. The question is, should I intervene in something that has a small chance of success? More fundamentally, in the economic system, there is uncertainty regarding what innovations will bring in the future. Some believe this can be handled by a price system—that is true, but only if everybody has the same information.[16]

Although only a small proportion of the population engages in the effort to obtain either price or quality information prior to obtaining health care services, an even smaller proportion uses that information. Consider the results of a survey asking people how much comparison shopping they have engaged in.[17] Asked if they had seen information on quality and price of hospitals, the respondents reported the following:

- On quality of hospitals, 13 percent said they saw such information; 4 percent said they used it.
- On quality of doctors, 10 percent said they saw such information; 6 percent said they used it.
- On hospitals' prices, 6 percent said they saw such information; 2 percent said they used it.
- On doctors' prices, 6 percent said they saw such information; 3 percent said they used it.

Trying to figure out why those who see the information and ignore it is enlightening. The effort to alter dietary behavior may throw some light on the subject. Presenting people with facts about the calories and fat they are about to ingest in eating fast food does not affect what they choose to eat. People admit to seeing the information and ignoring it. Transparency is apparently not enough.

Why people don't search for information deserves more attention than it has received. There is good reason to believe that the costs of engaging in a search are too high, too confusing, and too frustrating. The directive issued by the CMS requiring hospitals to list the prices they charge online serves as a case in point. The regulation went into effect January 1, 2019, so it is not clear how it will work at the time of this writing. However, there are clear indications that it will not bring about much transparency, for a long list of reasons. For a start, consumers will have a hard time interpreting the coded language and symbols hospitals use to describe a treatment or a procedure in their chargemasters. There is no standard language from one hospital to another, so comparing prices is nearly impossible. Compiling a price list for separate parts of the treatment may not identify all the goods and services associated with the treatment because the course of treatment can change in process. In the end, only uninsured consumers will be charged the listed prices. Everyone else will be charged the price their third-party payer has negotiated. Finally, while hospitals knew for months that this directive was coming, few had created links on their websites to their chargemasters by the date that it was supposed to happen, meaning that their chargemaster lists can't be found.

The fact is that it is very hard to achieve either price or quality transparency in the health care sector. The pharmaceutical sector serves as the poster child for distortion of information through upfront and over-the-top supplier-induced demand achieved through glossy advertising. This works in combination with concerted efforts to prevent transparency through out-of-court settlements of lawsuits charging that the companies withheld negative findings. The settlements are precisely aimed at preventing transparency of risk associated with the product. And then there was that First Amendment court case that ended up protecting outright lying about pharmaceutical products. Remember, the pharmaceutical sector comes closest to operating in ways consistent with the market-driven model. And it is also the sector in which the country is demanding to have government intervention. As I said in chapter 7, that is worth reflecting on.

Finally, what do those who argue for greater transparency expect to achieve? A number of states are working toward transparency on the prices of particular products. Not that full transparency is possible, but let's engage in a thought experiment: What would happen if all health care prices were suddenly to appear on publicly available lists? Would that bring about more competition and lower prices? What are the chances that it would result in the American propensity to assume that more expensive means better? Or would it lead to what might look much more like a regulated market with less reliance on competition? As far as I can tell, transparency is promoted as something that is highly desirable without laying out a game plan that includes a final result.

Moral Hazard

Advocates of market-based health care can be heard making the point that consumers who have health insurance coverage have little incentive to shop for less expensive health care goods and services because their health insurance will cover it. They also say that practitioners have little reason to attend to the cost of the tests they order because patients can expect to have most of the cost covered. That is the essence of moral hazard. Critics counter this claim by pointing out that consumers cannot be expected to determine when they need care, what kinds of care they need, and how to evaluate cost compared to quality. Critics also say that policies aimed at deterring the overuse of health care pose the threat of detrimental consequences when the consumer underuses care, that is, avoids spending money on services, when the problem is minor, and waits until the problem is more serious, when symptoms are more obvious and troubling, and of course more costly to treat. By then, it is not only the consumer who will be paying more but the whole health care apparatus will be spending more to take care of the problem—not to mention that the consumer is then sicker, which has a multitude of other socioeconomic consequences.

Some observers wonder whether the cure for moral hazard is likely to be worse than the disease.

At its core, the market-based health care argument is about turning patients into consumers. My reaction to this relabeling campaign is highly irreverent. As I see it, it amounts to changing the name of your miniature schnauzer from Fuzz Ball to Killer. The chances that the change will produce a significant alteration in Fuzz Ball's understanding of his new role are not great. Devoting considerable effort to training Fuzz Ball to behave in accordance with his new name is likely to be disappointing as well. Should the training take, can one really expect the big dogs down the street to give a whole lot of consideration to Fuzz Ball's newfound self-conception? Extending the analogy to its illogical extreme, is it likely that Fuzz Ball will be joining a highly motivated group treated to a similar name change with the intent of pursuing recognition of the shift in identity and the benefits associated with it any time soon?

Moving from irreverence to the ill-conceived, we are constantly being badgered to shop for health insurance as well as less expensive doctors, hospitals, drugs, and various kinds of medical services. Shopping in the face of inadequate knowledge about the products would be bad enough. In the case of health insurance, shopping is based on guessing how much health care we will need, if any, over the following year, which comes a lot closer to placing a bet. I can't see how that can be defined as highly desirable when it comes so much closer to gambling, which is not a well-regarded endeavor in this society. It's like going to a casino and knowing at some level that one is contributing to the casino's bottom line.

One is tempted to conclude that the main reason for justifying this burden, that is, trying to figure out the risks in placing this bet, is enhancing the opportunity for private sector organizations to earn a profit and allow shareholders to share in the profit.

PUBLIC OPTION REFORM PROPOSALS AND COMPETITION

Some policy experts have argued that employer-based health insurance is a drag on our economy because it locks people into jobs that they may want to escape but don't do so because they are afraid of losing their health insurance. Just think, not being dependent on employer-based health insurance would mean that people could leave their jobs altogether, choose to work fewer hours, engage in entrepreneurial adventures, and so on. Employers might be willing to hire more workers rather than force workers to accept overtime hours.

Medicare-for-all and single-payer proposals are in the news because a new wave of more liberal politicians are coming out in favor of these options. Those on the other side of the political divide continue to say that the proposals constitute government-run health care, that is, socialism, which they say calls for vigorous opposition because it will lead to the downfall of the country. In actuality, Medicare operates in more of a businesslike fashion than opponents want to admit. It contracts out with private vendors—called Medicare Administrative Contractors—who do the administrative work. Not only that, Medicare uses a bidding process, that is, competition, to get the best price.

Medicare-for-all and single-payer opponents regularly bring up the UK and Canada to make their point. The UK system is socialistic. The state owns the hospitals and pays everyone who works for the National Health Service. That is not true of the Canadian system. There the hospitals are privately owned nonprofits; doctors have traditionally been paid on a fee-for-service basis. The Canadian system, called Medicare, is a single-payer system. It operates like a single insurance company. The government is neither an owner of health care facilities nor an employer of health care personnel. Market-based health care facilities operate in both countries. They just don't play a major part.

Eight of nine proposals aimed at broadening access to health care focusing on expansion of "public option" alternatives to private health insurance were introduced during the 116th Congress.[18] Four bills propose Medicare-for-all. (We return to this topic in in the final pages of the book.)

The creative alternative offered by Jacob Hacker, a Yale University political science professor, employs an interesting perspective in acknowledging the value of competition rather than challenging it.[19] He takes the position that, if market-based advocates were really true believers in the superiority of the private sector approach to health insurance, you would think they would be ready to allow the government to put its product alongside theirs in the market. Hacker says that giving consumers a Medicare Part E (E for "everyone") choice would do exactly that. Hacker does not propose a government takeover. Instead, he advocates a gradual introduction offering the Medicare E option as an alternative to state health insurance exchanges. Further along he says that employers might be given the option of "pay or play." In other words, they could choose to contribute the share employees would pay for the Medicare E option or continue to provide health insurance coverage. Wouldn't that be in the true spirit of competition?

One may wonder, Is Hacker's proposal just another effort to bring socialized medicine in the back door? If it is, does that mean it will never fly? Or is it an idea whose time has come? As it happens, two months after the proposal appeared, the public was asked to assess it. The March 2018 Kaiser Tracking Poll asked respondents whether they favored a Medicare-for-all plan; 59 percent said yes, 39 percent said no.[20] But when asked, "Do you favor or oppose having a national Medicare-for-all plan open to anyone who wants it but people who currently have other coverage could keep what they have?" respondents were far more favorably inclined at 75 percent in favor and only

20 percent opposed. The value close to American sensibilities represented here is the right to choose based on need and preference. It's very much a "theoretical" right rather than an actual right, given that currently the choice is largely made by an employer for the vast majority of people.

The Medicaid buy-in is in some ways an even more radical idea that has only begun to gain traction.[21] The option is being lauded for solving the "bare" counties problem, that is, the problem of no sellers offering health insurance in some parts of the country. This proposal is in a very early stage as of early 2019, and there are no estimates on how much it would cost and who would be eligible.

There is no question that opening up Medicare and Medicaid to buy-in options would have a huge impact on private sector health insurance arrangements. Moving in this direction presents the challenge of figuring out the role competition is playing when the products on offer consist of government sponsored health insurance on the one hand and government-subsidized insurance on the other hand.

THE HEALTH POLICY DEBATE AND ROLE OF ECONOMICS

Debate about the US health care system has been on the political agenda for the past century. The debate has generally revolved around the question of privatization, whether the government should get out of the way and give greater control over health care to the private sector. The debate has gotten more bellicose over the past decade in the wake of passage of the ACA. While it is reasonable to think that people continue to be far more concerned about their health and the health care they do or do not receive than they are about politics of health and health care, allegiance to political party may be overcoming that reasonable assumption.

The disjointedness between health and health policy has clear implications for the nature of the debate and the public's reaction to what is said. According to some observers, policy debate is about values masquerading as debates about numbers and facts. "Each side hurls data and anecdotes at each other as if by identifying the killer data point, the other side would throw up its hands in surrender and declare: 'How could we ever have been so dumb?' Of course, this *never* (sic) happens in public policy debates."[22]

Other observers say that the facts and numbers are being tossed around in a way that reduces their value. "Several myths about health insurance interfere with the diagnosis of problems in the current system and impede the development of productive reforms. Although many are built on a kernel of truth, complicated issues are often simplified to the point of being false or misleading. Several stem from the conflation of health, health care, and health insurance, while others attempt to use economic arguments to justify normative preferences."[23]

Why numbers and anecdotes don't motivate people and values do is well understood. People do not "revise their beliefs in light of new information. On the contrary, they often stubbornly maintain their views. Certain disagreements stay entrenched and polarized." This phenomenon is known as confirmation bias: "This is the psychological tendency to favor information that confirms our beliefs and to disfavor information that counters them—a tendency manifested in the echo chambers and 'filter bubbles' of the online world."[24]

Efforts to prop up the argument favoring market-based health care invariably turn to economic theory. It is worth noting that the discipline is in the process of rethinking some basic tenets of mainstream economic theory that have long been grounded in a free-market perspective. Economics as a field has developed a new outlook labeled "behavioral economics" as reified by the Nobel Prize committee that awarded the prize to Robert Thaler in 2017 for his work. The Nobel Prize was awarded to Robert Shiller in 2013 for work in what he identified as "behavioral finance." These Nobel Prize–winning economists hold that rationality cannot be assumed when it comes to human behavior. Moreover, there is no guarantee that the accurate information necessary to make rational decisions actually exists. Shiller puts it this way: "I have argued that the theory makes little sense, except in fairly trivial ways. Of course, prices reflect available information. But they are far from perfect."[25]

I cannot resist adding the following far less theoretically sophisticated vignette to illustrate the relationship between pricing and the vaulted consumer rationality embraced by proponents of the free market. It is the story of the Payless retailer taking over a former Armani store and announcing that it was introducing a new line of high-end designer shoes created by Italian designer Palessi. The shoes were priced between $200 and $600. More than $3,000 in merchandise was sold during the first few hours. Buyers said that the shoes were "sophisticated" or "made with high-quality materials." The buyers were then informed that there is no such person as Palessi and that the shoes were regular stock usually priced between $20 and $40.[26] I know, one example does not prove that consumers are irrational. (I don't know what it says about the seller, which declared a second and final bankruptcy some months later in 2019.) On the other hand, I believe that we could collect many more examples of consumer irrationality.

The observation that rationality on the part of consumers cannot be assumed is reinforced by Reinhardt who observed that "much of the contemporary writing on health reform remains 'faith-based analysis.'"[27] That may explain how it is possible for economists to embrace contradictory thoughts regarding the successes of the market-based approach to health care in the country. That is also a point made by Reinhardt in charging fellow economists with "simultaneously deploring this monumental waste while celebrating the contribution of healthcare . . . to the American economy."[28]

Why economists are on the forefront of health care reform discussions may have something to do with the declaration made by John Kenneth Galbraith. Galbraith, a towering figure in economics a generation ago, once said, "Economists predict the future, not because they know what is going to happen, but because people ask them."

After considering all the evidence that we have reviewed in preceding chapters, including the observations made by health economists whose discipline is being used as the foundation on which the market-based approach is built, it is hard to understand how the views of economists who are most knowledgeable about how the health system works can be ignored.

FORECASTING NATIONAL HEALTH EXPENDITURES

Also worth attending to is the work of another category of experts, which rests on an economic accounting framework to track national health expenditures for forecasting purposes.[29] These are the analysts who project that the 17.9 percent share of GDP going to health care in 2016 will increase to 19.7 percent—nearly 20 percent—by 2026.

The use of National Health Accounts dates back to 1929. The tool was designed "to answer three critical questions: What is being spent on health care? Where is it being spent? Who is paying?" The historical overview as presented in graphs documents the maturation of the US economy. This allows for comparison of health expenditures to other forms of personal consumer expenditures over time.

What the accounting framework cannot do is address variations on the critical questions that it is designed to answer. The accounts cannot say whether

(1) we are spending the "right" amount on health, (2) we are spending on the right people and things, (3) we are measuring the right things, and (4) we are paying the right prices. Elaboration on the last question reveals the following.

> Price inflation for health care goods and services has largely outpaced that for other consumer services and that for consumer goods. . . . To some extent this reflects Baumol's model of unbalanced growth, but it also reflects the unique nature of the health care market. Given that health care fails virtually every condition needed for market efficiency—free entry and exit, symmetric information, absence of externalities, impartial agency, and so on—there is no reason to assume that pricing is proper. [The Baumol model determines the firm's optimum cash balance.][30]

Emphasis on technical tools designed to capture spending patterns continues to occupy a considerable amount of attention on the part of health policy makers, because the tools capture important facts represented in clear numerical form. But health policy requires answers to the questions raised by those numbers. In responding to presentations at a conference focusing on why health care prices are so high, Lawrence Brown identifies five such questions.

1. Who is covered by health insurance? This raises questions about universality of coverage.
2. What is covered? What should be covered by a basic plan and what can be addressed by supplementary plans?
3. Where is the money coming from? General revenues?
4. What does the supply side look like? How many doctors are needed? How many hospitals?
5. How will providers be paid? Uniform prices are essential.[31]

He argues that it doesn't matter what form the health care system takes—single-payer, government sponsored, mixed private and public sector—someone must develop health policies that respond to these questions. Otherwise there is disorganization. He concludes by saying that we keep having this discussion. Another way of putting it: it's déjà vu all over again.

Forecasting future gains and losses invites argument because it can be approached in so many different ways. For example, deciding to focus on the potential impact of chronic disease on the nation's economy rather than all causes of illness results in some impressive findings. A report issued by the Milken Institute in 2007 starts by saying that more than half of all Americans suffer from one or more chronic illnesses. The researchers predicted a 42 percent increase in seven major chronic diseases by 2023. They concluded that investing in preventive treatment—upstream before the onset of chronic illness—"could reduce the economic impact by 27 percent, or $1.1 trillion annually; we could increase the nation's GDP linked to productivity gains; we could also decrease treatment costs by $218 billion per year." The report concludes with a very clear message, a projection, that investment in approaches designed to avoid expensive health care services associated with treatment of avoidable chronic illness is not only beneficial to patients but is certain to benefit "employers, the government and the nation's economy."[32]

THE EFFECTS OF GETTING GOVERNMENT OUT OF THE WAY

Now that we are nearing the end of this long and complicated story, replete with unanswered questions, where do you stand on the initial question that inspired this discussion: Is getting the government out of the way the solution? Would that bring more choice and lower prices as private sector proponents say it will? Or is it that market-based health care is grounded in an ideology that does not work the way its proponents say it works, and that is exactly what is causing both high prices and complexity? The debate does not look like it will be settled anytime soon.

I am certain that it could be settled a little sooner if policy makers, as opposed to policy analysts who keep suggesting it, would be willing to look at how other economically advanced countries—which have managed to keep health costs so much lower the United States, provide universal health insurance coverage, and attain higher life expectancy than the United States does— have organized their health care arrangements. Virtually all of these countries have made accommodations to private sector participation in the provision of health insurance. The option typically allows consumers who have the money to pay for getting a place closer to the head of the line in receiving care. It is just that the extent of the private sector participation is lower in most economically advanced countries than in the United States. The small number of countries in which private health insurance is the norm are characterized by socioeconomic arrangements that make those societies and the policies related to health care very different from the way they are in the United States.

Comparison of health care systems across economically advanced countries, even countries that are not so rich, requires more attention to detail than we can take up here. However, it is a discussion well worth having. Discussion is most productive when it takes place among knowledgeable persons who bring both expertise and data to the table. I recommend sitting in on exactly that kind of event, the one that was captured in a 2018 webcast monitored by Lawrence Brown and produced by the Kaiser Family Foundation and Peterson Center on Healthcare, which was cited earlier.[33]

As it happens, there is a social experiment taking place that may not provide a complete answer but is sure to provide valuable and provocative insights on the effort to get the government out of way. It is clear that the majority political party in charge of the government at the end of the teens has taken the idea of getting the government out of the way to heart. We can see evidence of politicians in Washington actively engaged in working to dismantle the ACA, which serves as the battleground for getting the government out of the way. Although one branch of government, Congress, failed to get the job done, the executive branch of government is moving forward issuing a series of directives aimed at doing so. What the directives have accomplished is to open the door for politicians at the state level to become more engaged. Efforts aimed at getting the government out of the way at the federal level is bringing in new legislation, regulations, and bureaucratic procedures at the state level.

To illustrate, consider the fact that the individual mandate was overturned in 2017. A closer look at this decision reveals that it eliminated the penalty for not enrolling in health insurance, but it did not eliminate the requirement until 2019. The upshot is that politicians in some states passed new legislation requiring everyone in their state to obtain health insurance and reinstituted the fine. Politicians in other states, encouraged by the edicts issued by the executive branch, have moved in the opposite direction, passing legislation that has the effect of discouraging people from obtaining health insurance. For example, they have introduced restrictions through Medicaid waivers and welcomed health insurance sellers willing to offer plans that are not in compliance with the ACA, which is in violation of the law since the law has not been overturned. These activities have served to bring in the third branch of government, the judicial branch, which is being pressed into working out how the law should be interpreted and whose rights are to be upheld.

An apt example of the effect that courts can have is the lawsuit, mentioned in chapter 8, brought by twenty Republican attorneys general and two governors in a Texas court early in 2018. It was settled, at least in part, in December 2018. The Texas judge found the entire ACA law to be unconstitutional because of the earlier decision to drop the penalty associated with the individual mandate. While many experts say that the judge's ruling is incorrect and will be reversed upon appeal, that will take time. However, the fact that the law is outlined in over 2,300 pages plus thousands of pages of regulations introduced over following years (as mentioned in chapter 3) means that virtually everyone in the country is affected by this court's decision. And since the law has been in effect for nearly a decade, health care organizations both public and private have put in place processes and procedures required by the law over that time. All of those arrangements are now threatened by a great deal of uncertainty and disruption. We will just have to watch and see how this turns out.

In short, the effort to get government out of the way on the part of some participants is having the unanticipated consequence of producing an avalanche of government activity and intervention in health care matters. Indeed, we have entered what is turning out to be a transformative era. The level of political and legislative activity shouldn't be surprising, given the amount of money circulating in the health care arena and the number of occupations and organizations that have developed a stake in system operations, which translates, at least in some cases, into raking in a share of the money.

It is also true that transformation is occurring in some sections of the health marketplace with less fanfare than might be expected, given the antagonism to the ACA before it was passed. Sellers of health care goods and services, who voiced strong opposition to the changes introduced by the ACA seem to have quietly accommodated requirements that they initially resisted. More importantly, they are now unwilling to abandon those accommodations. In a surprising turn of events, the attempt to repeal and replace the ACA has run up against strong resistance from the private sector insurance companies. The overt reason according to the companies is that they would have to raise prices in the face of withdrawal of funding for cost subsidies—which is exactly what they did. But they had another reason to oppose repeal, a reason that they did not emphasize. Consider the fact that in 2016, Medicare and

Medicaid, the two biggest government-sponsored health insurance programs, accounted for 60 percent of health care revenues reported by the nation's five largest health insurance companies. Revenue going to private sector insurance companies contracted to manage public health insurance plans has more than doubled since passage of the ACA, "growing from a combined total of $92.5 billion in 2010 to $213.1 billion in 2016."[34]

Market-based health care proponents, politicians and others who argue that the government should get out of the way have simply not caught up with the shift in the stance toward government munificence that private sector insurers are ready to accept. Insurers are not at all interested in raising objections about tax dollars going to support public health insurance programs.

WHAT MATTERS: INNOVATIVE REIMBURSEMENT OR PATIENT HEALTH?

There is so much change taking place currently that it is hard to keep track. It doesn't help that what constitutes positive results is in the eye of the beholder. An organization introduced by the ACA, the Center for Medicare and Medicaid Innovation (CMMI) provides a good example. It has not received much public attention, but its work is certainly attracting the attention of physicians and other health care providers. It holds the potential for introducing a lot of health system change. The organization was established to support the development of innovative reimbursement arrangements, forty of which have been established in various parts of the country and are now being watched and evaluated with the potential of being adopted by other entities. According to Alan Weil, editor of *Health Affairs*, the single most important health policy journal, "Innovation is the hottest word in health care."[35]

A proposal offered by the Physicians Foundation in response to the CMMI's call for "patients over paperwork" and "measures that matter" serves as an interesting example. It is special in that it begins with what the authors admit is a radical statement coming from an organization representing physicians.[36] The Foundation states that "medical care, it turns out, doesn't always lead to better health."

The origins of the Physicians Foundation, founded in 2003, are worth noting. It grew out of winning a class-action lawsuit brought by physicians affiliated with nineteen state medical societies and three county medical societies against private third-party payers. The settlement provided the resources for the Foundation to become the voice of physicians across the country. It is certainly the voice of those who feel that established professional organizations such as the AMA are not doing a good job representing their views.

The authors of the "patients over paperwork" proposal praise the CMMI initiative calling for greater emphasis on the needs of patients but say the following:

> The Innovation Center has developed and tested many promising models, but the market often experiences them as uncoordinated efforts. The proliferation of models creates complex and burdensome regulatory and reporting requirements that make it harder, not easier, to achieve a person-centered system that delivers health. We know that for every hour physicians spend providing direct clinical care to patients, they spend nearly two additional hours on administrative and regulatory work, which affects patient care and is a significant driver of increasing physician burnout.[37]

The Physicians Foundation urges CMS, the agency that has the greatest influence over reimbursement arrangements, to build on its Comprehensive Primary Care Model. It places emphasis on screening and navigation for health-related social needs with the aim of "patient-centered" care. The rationale is backed up by the results reported in what is now an enormous body of literature finding that variation in health status—70 percent of it, according to the Physicians Foundation—is attributable to what has become known as the "social determinants of health." The Foundation puts it this way:

> Building on this, we urge the inclusion of health-related social needs as a guiding design principle for all future Innovation Center payment and care delivery models—and revisions to its current models. By doing so, the Innovation Center would send a powerful signal to the market that the goal is achieving health, not only treating and managing illness.

The issue of *Health Affairs* with the message that innovation is the hottest word in health care offers a narrative that captures the essence of "patient-centered" care. It takes place in a small corner of the health care arena, a start-up clinic built by an agricultural company in Southern California. The physician telling the story describes a "shared medical appointment program" for diabetic and prediabetic patients. The medical visit lasts one to two hours. It involves eight to fifteen patients. Patients help each other weigh in and check blood pressure. A staff member checks finger stick glucose levels and records results.

[The visit] couples brief medical exams, prescription refills, and other medical care with education on topics such as the complications of diabetes. But at the crux of the program is peer interaction and sharing experiences, strength, and hope—akin to a twelve-step program.[38]

The shared medical appointment addresses two sets of needs: first, the needs of patients who, in this case, are "affected by social isolation, economic challenges, lack of education, or poor health literacy"; and second, the needs of physicians who seek to avoid burnout that comes from being required to see too many patients in too short a time. The physician who is offering this account illustrates the problem by recalling her days as a clinical preceptor:

I witnessed the same dilemma when working with residents. They would plop down next to me, heave a deep sigh, and speak with hopelessness about treating the triad of diagnoses in patients who presented with diabetes, hypertension, and hyperlipidemia. They'd spend a long time discussing diet and medication adherence with their patients, yet they wondered if anything was "sinking in." Invariably, a medical assistant would interrupt the precepting session and remind the resident that the next patient was outside the exam room, pacing the hall, irritated with the delay.[39]

At the health policy level, the shared medical appointment approach meets basic health policy objectives in providing access and quality without increasing costs. But it does much more. It provides this group of patients with an invaluable resource: a sense of belonging to a community that cares. The community is a resource that can provide assistance outside of the appointment with transportation, reminders of meetings, and a range of other benefits that come with friendship. It relieves the physician of trying to deal with so many of the ancillary issues that must be addressed during a very short visit.

Consider what is innovative about the shared appointment story. It is grounded in cooperation rather than competition. Competition is expected, encouraged, and generally celebrated when it is embraced by organizations that sell health products. Cooperation among for-profit organizations would be viewed as collusion and is prohibited by law. However, the extent to which the market-based approach, grounded in the commitment to competition, has been embraced by the health care sector has transformed the sector. It has monetized all interaction. It is this commitment that requires turning patients into consumers.

Eli Ginzberg, a health economist who served as an advisor to nine presidents, made clear the threat that monetarization poses. The risk, he said, was turning medicine from a profession into a business. He blamed faulty policy for creating opportunities, "for those with money-making proclivities to establish a strong niche in what was formerly a quasi-eleemosynary [charitable] sector."

> The American public cannot continue indefinitely down the path that it has been following—that is, to devote an ever larger share of its gross national product to health care. But only the naïve believe that the goals that must be pursued—innovation, quality, access, and equity at an affordable cost—can be achieved either by greater reliance on the for-profit sector or by radically constraining its growth.
>
> To secure its long-term financial foundation, American medicine will require a combination of political leadership and professional cooperation that is not yet visible on the horizon. The great danger is that such cooperation will be delayed past the point at which intervention can be effective.[40]

He issued this warning in 1984. Since then the proportion of the gross national product going to health care has risen dramatically. And the number of parties "with money-making proclivities" has expanded exponentially.

Patients come to the health sector seeking *health*, which involves obtaining health care goods and services—not the other way around. Success in shopping and getting the best health products has only a tenuous connection to improving health status—presumably the ultimate objective of everyone who seeks health care. The market approach fails to deal with significant realities affecting health as opposed to realities surrounding the purchase of health products. It ignores the "health-related social needs and associated behaviors" that the Physicians Foundation mentioned above points to. And it ignores the fact that patients' choices are constrained by the health insurance coverage they have, which is itself heavily influenced by various personal characteristics such as employment status, age, and poverty level. These realities violate the notion that individuals in the role of health care consumers are in a position to buy products based on their needs and preference. Which, in turn, makes the notion that their behavior will influence the price, quantity, and quality of health care goods and services, resulting in a consumer-driven health care system, unconvincing.

PHYSICIANS AND CONSUMER-DRIVEN VERSUS PATIENT-CENTERED CARE

Turning to the role physicians play, the assumption built into the market-based approach is that physician behavior is best shaped through financial incentives and that monetary rewards will cause physicians to take steps to contain costs and increase quality. Encouraging physicians to accept some financial risk in reimbursement arrangements is among the most recent innovations being lauded as a step forward in the effort to contain costs. However, financial reimbursement arrangements do not address the main complaint being registered by physicians, which is time pressure: time required to deal with electronic record keeping, limits on time allocated to patient visits, time involved in responding to quality measures, and so on. Time pressure has become the leading cause of physician burnout, a rising matter of concern among physicians. According to the president of the AMA, the 2018 annual survey of physicians found half of all physicians saying that they were feeling burned out.[41] It is not a minor complaint. It has serious effects. According to Dr. Khatri, who is issuing a 911 call to deal with current health care arrangements, "close to half of U.S physicians suffer from burnout—far more than other American workers." The level of stress, he points out, is leading to a higher suicide rate than any other profession in the country.[42]

The National Academy of Medicine, the former IOM, has launched what it describes as the

> first-of-its kind comprehensive resource repository on clinician burnout and well-being. . . . a resource center that includes peer-reviewed research news articles, blog posts, toolkits, reports, and briefs. . . . The knowledge hub provides a central source for health system leaders, clinicians, and trainees, to not only better understand what's causing burnout, but to adopt solutions that promise a brighter, healthier future.[43]

Reimbursement arrangements orchestrated through a market-based approach to health care is what is fueling physician burnout. The underlying assumption is that what doctors do is all about the money, which diminishes the reasons that most physicians say they go into medicine in the first place. A statement made by the former editor of the *Journal of the American Medical Association*, Catherine DeAngelis, speaks to this point:

> Physicians have long been quick to point to the social contract they have with their patients and the community in which they live. Sadly, several baser trends have gathered steam that have the potential to diminish the nobler aspects of the medical profession.
>
> For example, the ever-increasing commercialization of health care has resulted in the perception that medicine is now primarily a business rather than a vocation. . . . So what must be done? The simple answer is for all doctors to remember why they chose medicine as a profession. As a medical educator for more than 40 years, I know that medical students' stated reasons for entering medicine have not changed one bit. They, like the majority of doctors, want to have a noble profession of taking care of patients. . . .
>
> If physicians are truly allowed to care for patients, they must refuse to take less time with patients than needed, to order unnecessary tests, to prescribe unnecessary drugs when generic or other less expensive drugs would work as well, to accept gifts from pharmaceutical and device representatives, to publish articles that contain tainted data, and to complete forms that do little or nothing for patient care.[44]

This is not to deny that physicians want a good income or that a notable few are willing to accept vast amounts of money from pharmaceutical companies for touting their products. But on the whole, physicians, like everyone else, want to enjoy a comfortable living. Physicians want to pay down their educational debt, cover malpractice insurance, and provide for their families. Nonetheless, the fact that there are so many examples of physicians engaging in activities for which there is little financial incentive—taking time off to work in storm-ravaged communities, war-torn settings, clinics for the underserved—suggests that those physicians are motivated by something other than the wish to get rich.

Medical students choose to specialize in pediatrics and primary care knowing very well that they will be earning far less than their peers who opt for high-paying specialties. Money is clearly not playing the critical role in determining choice in those cases.

Connecting rewards to what physicians define as rewarding makes a lot more sense than endless schemes based on innovations in financial incentive arrangements. Support for efforts that allow doctors and patients to develop innovative approaches for delivering "patient-centered" health care services is sure to be far more satisfying to both, to more likely produce positive health outcomes, and to ultimately cost less. This requires moving away from the commitment to consumer-driven health care and competition toward arrangements that allow for more time and cooperation between the individuals most closely involved in the cause of health, that is, doctors and patients. That is "patient-centered" care.

FINAL THOUGHTS

Curiously it seems that it is only within the last few pages of this book that the question of what we want to achieve in turning to market-based health care has broken through. That requires me to return to what my students were telling me that first day of class. While they did not make this explicit, they were clearly voicing support for health care arrangements reflecting cherished American values grounded in competition and individual choice. They were invoking the strong and healthy, self-sufficient, hardworking individual imagery that Americans like to project. The imagery is linked to the "means" not the "ends" for seeking health care. That is, it addresses the challenge of designing a structure for managing health care occupations, organizations, and reimbursement arrangements.

What does the market-based approach have to say about the "ends" or goals it seeks to achieve? Cost containment is regularly mentioned, far more often than access to or quality of care. And at the same time, increasing economic rewards, that is, profit, is certainly another important organizational if not health system goal, one generally not invoked in discussions focusing on market-based health care. Health care arrangements, not the health of the individual seeking health care, is the core issue. Health per se or "achieving health" (as outlined by the Physicians Foundation discussed above) is not addressed by advocates of a market-based approach to health care.

However, the "means" involved in market-based health care does affect the "end" of "achieving health." Recognizing that research on the "social determinants of health" finds that social factors have an enormous impact on individual health status means that the health care delivery system has an enormous effect on health.[45] And as the report on the impact of chronic illness mentioned above makes clear, it has an enormous impact on the economy as well but not necessarily the impact publicized by market-based health care proponents. Health care arrangements are after all unambiguously socially constructed arrangements. In emphasizing competition, individualism, interactions between buyers and sellers as opposed to cooperation, sense of belonging in a supportive community, trust, and interaction between doctors and patients, market-based health care creates a scenario that operates as a significant social determinant of health. It has the effect of detracting from rather than advancing health.

NOTES

1. *National Tracking Poll #171011*, Morning Consult, October 19–23, 2017, https://morningconsult.com/wp-content/uploads/2017/10/171011_crosstabs_POLITICO_v1_AP-2.pdf.

2. Sara Collins, Munira Gunja, and Michelle Doty, "Following the ACA Repeal-and-Replace Effort, Where Does the U.S. Stand on Insurance Coverage?" Commonwealth Fund, September 7, 2017, https://www.commonwealthfund.org/publications/issue-briefs/2017/sep/following-aca-repeal-and-replace-effort-where-does-us-stand.

3. Drew Altman, "One Big Thing People Don't Know About Single Payer," Axios, November 2, 2017, https://www.axios.com/one-big-thing-people-dont-know-about-single-payer-1513306567-26ab72cc-0fa9-4fcc-82c1-835a1793698d.html.

4. Rachel Dolan, "From the Archives: Prices and Consumer Shopping," *Health Affairs Blog*, July 19, 2017, https://www.healthaffairs.org/do/10.1377/hblog20170719.061105/full/; Paul Ginsburg, "Shopping for Price in Medical Care," *Health Affairs*, Feb. 6, 2007, https://www.healthaffairs.org/doi/pdf/10.1377/hlthaff.26.2.w208.

5. Dolan, "From the Archives."

6. Joseph Dieleman et al., "Factors Associated with Increase in U.S. Health Spending, 1996–2013," *Journal of the American Medical Association*, November 7, 2017.

7. Gary Claxton et al., "How Have Health Care Prices Grown in U.S. over Time?" Peterson-Kaiser Health System Tracker, May 8, 2018, https://www.healthsystemtracker.org/chart-collection/how-have-healthcare-prices-grown-in-the-u-s-over-time/#item-start.

8. Drew Altman, "Public vs. Private Health Insurance on Controlling Spending," *Washington Wire, Wall Street Journal*, April 16, 2015, https://blogs.wsj.com/wash wire/2015/04/16/public-vs-private-health-insurance-on-controlling-spending/.

9. "Concentration of Health Care Spending in the U.S. Population, 2010," Kaiser Family Foundation, March 13, 2013, https://www.kff.org/health-costs/slide/concen tration-of-health-care-spending-in-the-u-s-population-2010/.

10. David Himmelstein and Steffie Woolhandler, "The Current and Projected Taxpayer Shares of US Health Costs," *American Journal of Public Health* 106, no. 3 (2016): 449–52.

11. Robert Evans, "Waste, Economists and American Healthcare," *Healthcare Policy* 9, no. 2 (2013): 12–20.

12. Evans, "Waste, Economists and American Healthcare."

13. Daniel O'Neill and David Scheinker, "Wasted Health Spending: Who's Picking Up the Tab?" *Health Affairs Blog*, May 31, 2018, https://www.healthaffairs.org/do/ 10.1377/hblog20180530.245587/full/; Donald Berwick and Andrew Hackbarth, "Eliminating Waste in US Health Care," *Journal of the American Medical Association* 307, no. 14 (2012.): 1513–16.

14. Bradley Herring, "An Unfortunate Inconsistency between Value-based Purchasing and Price Transparency," *Health Affairs Blog*, August 21, 2018, https:// www.healthaffairs.org/do/10.1377/hblog20180817.858519/full/.

15. Asher Schechter, "'There is Regulatory Capture, but It Is by No Means Complete,'" *ProMarket Blog*, March 15, 2016, https://promarket.org/there-is -regulatory-capture-but-it-is-by-no-means-complete/.

16. Schechter, "'There is Regulatory Capture.'"

17. Drew Altman, "Few Consumers Use Information on Health Provider Quality or Price," Kaiser Family Foundation, April 27, 2015, https://www.kff.org/health-costs/ perspective/few-consumers-use-information-on-health-provider-quality-or-price/.

18. Sara Collins, "The 'Medicare for All' Continuum: A New Comparison Tool for Congressional Health Bills Illustrates the Range of Reform Ideas," Commonwealth Fund, March 12, 2019, https://www.commonwealthfund.org/blog/2019/medicare-all -continuum.

19. Jacob Hacker, "The Road to Medicare for Everyone," *American Prospect*, January 3, 2018, https://prospect.org/article/road-medicare-everyone.

20. Ashley Kirzinger, Bryan Wu, and Mollyann Brodie, "Kaiser Tracking Poll—March 2018: Views on Prescription Drug Pricing and Medicare-for-all Proposals," Kaiser Family Foundation, March 23, 2018, https://www.kff.org/health-costs/poll-finding/kaiser-health-tracking-poll-march-2018-prescription-drug-pricing-medicare-for-all-proposals/.

21. David Anderson and Emma Sandoe, "A Framework for Evaluating Medicaid Buy-In Proposals," *Health Affairs Blog*, March 23, 2018, https://www.healthaffairs.org/do/10.1377/hblog20180320.297250/full.

22. John McDonough, "Health and Taxes and the Values at Stake in the ACA Debate," *Milbank Quarterly*, March 2017, https://www.milbank.org/quarterly/articles/health-taxes-values-stake-aca-debate/.

23. Katherine Baicker and Amitabh Chandra, "Myths and Misconceptions about U.S. Health Insurance," *Health Affairs* 27, no. 6 (2008): 533–43, https://www.healthaffairs.org/do/10.1377/hblog20180320.297250/full/.

24. Ben Tappin, Leslie Van Der Leer, and Ryan McKay, "You're Not Going to Change Your Mind," *New York Times*, May 27, 2017.

25. Robert Shiller, "We'll Share the Honors, and Agree to Disagree," *New York Times*, October 27, 2013, p. 6.

26. Emily Price, "Payless Opened a Fake Luxury Store with $600 Shoes," *Fortune*, November 28, 2018.

27. Stuart Altman, "In Remembrance of Uwe Reinhardt," *Health Affairs Blog*, November 27, 2017, https://www.healthaffairs.org/do/10.1377/hblog20171121.406306/full/.

28. Evans, "Waste, Economists and American Healthcare."

29. Daniel Waldo, "National Health Accounts: A Framework for Understanding Health Care Financing," *Health Affairs* 37, no. 3 (2018): 1–6.

30. Waldo, "National Health Accounts."

31. Lawrence Brown, "Webcast: Why Are Healthcare Prices So High, and What Can Be Done About Them?" Peterson-Kaiser Health System Tracker, May 9, 2018, https://www.healthsystemtracker.org/may-9-webcast-why-are-healthcare-prices-so-high-and-what-can-be-done-about-them/.

32. Ross DeVol et al. "An Unhealthy America: The Economic Burden of Chronic Disease—Charting a New Course to Save Lives and Increase Productivity and

Economic Growth," Milken Institute, October 1, 2007, https://www.milkeninstitute
.org/publications/view/321.

33. Brown, "Webcast: Why Are Healthcare Prices So High?"

34. "Medicaid and Medicare Accounted for 59 Percent of Health Care Revenue
for the Five Largest U.S. Insurers in 2016, More Than Doubling Since 2010,"
Commonwealth Fund, December 4, 2017, https://www.commonwealthfund.org/
press-release/2017/medicaid-and-medicare-accounted-59-percent-health-care
-revenue-five-largest-us.

35. Alan Weil, "Diffusion of Innovation," *Health Affairs* 37, no. 2 (2018): 175.

36. Walker Ray and Tim Norbeck, "Physicians' Broader Vision for the Center for
Medicare and Medicaid Innovation's Future: Look Upstream," *Health Affairs Blog*, 2,
2018, https://www.healthaffairs.org/do/10.1377/hblog20180227.703418/full/.

37. Ray and Norbeck, "Physicians' Broader Vision."

38. Maureen Mavrinac, "Rethinking the Traditional Doctor's Visit," *Health Affairs*
37, no. 2 (2018): 325–28.

39. Mavrinac, "Rethinking the Traditional Doctor's Visit."

40. Eli Ginzberg, "The Monetarization of Medical Care," *New England Journal of
Medicine* 310, no. 18 (1984.): 1162–65.

41. David Barbe, "Dousing the Physician Burnout Epidemic: An AMA Perspective,"
Practical Pain Management, August 7, 2018, https://www.practicalpainmanagement.
com/resources/practice-management/dousing-physician-burnout-epidemic-ama
-perspective.

42. Bhupendra Khatri, *Healthcare 911* (Milwaukee, WI: Hansa House Publishing,
2018).

43. "Communications Toolkit: Clinician Well-Being Knowledge Hub," National
Academy of Medicine, https://nam.edu/resource-toolkit-clinician-well-being
-knowledge-hub/.

44. Catherine DeAngelis, "Medicine: A Profession in Distress," *Milbank Quarterly*,
November 2017, https://www.milbank.org/quarterly/articles/medicine-profession
-distress/.

45. "Health Impact Assessment," World Health Organization, https://www.who.int/
hia/evidence/doh/en/.

Epilogue
Some Reflections on Solutions

The market-based approach to health care has had over four decades (I am dating it to the effort to promote HMOs) to prove that competition will lower costs. That objective is still nowhere near being attained. In fact, it is during this time period that the United States increased its spending to about twice as much as other economically developed countries. At the same time, all those other countries have succeeded in providing access to health care for everyone, with their people using more health services than we do (they see their doctors more often). And they live longer than Americans do. The United States differs from those other countries in one other important way: none of those countries employs the kind of market-based approach to the delivery of health care that is used by the United States.

Interest in health care reform has come in waves. Interest is high at this time, as the midterm elections of 2018 attest. The focus, as has been true of each earlier wave of interest, is on the high cost of health care. There is little disagreement about "what" is to be achieved, namely, access, cost containment, and quality. There is much disagreement about the "how."

The options we have before us now are not that different from the options that have been before us all along. On the one hand, there are proposals designed to do a better job of correcting for the flaws in the market-based approach that require working within the framework employed by that approach. On the other hand, there are proposals that aim to abandon the market-based approach in order to move on to a new approach.[1]

OPTION 1: WORKING WITHIN THE FRAMEWORK

Improving on the functioning of the market-based approach requires getting both sides in the exchange, the sellers and the buyers, to perform their respective roles in the way the model lays out those roles. That means continuing to work on proposals and initiatives aimed at sellers, primarily health care providers, and designed to incentivize them. This involves creating newer and better schemes to calculate costs and measures of quality. It requires coming up with better formulas for linking the results to financial rewards and/or penalties in the expectation that this will result in lower costs and higher quality. In the case of hospitals, it means continuing efforts aimed at designing an assessment tool that will succeed in separating the efficient from the inefficient hospitals and a formula linking those results to financial rewards or penalties. The incentives directed to health insurance companies have taken the form of subsidies (paying them) to stay in the market (to ensure access) and compete with each other for customers (to achieve cost containment). Since this arrangement appears to be a slippery slope, it requires making continuing adjustments to ensure that the companies will in fact stay in the market and perform the role they have been assigned. Pharmaceutical companies have succeeded in escaping from efforts to incentivize them to perform the role envisioned for them in market-based health care theory. They just keep finding ways to raise prices and hide problems related to questionable quality.

The search for new measures and new incentive arrangements is never-ending, because (1) the schemes don't produce the results they say they will produce and (2) the sellers of health care goods and services continue to object, pointing out flaws in the measures and incentive arrangements.

On the other side, in the effort to help consumers play the role the market-based approach expects of them, a growing industry of groups has come into existence. The groups aim to provide information designed to help consumers select a provider or insurer and evaluate the drugs they have been prescribed. Developed accurately, such information is beneficial. Depending on consumers to use the information to affect the market is where things go astray. The expectation that the majority of consumers have the capacity to search out and find the information, understand it, and be in a position to use it is unrealistic.

Continuing to rely on the market-based health care approach has clearly been disappointing. Thus a greater number of Americans have begun to warm to the idea of shifting to a single-payer or Medicare-for-all plan. There is good reason to think that many who take this position are just upset about the arrangements that we currently have in place and do not really know a lot about what they say they are ready to support. It is also true that the public will be hearing a lot more about this alternative.

OPTION 2: MOVING TO AN ALTERNATIVE FRAMEWORK

The Medicare-for-all approach to health care is well laid out in seven proposals that aim to shift health care arrangements from a market-based, private sector approach to a public sector approach, and both are up for deliberation in the halls of government, that is the 116th Congress, in 2019. One other proposal outlines greater private health plan and provider regulation.[2]

Two bills presented in 2018 during the 115th Congress have been reviewed by policy experts. I would like to focus on those. One is in the Senate (S. 1804), the Medicare for All Act, and the other is in the House of Representatives (H.R. 676), the Expanded & Improved Medicare for All Act. It is interesting to see what the two bills have in common and how they differ. But it is the contrast between the Medicare-for-all proposals and the market-based approach we have been relying on for more than half a century that deserves special attention.

Medicare-for-All

Both the Senate and House Medicare-for-all alternatives proposed in 2018 advocate universal health care coverage, that is, access to care for everyone. And they both aim to replace the array of both public and private health insurance plans we have now with a single-payer plan. They differ in how the single-payer plan will operate.

The objection that is quick to follow any mention of Medicare-for-all is that it would cost too much. That charge has now been thoroughly investigated and soundly refuted by a team of economists associated with the Political Economy Research Institute (PERI).[3] The following discussion is largely based on the PERI report. A YouTube version with easy-to-understand statistics is "The Sanders Institute—Medicare For All—How We Pay for It" (https://www.youtube.com/watch?v=MaTcUsPmhks).

The PERI analysis concentrates on the Senate version. Here's what the researchers have to say about it. The plan would provide health care for everyone, that is, universal coverage, with no cost sharing. The researchers acknowledge that this would increase utilization. They note, however, that it is unlikely that many people will be volunteering for expensive surgery that they don't need. Increased utilization can be expected to take the form of seeking medical care in an office setting, a far less expensive form of care. The analysts provide data showing that the savings achieved by Medicare-for-all would not only compensate for that but would result in a 19 percent drop in overall health care costs.

The authors of the report identify four arenas in which cost savings would occur, providing estimates of the amount of money that would be saved in each case. First, the biggest source of savings would come from reduction in administrative costs. The second would be pharmaceutical pricing. Third would be establishing uniform rates for hospitals, physicians, and clinics. Fourth, fraud and waste would be reduced.

The PERI report is extensive. It responds to a number of practical concerns, such as how a single-payer plan would affect the business community. The authors estimate that the business sector would save 8 percent by switching from higher-priced private insurance to Medicare-for-all. And it would be pleased to be rid of the hassle of the need to deal with insurance.

One big question the Senate bill takes up is, What about all the people employed by insurance companies and by providers now involved in processing health insurance paperwork? The Medicare for All Act guarantees them income for a full year, occupational training, and the assurance that the money now invested in pensions could not be touched by the employer. Transition costs are built into the bill.

How providers get paid is another crucial concern addressed by the Senate Medicare for All Act. The proposed bill reduces provider reimbursement rates by about 7.8 percent. But since doctors would no longer have to spend time checking with clerks, employed by different insurers, who are in charge of lists of covered procedures and rules governing who is entitled to receive those procedures, doctors would save about four hours per week in administrative work. The bill does little to discourage doctors from making up for the loss of income by offering more medical services and charging for them if they choose to do so.

The PERI economists who analyzed the Senate version of the bill go on to say that the Medicare for All Act would have macro-stabilizing effects that proceed from guaranteed access to health care: less personal anxiety, less bankruptcy, and less time off from work, which would add up to greater economic productivity.

The added socioeconomic benefits, as noted in the previous chapter, involve disconnecting health insurance from employment, giving people the freedom to leave their jobs to pursue entrepreneurial activities or creative interests, work part time, retire early, and so on. It is also hard to ignore the fact that the single-payer plan would release the public from the relentless pressure to spend time engaged in shopping for insurance and checking to see if the doctor is in a network covered by the insurance, in shopping for cheaper prescription drugs, and in dealing with surprise bills, just to name a few time-consuming and frustrating exercises.

Comparing the House and Senate Medicare-for-All Bills

A comparison of the Senate and the House Medicare-for-all bills is informative. The similarities and differences between the bills are thought-provoking. Both focus on extending access and reducing administrative costs. They differ in the extent to which they address provider reimbursement arrangements. The Senate bill does not alter to any great extent the per-patient billing system being used by private insurers as well as by Medicare. The House bill alters such arrangements significantly. The House bill recommends some very big changes in provider—both physician and hospital—reimbursement arrangements designed to address the "quantity" of care issue. It outlines three avenues of physician reimbursement: (1) fee-for-service, (2) salary under an institutional global budget, and (3) salary under an institutional capitation arrangement. The global budget refers to hospital reimbursement.

Capitation, Bundled Payments, and Global Budgets

The House bill does not eliminate fee-for-service reimbursement. However, because increasing numbers of physicians are moving to affiliate with a hospital, it states that it expects independent fee-for-service reimbursement arrangements to decline. It notes that physicians are readier to accept a salary or a capitation reimbursement arrangement. Capitation is reimbursement on the basis of the number of patients on the physician's list, regardless of whether the patients visit the doctor or not. That means physicians have no financial incentive to see more patients and perform more procedures than necessary. (It is an arrangement that exists in some other countries, so there is considerable evidence on how it affects health outcomes as well as costs.)

Bundled payment arrangements introduced by Medicare in recent years have achieved significant health cost savings. The bundled payment involves setting a reimbursement rate for all the goods and services associated with a specific procedure performed in the hospital, for example, a heart value replacement. The bundled reimbursement fee requires everyone involved in addressing the patient's problem to cooperate in ordering tests and providing treatment. The flaw is that the bundled payment arrangement doesn't work very well when the individual's problem cannot be resolved using a specific procedure and instead requires monitoring and dealing with the patient's chronic health problems over time.

Another criticism of the bundled payment reimbursement arrangement is that it is not a systematic solution to the challenge of cost containment because it is episodic. It involves individual cases. Bundling payments at the institutional level would have a much greater, systemic effect.

That moves us from talk about bundling payments for specific procedures to talk of global budgeting. Global budgeting means that the institution as a whole would have to operate under a preset budget to deal with all the health care that takes place under its roof. Everyone in the institution would have to cooperate in agreeing on how the allotted funds are distributed. This is obviously a huge challenge.

Such an approach reduces the chances of attaining greater financial gain through competition inherent in the market-based approach, because the amount of money available to the institution is fixed. Profit can no longer be the primary objective dictating the choices made by sellers of health care services, neither the doctors nor the health care facilities.

Under ideal circumstances, a bundled payment arrangement at the institutional level, the global budget, could have a positive effect on quality of care. Competition would not go away. It would shift to another standard in which earning a reputation for a high level of success would be the health care providers' reward. In the case of technical procedures performed in the hospital, the person who actually performs the procedure depends on prep work and testing carried by other members of the team. Ensuring that the patient does not return to the hospital a short while after the procedure is completed depends on the contribution of other personnel charged with follow-up. The existence of a team greatly advances quality. It insures transparency. The patient's file is open to a group of people. The contribution made by each member of the team can be evaluated.

A global budget presses providers into using institutional resources aimed at preventing patients from needing highly technical and expensive procedures. It works to discourage overtesting and overtreatment. That goes a long way toward improving quality of care while containing the costs of care.

Another bold recommendation in the House bill aimed at achieving cost containment calls for conversion to nonprofit status of all investor-owned facilities. (Just the opposite of what my students said they favored, as I noted in chapter 1!) The plan is to issue government bonds to buy out the facilities. This includes all for-profit hospitals, nursing homes, and clinics.

Strengths and Weaknesses of the House Bill Reimbursement Plan

While the PERI report does not focus on the House bill, it does review the evidence on strengths and weaknesses of global budgeting and capitation. The basic problem it identifies in the case of capitation involves "risk adjustment." To set a fair rate, it is important to calculate how many patients with serious rather than minor problems the physicians is treating. As to institutional global budgeting, the difficulty is determining the amount of funding needed to ensure that patients receive needed care without the institution receiving excessive funding. Under global funding arrangements at the hospital level, there is a tendency to shift care from the hospital to unregulated nonhospital settings. Moving to countrywide global budgeting, which occurs in some countries, may overcome that tendency, but it does not overcome the problem of setting institutional budgets.

Likelihood of a Shift from Market-Based to Medicare-for-All Arrangements

I want to make clear that I see this review of the two Medicare-for-all bills as an intellectual exercise. It is brief because Medicare-for-all bills are at a relatively early stage in the legislative process. More legislators would have to sign on. The bills would have to be aligned between Senate and House versions before Congress could actually pass a final version of the bill. There is a long way to go before any of that happens, which means there is no guarantee a Medicare-for-all bill will be considered for a vote. My purpose in reviewing the bills is not to suggest that I expect passage of Medicare-for-all to eliminate the problems inherent in the market-based health care delivery system we have now any time soon. It is a thought experiment meant to identify the strengths and weaknesses of the Medicare-for-all approach in contrast to the market-based approach. And it is to recognize that no health care system is perfect. The value of reviewing alternatives is to develop a better understanding of which approach one wants to support based on the strengths and weaknesses of each.

Finally, while I believe this thought experiment to be intellectually stimulating at the theoretical level, I want to acknowledge that any attempt to move in the direction of a single-payer plan will face tremendous opposition. Concerted effort launched in opposition is certain to come from the multitude of individuals and organizations that have a vested interest in protecting the tremendous financial gains they are reaping based on current arrangements.

NOTES

1. Sherry Glied and Jeanne Lambrew, "How Democratic Candidates for the Presidency in 2020 Could Choose among Public Health Insurance Plans," *Health Affairs* 37, no. 12 (2018): 2084–91.

2. Sara Collins, "The 'Medicare for All' Continuum: A New Comparison Tool for Congressional Health Bills Illustrates the Range of Reform Ideas," Commonwealth Fund, March 12, 2019, https://www.commonwealthfund.org/blog/2019/medicare-all-continuum.

3. Robert Pollin, James Heintz, Peter Arno, Jeannette Wicks-Lim, and Michael Ash, "Economic Analysis of Medicare for All," Political Economy Research Institute, University of Massachusetts, November 30, 2018, https://www.peri.umass.edu/publication/item/1127-economic-analysis-of-medicare-for-all.

Bibliography

Abelson, Reed. "Bigger May Be Better for Health Insurers, but Doubts Remain for Consumers." *New York Times*, August 3, 2015.

Abelson, Reed. "To Fend Off Competition, Hospitals Consolidate." *New York Times*, December 19, 2017.

Almashat, Sammy. "Pharmaceutical Lobby Reigns Supreme in Washington." Public Citizen, June 2014. https://www.citizen.org/our-work/health-and-safety/health-letter-pharmaceutical-lobby-reigns-supreme-washington.

Almashat, Sammy, and Michael Carome. "Withholding Information on Unapproved Drug Marketing Applications." *Journal of Law, Medicine & Ethics*, January 10, 2018.

Almashat, Sammy, Sidney M. Wolfe, and Michael Carome. *Twenty-Five Years of Pharmaceutical Industry Criminal and Civil Penalties: 1991 through 2015*. Public Citizen, March 31, 2016. https://www.citizen.org/sites/default/files/2311_0.pdf.

Altman, Drew. "Few Consumers Use Information on Health Provider Quality or Price." Kaiser Family Foundation, April 27, 2015. https://www.kff.org/health-costs/perspective/few-consumers-use-information-on-health-provider-quality-or-price/.

Altman, Drew. "One Big Thing People Don't Know About Single Payer." Axios, November 2, 2017. https://www.axios.com/one-big-thing-people-dont-know-about-single-payer-1513306567-26ab72cc-0fa9-4fcc-82c1-835a1793698d.html.

Altman, Drew. "Public vs. Private Health Insurance on Controlling Spending." *Washington Wire, Wall Street Journal*, April 16, 2015. https://blogs.wsj.com/washwire/2015/04/16/public-vs-private-health-insurance-on-controlling-spending/.

Altman, Stuart. "In Remembrance of Uwe Reinhardt." *Health Affairs Blog*, November 27, 2017. https://www.healthaffairs.org/do/10.1377/hblog2017 1121.406306/full/.

"Americans Are Paying More for Employer Health Coverage." Commonwealth Fund, December 18, 2018. https://www.commonwealthfund.org/publications/newsletter-article/2018/dec/americans-are-paying-more-employer-health -coverage.

Anderson, David, and Emma Sandoe. "A Framework for Evaluating Medicaid Buy-In Proposals." *Health Affairs Blog*, March 23, 2018. https://www.healthaffairs.org/do/10.1377/hblog20180320.297250/full/.

Andrews, Michelle. "Congress Urged to Cut Medicare Payments to Many Stand-Alone ERs." Kaiser Health News, April 17, 2018. https://khn.org/news/congressional -advisers-urge-medicare-payments-to-many-stand-alone-ers-be-cut/.

Angell, Marcia. *The Truth about the Drug Companies*. New York: Random House, 2005.

Appleby, Julie. "Brokers are Reluctant Players in a Most Challenging ACA Open-Enrollment Season." Kaiser Health News, November 13, 2017. https://khn.org/news/brokers-are-reluctant-players-in-a-most-challenging-aca-open-enrollment -season/.

Ash, Michael, and Jean Ann Seago. "The Effects of Registered Nurses' Unions on Heart-Attack Mortality." *IRL Review* 57, no. 3 (2004): 422–42.

Azar, Alex. "Remarks on Value-Based Transformation to the Federation of American Hospitals," HHS.gov, March 5, 2018. https://www.hhs.gov/about/leadership/secretary/speeches/2018-speeches/remarks-on-value-based -transformation-to-the-federation-of-american-hospitals.html.

Bai, Ge, and Gerard Anderson. "US Hospitals Are Still Using Chargemaster Markups to Maximize Revenues." *Health Affairs* 35, no. 9 (September 2016): 1658–64.

Baicker, Katherine, and Amitabh Chandra. "Myths and Misconceptions about U.S. Health Insurance." *Health Affairs* 27, no. 6 (2008): 533–43.

Barbe, David. "Dousing the Physician Burnout Epidemic: An AMA Perspective." *Practical Pain Management*, August 7, 2018. https://www.practicalpainmanagement .com/resources/practice-management/dousing-physician-burnout-epidemic-ama -perspective.

Barbey, Christopher, Nikhil Sahni, Robert Kocher, and Michael E. Chernew. "Physician Workforce Trends and Their Growth Implications for Spending Growth." *Health Affairs Blog*, July 28, 2017. https://www.healthaffairs.org/ do/10.1377/hblog20170728.061252/full/.

Barkholz, Dave. "Nation's Largest Investor-Owned Hospital Systems Are in Full Retreat." *Modern Healthcare*, January 28, 2017. https://www.modernhealthcare .com/article/20170128/MAGAZINE/301289983/nation-s-largest-investor-owned -hospital-systems-are-in-full-retreat.

Batty, Michael, and Benedic Ippolito. "Mystery of the Chargemaster: Examining the Role of Hospital List Prices in What Patients Actually Pay." *Health Affairs* 36, no. 4 (2017): 689–96.

Berchick, Edward R., Emily Hood, and Jessica C. Barnett. "Health Insurance Coverage in the United States: 2017." United States Census Bureau, September 12, 2018. https://www.census.gov/library/publications/2018/demo/p60-264.html.

Berwick, Donald, and Andrew Hackbarth. "Eliminating Waste in US Health Care." *Journal of the American Medical Association* 307, no. 14 (2012.): 1513–16.

Bingham, Amy. 2011. "Tea Party Debate Audience Cheered Idea of Letting Uninsured Patients Die." ABC News, September 13, 2011. https://abcnews.go .com/blogs/politics/2011/09/tea-party-debate-audience-cheered-idea-of-letting -uninsured-patients-die/.

Blumenthal, David. "The Decline of Employer-Sponsored Health Insurance." Commonwealth Fund, December 7, 2017. https://www.commonwealthfund.org/ blog/2017/decline-employer-sponsored-health-insurance.

Blumenthal, David. "The Three R's of Health Insurance." Commonwealth Fund, March 5, 2014. https://www.commonwealthfund.org/blog/2014/three-rs-health -insurance.

Blumenthal, David, and David Squires. "Drug Price Control: How Some Government Programs Do It." Commonwealth Fund, May 10, 2016. https://www .commonwealthfund.org/blog/2016/drug-price-control-how-some-government -programs-do-it.

Boccuti, Cristina, Gretchen Jacobson, Kendal Orgera, and Tricia Neuman. "Medigap Enrollment and Consumer Protections Vary across States." Kaiser Family Foundation, July 11, 2018. https://www.kff.org/medicare/issue-brief/medigap -enrollment-and-consumer-protections-vary-across-states/.

Brooks, Megan. "Rare Disease Treatments Make Up Top 10 Most Costly Drugs," Medscape Medical News, May 2, 2017, https://www.medscape.com/view article/879422.

Brown, Lawrence. "Webcast: Why Are Healthcare Prices So High, and What Can Be Done About Them?" Peterson-Kaiser Health System Tracker, May 9, 2018. https://www.healthsystemtracker.org/may-9-webcast-why-are-healthcare-prices -so-high-and-what-can-be-done-about-them/.

Brownlee, Shannon. *Overtreated: Why Too Much Medicine Is Making Us Sicker and Poorer.* New York: Bloomsbury, 2008.

Budrys, Grace. *When Doctors Join Unions.* Ithaca, NY: Cornell University Press, 1997.

Bump, Philip. "The Hard-to-Answer Question at the Core of the Health-Care Fight: How Many More People Might Die?" *Washington Post,* June 27, 2017.

Buxbaum, Jason, John Mafi, and A. Mark Fendrick. "Tackling Low-Value Care: A New 'Top Five' For Purchaser Action." *Health Affairs Blog,* November 21, 2017. https://www.healthaffairs.org/do/10.1377/hblog20171117.664355/full/.

"Can You Trust Drug Ads on TV?" *Consumer Reports,* January 11, 2015. https:// www.consumerreports.org/cro/news/2015/01/can-you-trust-drug-ads-on-tv/ index.htm.

Capps, Cory, David Dranove, and Christopher Ody. "Physician Practice Consolidation Driven by Small Acquisitions, so Antitrust Agencies Have Few Tools to Intervene." *Health Affairs* 36, no. 9 (2017): 1556–63. https://www .healthaffairs.org/doi/10.1377/hlthaff.2017.0054.

Carome, Michael. "A Dangerous Gap in FDA Recall Authority." *Worst Pills, Best Pills News* 20, no. 9 (2014).

Carome, Michael. "New Report on Big Pharma Settlements Highlights Need for Tougher Enforcement." *Covering Health,* March 14, 2018. https:// healthjournalism.org/blog/2018/03/new-report-on-big-pharma-settlements -highlights-need-for-tougher-enforcement/.

Casalino, Lawrence, David Gans, Rachel Weber, Meagan Cea, Amber Tuchovsky, Tara F. Bishop, Yesenia Miranda, Brittany A. Frankel, Kristina B. Ziehler, Meghan M. Wong, and Todd B. Evenson. "US Physician Practices Spend More than $15.4 Billion Annually to Report Quality Measures." *Health Affairs* 35, no. 3 (2016.): 401–6.

Casselman, Ben. "Experts Foresee a U.S. Work Force Defined by Ever Widening Divides." *New York Times*, October 25, 2017, B3.

Castellucci, Maria, and Virgil Dickson. "Medicare ACO's Saved CMS $314 Million in 2017." *Modern Healthcare*, August 30, 2018. https://www.modernhealthcare.com/article/20180830/NEWS/180839987.

Center for Responsive Politics. "Ranked Sectors, 2018." Open Secrets.org. https://www.opensecrets.org/lobby/top.php?indexType=c&showYear=2018.

Center for Responsive Politics. "Who's Up, Who's Down?" OpenSecrets.org. https://www.opensecrets.org/lobby/incdec.php.

Chan, Gina. "Rising Drug Prices Put Big Pharma's Lobbying to the Test." *New York Times*, September 1, 2016.

Claxton, Gary, Matthew Rae, Larry Levitt, and Cynthia Cox. "How Have Health Care Prices Grown in U.S. Over Time?" Peterson-Kaiser Health System Tracker, May 8, 2018. https://www.healthsystemtracker.org/chart-collection/how-have-healthcare-prices-grown-in-the-u-s-over-time/#item-start.

Cohen, Robin, Michael Martinez, and Emily Zammitti. "Health Insurance Coverage: Early Release of Estimates from the National Health Interview Survey, January–March 2018." CDC/National Center for Health Statistics, August 2018. https://www.cdc.gov/nchs/data/nhis/earlyrelease/insur201808.pdf.

Cohen, Robin, Emily Zammitti, and Michael Martinez. "Health Insurance Coverage: Early Release of Estimates from the National Health Interview Survey, 2017." CDC/National Center for Health Statistics, May 2018. https://www.cdc.gov/nchs/data/nhis/earlyrelease/insur201805.pdf.

Collins, Sara. "The 'Medicare for All' Continuum: A New Comparison Tool for Congressional Health Bills Illustrates the Range of Reform Ideas." Commonwealth Fund, March 12, 2019. https://www.commonwealthfund.org/blog/2019/medicare-all-continuum.

Collins, Sara, Munira Gunja, and Michele Doty. "Following the ACA Repeal-and-Replace Effort, Where Does the U.S. Stand on Insurance Coverage?" Commonwealth Fund, September 7, 2017. https://www.commonwealthfund.org/publications/issue-briefs/2017/sep/following-aca-repeal-and-replace-effort-where-does-us-stand.

Collins, Sara, Munira Gunja, and Michelle Doty. "How Well Does Insurance Coverage Protect Consumers from Health Care Costs?" Commonwealth Fund, October 18, 2017. https://www.commonwealthfund.org/publications/issue-briefs/2017/oct/how-well-does-insurance-coverage-protect-consumers-health-care.

Collins, Sara, Munira Z. Gunja, Michelle M. Doty, and Herman K. Bhupal. "First Look at Health Insurance Coverage in 2018 Finds ACA Gains Beginning to Reverse." Commonwealth Fund, May 1, 2018. https://www.commonwealthfund.org/blog/2018/first-look-health-insurance-coverage-2018-finds-aca-gains-beginning-reverse.

"Communications Toolkit: Clinician Well-Being Knowledge Hub." National Academy of Medicine. https://nam.edu/resource-toolkit-clinician-well-being-knowledge-hub/.

"Concentration of Health Care Spending in the U.S. Population, 2010." Kaiser Family Foundation, March 13, 2013. https://www.kff.org/health-costs/slide/concentration-of-health-care-spending-in-the-u-s-population-2010/.

Consumers Union. "The Evidence Is Clear: Too Many Health Insurance Choices Can Impair, Not Help, Consumer Decision Making." *Consumer Reports*, November 1, 2012. https://advocacy.consumerreports.org/research/report-the-evidence-is-clear-too-many-health-insurance-choices-can-impair-not-help-consumer-decision-making/.

Cox, Cynthia, Gary Claxton, and Larry Levitt. "Explaining Health Care Reform: Risk Adjustment, Reinsurance, and Risk Corridors." Kaiser Family Foundation, August 17, 2016. https://www.kff.org/health-reform/issue-brief/explaining-health-care-reform-risk-adjustment-reinsurance-and-risk-corridors/.

Cox, Cynthia, Michelle Long, Ashley Semanskee, Rabah Kamal, Gary Claxton, and Larry Levitt. "2017 Premium Changes and Insurers Participation in the Affordable Care Act's Health Insurance Marketplaces." Kaiser Family Foundation, November 1, 2016. https://www.kff.org/health-reform/issue-brief/2017-premium-changes-and-insurer-participation-in-the-affordable-care-acts-health-insurance-marketplaces/.

DeAngelis, Catherine. "Medicine: A Profession in Distress." *Milbank Quarterly*, November 2017. https://www.milbank.org/quarterly/articles/medicine-profession -distress/.

Desai, Sunita, Laura A. Hatfield, Andrew L. Hicks, Anna D. Sinaiko, Michael E. Chernew, David Cowling, Santosh Gautam, Sze-jung Wu, and Ateev Mehrotra. "Offering a Price Transparency Tool Did Not Reduce Overall Spending among California Public Employees and Retirees." *Health Affairs* 36, no. 8 (2017): 1401–7.

De Vol, Ross, and Armen Bedroussian, with Anita Charuworn, Anusuya Chatterjee, In Kyu Kim, Soojung Kim, and Kevin Klowden. "An Unhealthy America: The Economic Burden of Chronic Disease—Charting a New Course to Save Lives and Increase Productivity and Economic Growth." Milken Institute, October 1, 2007. https://www.milkeninstitute.org/publications/view/321.

Dieleman, Joseph, Ellen Squires, Anthony L. Bui, Madeline Campbell, Abigail Chapin, Hannah Hamavid, Cody Horst, et al. "Factors Associated with Increase in U.S. Health Spending, 1996–2013." *Journal of the American Medical Association*, November 7, 2017.

Dolan, Rachel. "From the Archives: Prices and Consumer Shopping." *Health Affairs Blog*, July 19, 2017. https://www.healthaffairs.org/do/10.1377/hblog20170719 .061105/full/.

Emanuel, Ezekiel, Neera Tanden, Stuart Altman, Scott Armstrong, Donald Berwick, François de Brantes, Maura Calsyn, et al. "A Systemic Approach to Containing Health Care Spending." *New England Journal of Medicine* 367 (September 5, 2012): 949–54.

"Employment Projections." Bureau of Labor Statistics, October 24, 2017. https:// www.bls.gov/news.release/pdf/ecopro.pdf.

Evans, Robert. "Waste, Economists and American Healthcare." *Healthcare Policy* 9, no. 2 (2013): 12–20.

Fiedler, Matthew, Tim Gronniger, Paul B. Ginsburg, Kavita Patel, Loren Adler, and Margaret Darling. "Congress Should Replace Medicare's Merit-Based Incentive Payment System," *Health Affairs Blog*, February 26, 2018. https://www.health affairs.org/do/10.1377/hblog20180222.35120/full/.

Field, Robert. *Mother of Invention: How Government Created Free-Market Health Care.* New York: Oxford University Press, 2014.

"The First-Ever CMS Overall Hospital Quality Star Ratings Are Out. See How Hospitals Fared on Our Map." Advisory Board, July 28, 2016. https://www .advisory.com/daily-briefing/2016/07/28/cms-star-rating.

"First Release of the Overall Hospital Quality Rating on Hospital Compare." CMS, July 27, 2016. https://www.cms.gov/newsroom/fact-sheets/first-release-overall -hospital-quality-star-rating-hospital-compare.

Fowler, Annabelle, David C. Grabowski, Robert J. Gambrel, Haiden A. Huskamp, and David G. Stevenson. "Corporate Investors Increased Common Ownership in Hospitals and Postacute Care and Hospice Sectors." *Health Affairs* 36, no. 9 (2017): 1547–55.

Fox, Susannah. "Health Topics: 80% of Internet Users Look for Health Information Online." Washington, DC: Pew Research Center's Internet & American Life Project, February 1, 2011.

Frakt, Austin. "Missing from Medicare Advantage: True Competition." *New York Times*, May 2, 2016. https://www.nytimes.com/2016/05/03/upshot/missing-from -medicare-advantage-true-competition.html.

Frakt, Austin. "A Twist to Get Medicaid in Kentucky: Pass a Course." *New York Times*, January 23, 2018, A12.

Fuchs, Victor. *Health Economics and Policy*. New Jersey: World Scientific, 2018.

Fulton, Brent. "Health Care Market Concentration Trends in the United States: Evidence and Policy Responses." *Health Affairs* 36, no. 9 (2017): 1530–38.

Gani, Faiz, John Hundt, Michael Daniel, Jonathan E. Efron, Martin A. Makary, Timothy M. Pawlik. "Variations in Hospitals Costs for Surgical Procedures: Inefficient Care or Sick Patients." *American Journal of Surgery* 213, no. 1 (2017): 1–9.

Garrett-Peltier, Heidi. "Job Opportunity Cost of War." Watson Institute, Brown University, May 24, 2017. https://watson.brown.edu/costsofwar/files/cow/imce/ papers/2017/Job%20Opportunity%20Cost%20of%20War%20-%20HGP%20-%20 FINAL.pdf.

Gawande, Atul. "Why Doctors Hate Their Computers." *New Yorker*, November 12, 2018.

Gellad, Walid, Niteesh K. Choudhry, Mark W. Friedberg, M. Alan Brookhart, Jennifer S. Haas, and William H Shrank. "Variation in Drug Prices at Pharmacies:

Are Prices Higher in Poor Areas?" *Health Services Research* 44, no. 2 pt. 1 (2009.): 606–17.

Gelman, Lauren. "10 Wildly Overinflated Hospital Costs You Didn't Know About." *Reader's Digest*. https://www.rd.com/health/wellness/wildly-overinflated-hospital -costs/.

Ginzberg, Eli. "The Monetarization of Medical Care." *New England Journal of Medicine* 310, no. 18 (1984.): 1162–65.

Ginzburg, Paul. "Shopping for Price in Medical Care." Health Affairs, February 6, 2007. https://www.healthaffairs.org/foi/pdf/10.1377/hlthaff.26.2w208.

Giovanelli, Justin, and Emily Curran. "Efforts to Support Consumer Enrollment Decisions Using Total Cost Estimators: Lessons from the Affordable Care Act's Marketplaces." Commonwealth Fund, February 8, 2017. https://www.common wealthfund.org/publications/issue-briefs/2017/feb/efforts-support-consumer -enrollment-decisions-using-total-cost.

Giridharadas, Anand. *Winners Take All*. New York: Penguin Random House, 2018.

Glied, Sherry, and Stuart Altman. "Beyond Antitrust: Health Care and Health Insurance Market Trends and the Future of Competition." *Health Affairs* 36, no. 9 (2017): 1572–77.

Glied, Sherry, and Jeanne Lambrew. "How Democratic Candidates for the Presidency in 2020 Could Choose among Public Health Insurance Plans." *Health Affairs* 37, no. 12 (2018): 2084–91.

Gold, Jenny. "Accountable Care Organizations, Explained." Kaiser Health News, September 14, 2015. https://khn.org/news/aco-accountable-care-organization-faq/.

Goldstein, Amy. "Trump Administration Again Permits Kentucky to Impose Work Requirements for Medicaid Recipients," *Washington Post*, November 20, 2018. http://washingtonpost.com/national/health-science/trump -administration-again-permits-kectucky-to-impose-work-requirements -for-medicaid/2018/11/20/04a097cO-ed2b-11e8-96d4-Od23f2aaa09_story .html?noredirict=&_term=.6df1f4874420.

Goodman, John. *Priceless: Curing the Healthcare Crisis*. Oakland, CA: Independent Institute, 2012.

Goodnough, Abby. "Judge Blocks Medicaid Work Requirements in Two States." *New York Times*, March 28, 2019, A18.

Hacker, Jacob. "The Road to Medicare for Everyone." *American Prospect*, January 3, 2018. https://prospect.org/article/road-medicare-everyone.

Hakin, Danny. "Humira's Best-Selling Drug Formula: Start High. Go Higher." *New York Times*, January 6, 2018.

Hancock, Jay. "Everyone Wants to Reduce Drug Prices. So Why Can't We Do It?" *New York Times*, September 23, 2017.

Hancock, Jay. "Insurers' Flawed Lists Send Patients Scrambling." *New York Times*, December 4, 2016.

Hancock, Jay. "Obamacare Shopping Is Trickier than Ever. Here's a Cheat Sheet." Kaiser Health News, November 10, 2017. https://khn.org/news/obamacare -shopping-is-trickier-than-ever-heres-a-cheat-sheet/.

Harish, Nir, and Jennifer Wiler. "How the Freestanding Emergency Department Boom Can Help Patients." NEJM Catalyst, October 24, 2016. https://catalyst.nejm .org/how-the-freestanding-emergency-department-boom-can-help-patients/.

"Health Impact Assessment." World Health Organization. https://www.who.int/hia/ evidence/doh/en/.

Herring, Bradley. "An Unfortunate Inconsistency between Value-based Purchasing and Price Transparency." *Health Affairs Blog*, August 21, 2018. https://www .healthaffairs.org/do/10.1377/hblog20180817.858519/full/.

Herzlinger, Regina. *Market-Driven Health Care*. Cambridge, MA: Perseus Books, 1997.

Himmelstein, David, and Steffie Woolhandler. "The Current and Projected Taxpayer Share of U.S. Health Costs." *American Journal of Public Health* 106, no. 3 (2016): 449–52.

Hostetter, Martha, and Sarah Klein. "Health Care Price Transparency: Can It Promote High-Value Care?" Commonwealth Fund, 2012. https://www.common wealthfund.org/publications/newsletter-article/health-care-price-transparency -can-it-promote-high-value-care.

"How to Use the Searchable Medicare Physician Fee Schedule (MPFS)." https:// www.cms.gov/Outreach-and-Education/Medicare-Learning-Network-MLN/ MLNProducts/Downloads/How_to_MPFS_Booklet_ICN901344.pdf.

Hsiao, William, and Peter Heller. "What Should Macroeconomists Know About Health Care Policy?" Working Paper, International Monetary Fund, 2007.

Jacobson, Gretchen, Giselle Casillas, Anthony Damico, Tricia Neuman, and Marsha Gold. "Medicare Advantage 2016 Spotlight: Enrollment Market Update." Kaiser Family Foundation, May 11, 2016. https://www.kff.org/medicare/issue-brief/medicare-advantage-2016-spotlight-enrollment-market-update/.

Jewett, Christina, and Mark Alesia. "As Surgical Centers Boom, Patients Are Paying with Their Lives." Kaiser Health News, March 2, 2018. https://khn.org/news/medicare-certified-surgery-centers-are-expanding-but-deaths-question-safety/.

Johnson, Carolyn. "Hospitals Are Fed Up with Drug Companies, So They're Starting Their Own." *New York Times*, September 6, 2018.

Katz, Josh. "Drug Deaths in America Are Rising Faster than Ever." *New York Times*, June 5, 2017.

Kenney, Caitlin. "Shopping for an MRI." In *Planet Money*, podcast, November 6, 2009. https://www.npr.org/sections/money/2009/11/podcast_shopping_for_an_mri.html.

"Key Facts about the Uninsured Population." Kaiser Family Foundation, December 7, 2018. https://www.kff.org/uninsured/fact-sheet/key-facts-about-the-uninsured-population/.

Khatri, Bhupendra. *Healthcare 911*. Milwaukee, WI: Hansa House Publishing, 2018.

Kirzinger, Ashley, Elise Sugarman, and Mollyann Brodie. "Kaiser Tracking Poll: October 2016." Kaiser Family Foundation, October 27, 2016. https://www.kff.org/health-costs/poll-finding/kaiser-health-tracking-poll-october-2016/.

Kirzinger, Ashley, Bryan Wu, and Mollyann Brodie. "Kaiser Tracking Poll—March 2018: Views on Prescription Drug Pricing and Medicare-for-all Proposals." Kaiser Family Foundation, March 23, 2018. https://www.kff.org/health-costs/poll-finding/kaiser-health-tracking-poll-march-2018-prescription-drug-pricing-medicare-for-all-proposals/.

Koons, Cynthia. "The Shield of Patents Protects the World's Best-Selling Drug." Bloomberg Businessweek, September 7, 2017. https://www.bloomberg.com/news/articles/2017-09-07/this-shield-of-patents-protects-the-world-s-best-selling-drug.

Krugman, Paul. "Why Markets Can't Cure Healthcare." *New York Times*, July 25, 2009.

Ku, Leighton, Erika Steinmetz, Erin Brantley, Nikhil Holla, and Brian Bruen. "The American Health Care Act: Economic and Employment Consequences for States." Commonwealth Fund, June 14, 2017. https://www.commonwealthfund

.org/publications/issue-briefs/2017/jun/american-health-care-act-economic-and
-employment-consequences.

Kunneman, Marleen, Victor Montori, and Nilay Shah. "Measurement with a Wink."
    BMJ Quality and Safety 26, no. 10 (October 2017): 849–51. https://qualitysafety
    .bmj.com/content/26/10/849?utm_source=trendmd&utm_medium=cpc&utm
    _campaign=bmjqs&utm_content=consumer&int_source=trendmd&int
    _medium=trendmd&int_campaign=trendmd.

Lewis, Valerie, Thomas D'Aunno, Genevra F. Murray, Stephen M. Shortell, and
    Carrie H. Colla. "The Hidden Roles that Management Partners Play in
    Accountable Care Organizations." *Health Affairs* 37, no. 2 (February 2018): 292–98.

Loewenstein, George, and Saurabh Bhargava. "The Simple Case against Health
    Insurance Complexity." NEJM Catalyst, August 23, 2016. https://catalyst.nejm
    .org/simple-case-health-insurance-complexity/.

Lowes, Robert. "Malpractice Insurance Premiums Nudge Down Again." Medscape,
    October 13, 2014. https://www.medscape.com/viewarticle/833151.

Luthra, Shefali. "For Hospitals, Sleep and Patient Satisfaction May Go Hand in
    Hand." Kaiser Health News, August 17, 2017. https://khn.org/news/for-hospitals
    -sleep-and-patient-satisfaction-may-go-hand-in-hand/.

Mandel, Michael. "Rising Labor Costs Accounted for 47 Percent of Increased
    Personal Health Care Spending in 2015." *Blog*, Progressive Policy Institute,
    September 30, 2016. https://www.progressivepolicy.org/blog/rising-labor-costs
    -accounted-47-percent-increased-personal-health-care-spending-2015/.

"Market Effectuated Enrollment and Financial Assistance." Kaiser Family
    Foundation. https://www.kff.org/other/state-indicator/effectuated-marketplace
    -enrollment-and-financial-assistance/?currentTimeframe=0&selectedRows=%7
    B%22states%22:%7B%22all%22:%7B%7D%7D,%22wrapups%22:%7B%22united
    -states%22:%7B%7D%7D%7D&sortModel=%7B%22colId%22:%22Location%22,
    %22sort%22:%22asc%22%7D.

Martinez, Michael, Emily Zammitti, and Robin Cohen. "Health Insurance Coverage:
    Early Release of Estimates from the National Health Insurance Survey, January—
    September 2017." CDC/National Center for Health Statistics, February 2018.
    https://www.cdc.gov/nchs/data/nhis/earlyrelease/insur201802.pdf.

Mavrinac, Maureen. "Rethinking the Traditional Doctor's Visit." *Health Affairs* 37,
    no. 2 (2018): 325–28.

McCaughan, Mike. "Patent Settlements." Health Policy Briefs. *Health Affairs*, July 21, 2017. https://www.healthaffairs.org/do/10.1377/hpb20170721.583967/full/.

McDonough, John. "Health and Taxes and the Values at Stake in the ACA Debate." *Milbank Quarterly*, March 2017. https://www.milbank.org/quarterly/articles/health-taxes-values-stake-aca-debate/.

"Medicaid and Medicare Accounted for 59 Percent of Health Care Revenue for the Five Largest U.S. Insurers in 2016, More Than Doubling Since 2010." Commonwealth Fund, December 4, 2017. https://www.commonwealthfund.org/press-release/2017/medicaid-and-medicare-accounted-59-percent-health-care-revenue-five-largest-us.

"Medicare Provider Utilization and Payment Data: Physician and Other Supplier PUF—Frequently Asked Questions." Centers for Medicare and Medicaid Services, updated May 4, 2018. https://www.cms.gov/Research-Statistics-Data-and-Systems/Statistics-Trends-and-Reports/Medicare-Provider-Charge-Data/Downloads/Physician_FAQ.pdf.

Mehr, Stanton. "More Adalimumab News, AbbVie Signs a Licensing Deal with Coherus, Coherus Sues Amgen for Patent Infringement." BR&R, January 28, 2019. https://biosimilarsrr.com/2019/01/28/more-adalimumab-news-abbvie-signs-a-licensing-deal-with-coherus-coherus-sues-amgen-for-patent-infringement/.

Melnick, G. A., and K. Fonkych. "Hospital Prices Increase in California, Especially among Hospitals in the Largest Multi-Hospital Systems." Inquiry 53 (June 9, 2016): 1–7.

Misfeldt, Dayton, and James Robinson. "Orphan Diseases or Population Health? Policy Choices Drive Venture Capital Investments." *Health Affairs Blog*, July 21, 2017. https://www.healthaffairs.org/do/10.1377/hblog20170721.061150/full/.

Morgenson, Gretchen. "A Costly Drug, Missing a Dose of Disclosure." *New York Times*, January 27, 2017. https://www.nytimes.com/2017/01/27/business/gretchen-morgenson-mallinckrodt-drug-disclosures.html

Mullins, Joe. "Judge Throws Out Allergen Patent, Slams Company's Native American Deal." ARS, http://arstechnica.com/tech-polcy/2017/10/judge-throws-out-allergan-patent-slame-company's-native-american-deal.

Munro, Dan. "Avoiding Healthcare Cost with Pricing Transparency Hype." *Forbes*, April 22, 2014. https://www.forbes.com/sites/danmunro/2014/04/22/avoiding-healthcare-cost-with-pricing-transparency-hype/#5ae0d7f933bd.

National Center for Chronic Disease Prevention and Health Promotion (NCCDPHP). "Chronic Diseases in America." Last reviewed November 19, 2018. https://www.cdc.gov/chronicdisease/about/index.htm.

National Center for Health Statistics. "International Classification of Diseases, (ICD-10-CM-PCS) Transition—Background." CDC/National Center for Health Statistics. http://www.cdc.gov/nchs/icd/icd10cm_pcs_background.htm.

National Center for Health Statistics. "Table 89. Hospitals, Beds, and Occupancy Rates, by Type of Ownership and Size of Hospital: United States, Selected Years, 1975–2014." CDC/National Center for Health Statistics, 2017. https://www.cdc.gov/nchs/data/hus/2016/089.pdf.

National Center for Health Statistics. "Table 93. Gross Domestic Product, National Health Expenditures, Per Capita Amounts, Percent Distribution, and Average Annual Percent Change: United States, Selected Years 1960–2015." CDC/National Center for Health Statistics, 2016. https://www.cdc.gov/nchs/data/hus/2016/093.pdf.

National Center for Health Statistics. "Table 102. Private Health Insurance Coverage among Persons under Age 65, by Selected Characteristics: United States, Selected Years 1984–2016." CDC/National Center for Health Statistics, 2017. https://www.cdc.gov/nchs/data/hus/2017/102.pdf.

National Center for Health Statistics. "Table 103. Private Health Insurance Obtained through the Workplace among Persons under Age 65, by Selected Characteristics: United States, Selected Years 1984–2015." CDC/National Center for Health Statistics, 2016. https://www.cdc.gov/nchs/data/hus/2016/103.pdf.

National Center for Health Statistics. "Table 105. No Health Insurance Coverage among Persons under Age 65, by Selected Characteristics: Selected Years 1984–2016." CDC/National Center for Health Statistics, 2018. https://www.cdc.gov/nchs/data/hus/2017/105.pdf.

"National Survey Examines Perceptions of Health Care Provider Quality." National Opinion Research Center, July 20, 2014. http://www.norc.org/NewsEventsPublications/PressReleases/Pages/national-survey-examines-perceptions-of-health-care-provider-quality.aspx.

National Tracking Poll #171011. Morning Consult, October 19–23, 2017. https://morningconsult.com/wp-content/uploads/2017/10/171011_crosstabs_POLITICO_v1_AP-2.pdf.

Newman, Patricia, and Gretchen Jacobson. "Medicare Advantage Checkup." *New England Journal of Medicine* 379, no. 11 (November 4, 2018): 2163–72. https://www.nejm.org/doi/full/10.1056/NEJMhpr1804089.

"Number of Americans with Inadequate Health Insurance Coverage Rose Sharply in 2016." Commonwealth Fund, October 30, 2017. https://www.commonwealthfund.org/publications/newsletter-article/2017/oct/number-americans-inadequate-health-insurance-coverage-rose.

O'Neill, Daniel, and David Scheinker. "Wasted Health Spending: Who's Picking Up the Tab?" *Health Affairs Blog*, May 31, 2018. https://www.healthaffairs.org/do/10.1377/hblog20180530.245587/full/.

Ornstein, Charles, Mike Tigas, and Ryann Grochowski Jones. "Now There's Proof: Docs Who Get Company Cash Tend to Prescribe More Brand-Name Meds." ProPublica, March 17, 2016. https://www.propublica.org/article/doctors-who-take-company-cash-tend-to-prescribe-more-brand-name-drugs.

Patel, Yash, and Stuart Guterman. "The Evolution of Private Plans in Medicare." Commonwealth Fund, December 8, 2017. https://www.commonwealthfund.org/publications/issue-briefs/2017/dec/evolution-private-plans-medicare.

Pearl, Robert. "Why This Is the Hardest of Times to Be a Physician in America." *Forbes*, August 6, 2015.

"Persuading the Prescribers: Pharmaceutical Industry Marketing and Its Influence on Physicians and Patients." Pew Charitable Trusts, November 11, 2013. https://www.pewtrusts.org/en/research-and-analysis/fact-sheets/2013/11/11/persuading-the-prescribers-pharmaceutical-industry-marketing-and-its-influence-on-physicians-and-patients.

"Physician Fee Schedule Look-Up Tool." Centers for Medicare and Medicaid Services, updated March 8, 2019. https://www.cms.gov/Medicare/Medicare-Fee-for-Service-Payment/PFSlookup.

Physicians Foundation. *2016 Survey of American's Physicians: Practice Patterns and Perspectives*. September 21, 2016. https://physiciansfoundation.org/wp-content/uploads/2018/01/Biennial_Physician_Survey_2016.pdf.

Pollin, Robert, James Heintz, Peter Arno, Jeannette Wicks-Lim, and Michael Ash. "Economic Analysis of Medicare for All." Political Economy Research Institute,

University of Massachusetts, November 30, 2018. https://www.peri.umass.edu/
    publication/item/1127-economic-analysis-of-medicare-for-all.

Pollitz, Karen, Jennifer Tolbert, and Rosa Ma. "2015 Survey of Health Insurance
    Marketplace Assister Programs and Brokers." Kaiser Family Foundation, August
    6. 2015. https://www.kff.org/health-reform/report/2015-survey-of-health-insur
    ance-marketplace-assister-programs-and-brokers/.

"Premiums for Employer-Sponsored Family Health Coverage Rise 5% to Average
    $19,616; Single Premiums Rise 3% to $6896." Kaiser Family Foundation, October 3,
    2018. https://www.kff.org/health-costs/press-release/employer-sponsored-family
    -coverage-premiums-rise-5-percent-in-2018/.

Price, Emily. "Payless Opened a Fake Luxury Store with $600 Shoes." *Fortune*,
    November 28, 2018.

Rae, Matthew, Gary Claxton, and Larry Levitt. "Do Health Plan Enrollees Have
    Enough Money to Pay Cost Sharing?" Kaiser Family Foundation, November 3,
    2017. https://www.kff.org/health-costs/issue-brief/do-health-plan-enrollees-have
    -enough-money-to-pay-cost-sharing/.

Ray, Walker, and Tim Norbeck. "Physicians' Broader Vision for the Center
    for Medicare and Medicaid Innovation's Future: Look Upstream." *Health
    Affairs Blog*, March 2, 2018. https://www.healthaffairs.org/do/10.1377/
    hblog20180227.703418/full/.

Reinhardt, Uwe. "The Pricing of U.S. Hospital Services: Chaos Behind a Veil of
    Secrecy." *Health Affairs* 25, no. 1 (2006): 57–69.

Relman, Arnold. "Shattuck Lecture—The Health Care Industry: Where Is It Taking
    Us?" *New England Journal of Medicine* 325, no. 10 (September 1991): 854–59.

Rice, Sabriya. "Experts Raise Questions about Hospital Raters' Methods and Lack
    of Transparency." *Modern Healthcare*, May 31, 2014. https://www.modern
    healthcare.com/article/20140531/MAGAZINE/305319980/experts-question
    -hospital-raters-methods.

"The Rising Cost of Generic Drugs." *Worst Pills, Best Pills News* 22, no. 12 (2016).

Robeznieks, Andis. "More Patients Chose Specialists over Primary-Care Docs in
    2013." *Modern Healthcare*, April 21, 2014. https://www.modernhealthcare.com/
    article/20140421/blog/304219936.

Romm, Sylvia. "How Many Doctors Does It Take to Read a Hospital Bill?" Costs of Care, June 30, 2018. https://costsofcare.org/how-many-doctors-does-it-take-to -read-a-hospital-bill/.

Rosenthal, Elizabeth. *An American Sickness*. New York: Penguin Press, 2017.

Rosenthal, Elizabeth. "Good Deals on Pills? It's Anyone's Guess." *New York Times*, November 10, 2013.

"Same Generic Drug, Many Prices." *Consumer Reports*, May 2013. https://www .consumerreports.org/cro/magazine/2013/05/same-generic-drug-many-prices/ index.htm.

Sawyer, Bradley, Cynthia Cox, and Gary Claxton. "An Analysis of Who Is Most at Risk for High Out-of-Pocket Spending." Peterson-Kaiser Health System Tracker. https://www.healthsystemtracker.org/brief/who-is-most-at-risk-for-high-out-of -pocket-health-spending/.

Schechter, Asher. "'There is Regulatory Capture, but It Is by No Means Complete.'" *ProMarket Blog*, March 15, 2016. https://promarket.org/there-is-regulatory- capture-but-it-is-by-no-means-complete/.

Scheffer, Richard, and David Arnold. "Insurers Market Power Lowers Prices in Numerous Concentrated Provider Markets." *Health Affairs* 36, no. 9 (September 2017):1539–46.

Schencker, Lisa. "Muscular Dystrophy Drug Launch on Hold." *Chicago Tribune*, February 14, 2017, Business 1.

Schwarz, Alan. "The Selling of Attention Deficit Disorder." *New York Times*, December 15, 2013.

Semanskee, Ashley, Gary Claxton, and Larry Levitt. "How Premiums are Changing in 2018." Kaiser Family Foundation, November 29, 2017. https://www.kff.org/ health-costs/issue-brief/how-premiums-are-changing-in-2018/.

Shay, Julie. "What is Coding & Understanding the Difference Between CCA, CCS CPC." http://dept.sfcollege.edu/business/hitprograms/content/PDFs/ codingpresentation.pdf.

Shiller, Robert. "We'll Share the Honors, and Agree to Disagree." *New York Times*, October 27, 2013.

Smoldt, Robert, Denis Cortese, Natalie Landman, and David Gans. "Medicare Physician Payment: Why It's Still A Problem, And What to Do Now." *Health Affairs Blog*, January 27, 2017. https://www.healthaffairs.org/do/10.1377/hblog20170127.058490/full/.

Sood, Neeraj, Tiffany Shih, Karen Van Nuys, and Dana P. Goldman. "Follow the Money: The Flow of Funds in the Pharmaceutical Distribution System." *Health Affairs Blog*, June 13, 2017. https://www.healthaffairs.org/do/10.1377/hblog20170613.060557/full/.

Sorkin, Andrew Ross. "C.E.O.s Voice Confidence, but Deals Say Otherwise." *New York Times*, June 13, 2017.

Squires, David, and David Blumenthal. "Do Small Physicians Practices Have a Future?" Commonwealth Fund, May 26, 2016. https://www.commonwealthfund.org/blog/2016/do-small-physician-practices-have-future.

Strauss, Mark. "Most Patients in U.S. Have High Praise for Their Health Care Providers." Pew Research Center, August 2, 2017. http://www.pewresearch.org/fact-tank/2017/08/02/most-patients-in-u-s-have-high-praise-for-their-health-care-providers/.

Swanson, Ana. "Big Pharmaceutical Companies Are Spending Far More on Marketing than Research." *Time*, February 11, 2015.

Tappin, Ben, Leslie Van Der Leer, and Ryan McKay. "You're Not Going to Change Your Mind." *New York Times*, May 27, 2017.

"10 Essential Facts about Medicare and Prescription Drug Spending." Kaiser Family Foundation, November 10, 2017. https://www.slideshare.net/KaiserFamilyFoundation/10-essential-facts-about-medicare-and-prescription-drug-spending.

Terhune, Chad. "The $109K Heart Attack Bill is Down to $332. What About Other Surprise Bills?" Kaiser Health News, August 31, 2018. https://khn.org/news/the-109k-heart-attack-bill-is-down-to-332-what-about-other-surprise-bills/.

Thomas, Katie. "Health Law Drug Plans Are Given a Check-Up." *New York Times*, October 8, 2014, B1.

Thomas, Katie. "Patents for Restasis Are Invalidating Opening Door to Generics." *New York Times*, October 16, 2017.

Thomas, Katie. "Three Drug Makers Are Accused of Conspiring to Raise Insulin Prices." *New York Times*, January 31, 2017, A22.

"Three Firms Account for Over Half of All Medicare Part D Enrollees in 2018, and Pending Mergers Would Further Consolidate the Marketplace." Kaiser Family Foundation, May 17, 2018. https://www.kff.org/medicare/press-release/three -firms-account-for-over-half-of-all-medicare-part-d-enrollees-in-2018-and -pending-mergers-would-further-consolidate-the-marketplace/.

Tigas, Mike, Ryann Grochowski Jones, Charles Ornstein, and Lena Groeger. "Dollars for Docs." ProPublica, December 13, 2016. https://projects.propublica .org/docdollars/.

"Trump Announces Plan to Lower 'Unfair' Prescription Drug Prices." CBS News, updated Oct. 25, 2018. http://cbsnews.com/news/trump-prescription-drug -pricing-costs-speech-today-10-25-18-live-stream-updates.

"Underinsured Rate Increased Sharply in 2016; More Than Two of Five Marketplace Enrollees and a Quarter of People with Employer Health Insurance Plans Are Now Underinsured." Commonwealth Fund, October 18, 2017. https://www.com monwealthfund.org/press-release/2017/underinsured-rate-increased-sharply -2016-more-two-five-marketplace-enrollees-and.

"Updated Physician Practice Acquisition Study: National and Regional Changes in Physician Employment 2012–2016." Physician Advocacy Institute, March 2018. http://www.physiciansadvocacyinstitute.org/Portals/0/assets/docs/2016-PAI -Physician-Employment-Study-Final.pdf.

US Government Accountability Office, "Profits, Research and Development Spending, and Merger and Acquisition Deals." GAO-18-40. GAO, November 17, 2017. https://www.gao.gov/products/GAO-18-40.

"U.S. Patent and Trademark Office, Hiring Efforts Are Not Sufficient to Reduce Patent Application Backlog." U.S. Government Accountability Office, September 2007.

Ventola, C. Lee. "Direct-to-Consumer Pharmaceutical Advertising: Therapeutic or Toxic?" *Pharmacy and Therapeutics* 36, no. 10 (2011): 681–84.

Verma, Seema. "Empowered Patients Are the Future of Health Care." RealClear Health, May 3, 2018. https://www.realclearhealth.com/articles/2018/05/03/ empowered_patients_are_the_future_of_health_care_110784.html.

Vokinger, Kerstin, Aaron Kesselheim, and Jerry Avorn. "Strategies That Delay Market Entry of Generic Drugs," *Journal of the American Medical Association, Internal Medicine* 177, no. 11 (2017): 1665–69.

Wagner, John, Lenny Bernstein, and Scott Higham. "Trump Drug Czar Nominee Is Withdrawing; Administration 'Very Concerned' about Law He Championed." *Washington Post*, October 17, 2017.

Waldman, Deane. "Administrative Job Growth in Healthcare Isn't Good for America." The Hill, May 8, 2017. https://thehill.com/blogs/pundits-blog/healthcare/332372-administrative-job-growth-in-healthcare-isnt-good-for-america.

Waldo, Daniel. "National Health Accounts: A Framework for Understanding Health Care Financing." *Health Affairs* 37, no. 3 (2018): 1–6.

Waxman, Henry, Bill Corr, Kristi Martin, and Sophia Duong. "Getting to the Root of High Prescription Drug Prices." Commonwealth Fund, July 10, 2017. https://www.commonwealthfund.org/publications/issue-briefs/2017/jul/getting-root-high-prescription-drug-prices.

"Web Briefing for Journalists: A Closer Look at the Evolving Landscape of Medicaid Waivers." Kaiser Family Foundation, February 2, 2018. https://www.kff.org/medicaid/event/web-briefing-for-journalists-evolving-landscape-medicaid-waivers/.

Weil, Alan. "Diffusion of Innovation." *Health Affairs* 37, no. 2 (2018): 175.

Weintraub, Arlene. "Shrekli is Out as Shareholder and Influencer of KaloBios—Well Almost." *Forbes*, July 7, 2016. http://forbes.com/sites/arleneweintraub/2016/07/07/shkreli-is-out-as-a-shareholder-and-influencer-of-kalobios-well-almost/#17c69ca5754.

Welch, Gilbert. *Less Medicine, More Health*. Boston: Beacon Press, 2015.

Wible, Pamela. "Depressed Doctor: 'I'm Angry and Frustrated and Lost,'" *Patient Care*, September 16, 2015, https://www.patientcareonline.com/blog/depressed-doctor-im-angry-and-frustrated-and-lost.

Williams, Lawrence and John Bargh. "Experiencing Physical Warmth Promotes Interpersonal Warmth." *Science* 322 (October 24, 2008): 606–7.

Wishner, Jane, Patricia Solleveld, Robin Rudowitz, Julia Paradise, and Larisa Antonisse. "A Look at Rural Hospital Closures and Implications for Access to Care: Three Case Studies." Kaiser Family Foundation, July 7, 2016. https://www.kff.org/medicaid/issue-brief/a-look-at-rural-hospital-closures-and-implications-for-access-to-care/.

Wolfe, Sidney. "Direct-to-Consumer Advertising: Education or Emotion Promotion?" *New England Journal of Medicine* 346, no. 7 (2002): 524–26.

Wolfe, Sidney. "Pharma's Foreign Corrupt Practices Accompany Its Domestic Violations." *Worst Pills, Best Pills News* 19, no. 10 (2013): 2.

Wynne, Billy. "Breaking Down the MACRA Final Rule." *Health Affairs Blog*, November 9, 2017. https://www.healthaffairs.org/do/10.1377/hblog20171109 .968225/full/.

Xu, Susan, and Atul Grover. "CMS' Hospital Quality Star Ratings Fail to Pass the Common Sense Test." *Health Affairs Blog*, November 14, 2016. https://www .healthaffairs.org/do/10.1377/hblog20161114.057512/full/.

Young, Aaron, Humayun J. Chaudhry, Xiaomei Pei, Katie Arnhart, Michael Dugan, and Gregory B. Snyder. "A Census of Actively Licensed Physicians in the United States, 2016." *Journal of Medical Regulation* 103, no. 2 (2017): 7–21.

Yun, Jonathan, Kathryn Oehlman, and Michael Johansen. "Per Visit Emergency Department Expenditures by Insurance Type, 1996–2015." *Health Affairs* 7 (July 2018): 1109–14.

Zuckerman, Stephen, Laura Skopee, and Stuart Guterman. "Do Medicare Advantage Plans Minimize Costs? Investigating the Relationship between Benchmarks, Costs, and Rebates." Commonwealth Fund, December 21, 2017. https://www.com monwealthfund.org/publications/issue-briefs/2017/dec/do-medicare-advantage -plans-minimize-costs-investigating.

Index

Lightning Source UK Ltd.
Milton Keynes UK
UKHW010954260719
346787UK00009BB/71/P